D1426926

EMPEROR HIROHITO

AND

THE PACIFIC WAR

Emperor Hirohito in the uniform of army commander in chief, ca. 1928–29

EMPEROR HIROHITO

AND

THE PACIFIC WAR

NORIKO KAWAMURA

UNIVERSITY OF
WASHINGTON PRESS
Seattle and London

© 2015 by the University of Washington Press
Printed and bound in the United State of America
Composed in Warnock, a typeface designed by Robert Slimbach
19 18 17 16 15   5 4 3 2 1

UNIVERSITY OF WASHINGTON PRESS
www.washington.edu/uwpress

Library of Congress Cataloging-in-Publication Data

Kawamura, Noriko, 1955–
Emperor Hirohito and the Pacific war / Noriko Kawamura.
pages   cm
Includes bibliographical references and index.
ISBN 978-0-295-99517-5 (hardback : alk. paper) 1. Hirohito, Emperor of Japan, 1901–1989. 2. World War, 1939–1945—Japan.
I. Title.
DS889.8.K3959 2015
940.54'26—dc23

2015020141

The paper used in this publication is acid-free and meets the minimum requirements of American National Standard for Information Sciences—Permanence of Paper for Printed Library Materials, ANSI Z39.48–1984.∞

CONTENTS

ACKNOWLEDGMENTS

F ROM INCEPTION TO COMPLETION, THIS STUDY OF EMPEROR Hirohito and the Pacific War has covered many years of my career as a historian. Robert J. C. Butow first encouraged me to pursue the topic and warmly supported me throughout the process. Without his encouragement and advice, I would not have been able to bring this project to a successful conclusion. Wilton B. Fowler offered me the foundational training that shaped me as a diplomatic historian with keen interests in historical issues of war and peace. Kenneth B. Pyle guided me in the study of modern Japanese history in the English-speaking world. In the early stage of my research in Japan, Akira Yamada and Hisashi Takahashi showed me divergent ways to approach the project and helped me with archival research. I also want to thank numerous people who assisted me at the National Diet Library of Japan, the National Institute for Defense Studies (Boeikenkyujo), and the Imperial Household Agency (Kunaicho). As this project progressed, many scholars gave me helpful suggestions and comments. I want to especially thank E. Bruce Reynolds, Michael A. Barnhart, Barton J. Bernstein, and Fredrick Dickenson. I would also like to express my deep gratitude to Richard H. Minear for reading the entire manuscript and giving me useful suggestions. In addition, I would like to extend my heartfelt thanks to Lorri Hagman of the University of Washington Press for her kind support and to Alice Davenport, Ernst Schwintzer, and my husband, Roger Chan, for editorial assistance.

EMPEROR HIROHITO

AND

THE PACIFIC WAR

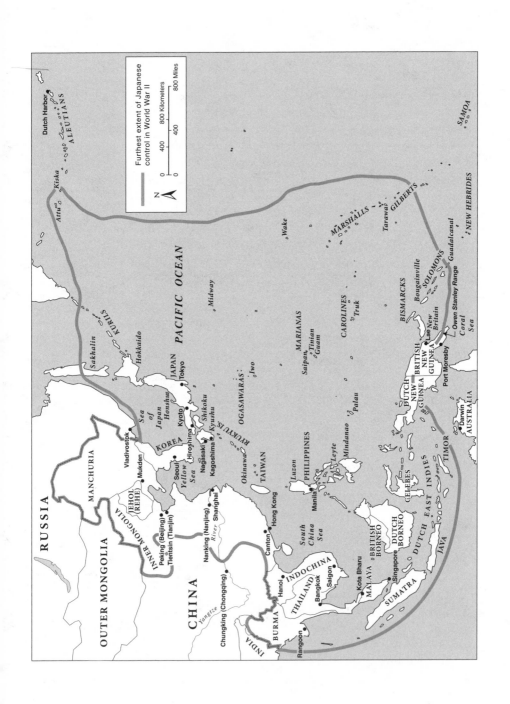

INTRODUCTION

WORLD WAR II CREATED MANY HEROES AND VILLAINS. Emperor Showa, better known in the United States as Emperor Hirohito, has been one of the most controversial figures in the history of the war that Japan waged in Asia and the Pacific.[1] Unlike US president Franklin D. Roosevelt and British prime minister Winston Churchill, both of whom were elected by their own peoples and held a democratic mandate to defend their countries during wartime, and unlike Adolf Hitler and Benito Mussolini, who emerged from political obscurity to seize dictatorial powers and to wage war, Emperor Hirohito was born to the throne and was trained from childhood to reign as monarch and to preserve the unbroken imperial line. Under the prewar Meiji Constitution of Japan, the emperor was both sovereign of the state and commander in chief of the Japanese imperial forces—but above all, he was the manifestation of divinity and a symbol of the national and cultural identity of Japan.[2]

Japan fought the Pacific War to the bitter end in order to preserve its *kokutai* (national polity), for which the myth of imperial rule served as core. Nevertheless, upon Japan's surrender to the Allied Powers, Hirohito, who renounced his divinity in his public "declaration of humanity," was altogether spared the postwar Tokyo war crimes trial. He continued to reign in postwar Japan until his death in January 1989, serving as "the symbol of the state and of the unity of the people" under the new democratic constitution, which was essentially written by the Americans who occupied Japan from 1945 to 1952. This dramatic shift—from a divine absolute monarch under the prewar constitution to a humanized symbolic emperor under the postwar democratic constitution—created numerous historical narratives of two diametrically opposed images of Hirohito, before and after Japan's war in Asia and the Pacific. These two contrasting images of Emperor Hirohito have fueled debates over his wartime responsibility, which remains a potentially explosive issue between Japan and former victims of Japanese military aggressions abroad, as well as a troublesome issue within domestic Japanese politics. Historians, in today's politically and ideologically partisan environment, continue to debate the power the emperor possessed and the role he played during the war.

As told from the United States' point of view, when Japan attacked Pearl Harbor and pulled the United States into what Americans call the Pacific War on December 7, 1941, Emperor Hirohito became the country's public enemy number one. Polls taken between 1943 and 1945 indicated that a third of the US public thought Hirohito should be executed, and even after Japan's surrender, the US Congress passed a joint resolution demanding that he be tried for war crimes.[3] However, General Douglas MacArthur—Supreme Commander for the Allied Powers (SCAP)—and his staff wanted to spare the emperor from the war trials and use him for their own political and military expediency.[4] Thus, the American occupiers were interested in finding the answers to one particular question: If the emperor possessed the power to stop the war on August 15, 1945 (as he did through his *seidan* [sacred imperial decision] to end the war), why did he permit the war to start in the first place?[5] Finding the answer to this particular question was vitally important to MacArthur and his staff and reflected their own assumptions and preoccupations.

In the end, the emperor was excluded from the entire process of the Tokyo war crimes trial and became the most useful ally of SCAP's reform efforts in occupied Japan. The Tokyo tribunal placed the blame for a reckless and aggressive war on the military, the ultranationalists, and the *zaibatsu* (financial cliques). The verdicts of the war crimes tribunal provided the basis for the postwar orthodoxy that portrayed Emperor Hirohito as a peace-loving constitutional monarch, who could not prevent the military from starting aggressive wars in Asia and the Pacific but who was nevertheless able to preserve his defeated nation from annihilation through his decision to end the war in August 1945. But the basic question—why did the emperor permit the war to begin in the first place?—was never fully answered at the time and haunted him thereafter.

Over the past seventy years, numerous analyses by Japanese scholars and journalists have kept within the bounds of the generally accepted postwar interpretation of the emperor, although their arguments reflect various shadings and show the authors' sensibilities to the complexity and nuances of the issue. Such Japanese studies explicitly or implicitly reinforce the orthodox view of Emperor Hirohito as a peace-minded constitutional monarch, and this view dominated the general public's perception of his role in the Pacific War. However, some conservative scholars, politicians, and news media—in an effort to revitalize Japanese nationalism—have taken this interpretation to the extreme, trying to perpetuate the myth of the emperor as a sacred monarch who saved the nation of Japan.[6]

More recently, leftist historians in Japan have challenged what they call the "Tokyo Trial view" of history advocated by so-called palace group historians and have criticized the emperor's failure to take responsibility for starting the war. This leftist interpretation of Emperor Hirohito gained momentum after his death in January 1989. Utilizing primary sources that became available in the 1990s—including diaries, letters, memoirs by persons close to the emperor, and records of the emperor's own words—the postwar generation of leftist historians has been trying to bring the emperor to trial in the court of history. By focusing on his role as *daigensui* (commander in chief) and on his relationship with the military, these historians have been partially successful in portraying Hirohito as a more active military commander than the postwar Japanese public has traditionally been led to believe.[7]

Meanwhile, studies by Western scholars (that is, studies published in English but based on Japanese primary sources) tend to support a Tokyo Trial view of Emperor Hirohito's role in war decisions. These scholars have generally been more sympathetic to the dilemmas faced by the emperor than have been Japanese leftist historians. For example, Robert J. C. Butow, David A. Titus, Stephen S. Large, and Peter Wetzler all have aptly demonstrated that Japan's prewar decision-making process under the Meiji Constitution was a pluralistic and consensus-oriented system that involved the participation of ruling elite groups. These scholars all reflect Maruyama Masao's argument that under the pluralistic consensus-oriented system, each participant's individual responsibility was ambiguous throughout the process of negotiation and compromise that led to a final national-level decision.[8]

Butow's impressive works on Japan and the Pacific War have given us foundational arguments regarding Emperor Hirohito's role in Japan's war decisions. In *Tojo and the Coming of the War*, Butow showed that Emperor Hirohito was personally against going to war with the United States; but the same study also showed that the emperor's influence was limited and he could not reverse the unanimous decision for war by the military and the Tojo cabinet.[9] Butow's classic 1954 work, *Japan's Decision to Surrender*, offered a masterful narrative of the extraordinary circumstances in the summer of 1945 that allowed the emperor's decision to end the war to become a state decision. Butow provided an enduring definition of the nature of the emperor's power: "Although the trend of the decision should be ascribed to the personal preference of the man himself, the real significance of the role of the Emperor lies in *the influence of the Throne* and not in the authority or personality of its occupant. Despite the wording of the Constitution, the Emperor had never possessed the actual power to decide on war or peace. Even under the pressing circumstances of August 1945, the Emperor was only the instrument, and not the prime mover, of Japan's momentous decision."[10]

Another scholar, David A. Titus, has persuasively demonstrated several important points: first, that in 1941, with the lord keeper of the privy seal, Kido Koichi,[11] as a negotiator between the court and the government, the court "provided the all-important negotiation and ratification mechanism at the apex of the political process"; and second, that the emperor did play a role as the ultimate "ratifier" and "unifier" of national policies after his officials reached consensus. In Titus's argument, before the emperor ratified any policy, he made sure that the policy had been "thoroughly discussed and represented a genuine consensus among the policy makers." The palace, where the holder of the transcendental and immutable imperial will resided, was to serve as "an inviolable sanctuary for the resolution of political conflict." At the same time, Titus pointed out that the emperor "was kept from active and direct participation in the consensus-making process by formalities and precedents governing his relations with government leaders, individually and collectively." Therefore, Titus argued, "the palace acted as a brake on extremism throughout its prewar existence." However, Titus's study focused mostly on political decisions and did not offer a detailed examination of the emperor's role as *daigensui* (commander in chief) or of the emperor's relationship with the military. Although Peter Wetzler illuminated Emperor Hirohito's active involvement in the military decision-making process (as the commander in chief), Wetzler did not deny the interpretation of pluralistic and consensus-oriented decision making in prewar Japan.[12]

However, scholars and journalists critical of SCAP's decision to spare the emperor from the Tokyo Trial argue that the emperor, as the absolute monarch, was responsible for authorizing the war and that his hesitation to authorize war on the eve of the attack on Pearl Harbor was not because of his commitment to peace, but because of his fear of defeat by the United States. Reflecting this point of view, Herbert Bix's Pulitzer Prize–winning *Hirohito and the Making of Modern Japan* (2000) suggests that the emperor was a real war leader who was actively involved in the decision-making process prior to and throughout the war. Bix criticized the emperor for possessing a "stubborn personality" and argued that the emperor's obsession with the preservation of the imperial house and his own survival, in the end, prolonged Japan's hopeless war and caused more misery and suffering for the Japanese people.[13]

The contrast between these opposing interpretations of the role of Emperor Hirohito—both in Japan and the United States—is remarkable. This suggests that historical accuracy may have been compromised in the midst of a long-running and highly politicized partisan controversy. Because the prewar Meiji Constitution designated the emperor as sovereign head of state and commander in chief of the Japanese imperial forces, there is no doubt that the emperor—even as a ruler in name only—must share some responsibility for the war, on moral if not legal grounds. If his authority was derived primarily from his symbolic position, one could even argue that, precisely because of his symbolic value, the emperor should have taken a symbolic action to accept his responsibility for war—not as an individual, but as the head of the state. In other words, even if the power of the throne was symbolic, not actual, the emperor could have taken symbolic responsibility for the war, although there would still be a need to clarify what would constitute symbolic war responsibility. In fact, available sources suggest that the emperor himself was prepared to take responsibility and to abdicate if necessary but that the circumstances under the American occupation did not allow him to make his own choice.[14] The recent discovery of the emperor's unpublished apology to his people (drafted by Tajima Michiji, head of the Imperial Household Agency from 1948 to 1953) reveals that the emperor personally felt "a deep responsibility" for the tragic outcome of the war and felt sorry for "his lack of virtue."[15] Hirohito's lifelong public silence about his own war responsibility does not necessarily mean that he felt nothing about the subject, but his silence created unfortunate negative impressions among the Japanese people and among the victims of the war.

The purpose of this book is neither to examine Emperor Hirohito's war responsibility as it might be examined in a court of law nor to ask why he failed to take public responsibility for the war. Rather, its main objective is to reexamine and reevaluate Emperor Hirohito's role in the Pacific War and to offer a realistic reappraisal of two highly politicized and exaggerated interpretations of history: on the one hand, that the emperor was a pacifist constitutional monarch; and on the other hand, that he was an absolute monarch and commander in chief, who actively participated in Japan's war venture in Asia and the Pacific. It is also important for postwar generations to recognize that their views of Emperor Hirohito are still affected by the historical myths and propaganda that were promoted on both sides of the Pacific during the war years. For example, some may still be subtly influenced by photographs of Hirohito as "divine" commander in chief on a white horse inspecting his troops; and some may be influenced by seeing Hollywood war propaganda films, in which the emperor's image is lined up next to Adolf Hitler and Benito Mussolini, as three evils of the Axis Powers. And others may be influenced by images of a "humanized" emperor in modest civilian attire personally greeting individual Japanese in his tours of the defeated Japan.

Many scholars have pointed out that the emperor's dichotomous images—the divine and the humanized—stemmed from the ambiguous nature of the power he possessed under the prewar political system in Japan. In her book *The Dual-Image of the Japanese Emperor*, Kiyoko Takeda suggests that the reason for these diametrically opposing images lies in "the contradictory nature of the modern Japanese emperor system itself."[16] Before the war, Japanese political and military leaders were themselves divided between ultranationalists, who believed the emperor to be a living deity as well as the core of national polity (*kokutai*), and liberal intellectuals, who promoted constitutional monarchism under the so-called emperor organ theory: "The historical development of modern Japan demonstrates in some areas the harmony of the two approaches, sometimes in tension, sometimes in balance, under the leadership of a capable 'charioteer,' and in other areas we find disunity of disruption between the two, each viewpoint seeking, often violently, its own way according to its own logic."[17]

During the turbulent decades of the 1930s and 1940s, when "capable charioteers" disappeared from Japanese politics, it may be argued that the emperor himself was forced to act as the national charioteer. Although it is well known that Hirohito admired the British model of constitutional monarchy, historian Peter Wetzler observes that the emperor "advocated British constitutional norms not only as a model for governing but, more important, to preserve, protect, and legitimize in modern terms the imperial line and the supreme position of his house in Japanese society." Wetzler argues that Hirohito "participated in consensus decisions as a traditional leader in Japan often does: as an important member of a group of prewar power brokers who made political and military decisions." However, Wetzler adds, "at the same time the decision-making process precluded him [the emperor] from unilaterally determining policies as a president or dictator in the West would do. Therefore, Hirohito could simultaneously explain himself and justify his actions, or lack of action, in terms of Western constitutional monarchy."[18]

This study shares a general research perspective used by some other scholars, in that it places Emperor Hirohito within the unique, pluralistic decision-making process of the leadership of prewar Japan while acknowledging the contradictory and ambiguous powers he possessed. In order to understand the nature and extent of the power he could actually exercise to make war decisions in the political system of prewar Japan, it will be important to reexamine the reality of the power relations and negotiations between the emperor and the high-level political power centers that surrounded him and influenced his actions.

Japanese political historian Masumi Junnosuke, who tries to take a judicious middle approach, suggests that the prewar Japanese emperor was a robot neither of the government nor of the military. Masumi argues that Emperor Hirohito possessed far more power than a purely ceremonial constitutional monarch and that the emperor was, in fact, at the center of Japan's decision-making process. Masumi explains that during the final stages of governmental decision making, the emperor could draw on his own great authority, knowledge, and experience to influence the decisions by asking questions (*gokamon*) or by conveying his personal wishes during his audiences with government officials and military leaders.[19]

Although this study generally agrees with Masumi's interpretation, it modifies his argument on one important point. Compared to the almost unlimited power held by the throne under the Meiji Constitution, Emperor Hirohito, in reality, occupied a precarious and ambiguous position that existed above the highly complicated relations of a powerful political triangle composed of three sometimes competing power centers: court advisers and senior statesmen (*jushin*); government ministers and bureaucrats; and military leaders. Unlike his grandfather (Emperor Meiji) and his father (Emperor Taisho), Hirohito could not draw on guidance and support from the powerful Meiji oligarchs known as *genro* (senior statesmen), who had been the architects of the Meiji Restoration of 1868 and had continued to control all three power centers during the reigns of the Meiji and Taisho emperors. The triangular power struggle was further complicated by divisions within each group between the moderates and the hardline ultranationalists and militarists. To make the situation even more complicated, the military's decisions were constrained by a twofold division within the military organization—namely, a division stemming from interservice rivalry between the army and the navy, and another division between moderate senior officers and younger militant groups within each military branch.[20] Moreover, the power of each faction within the triangular relationship was influenced, not only by domestic conditions within Japan, but also by the situation on the war fronts of Asia and the Pacific islands and by an international environment over which Japan had little control.

Although some positions of the key individuals in these three groups overlapped (for example, Okada Keisuke, Konoe Fumimaro, Tojo Hideki, and Suzuki Kantaro), Hirohito, who was placed in the middle of these competing forces, many of which were trying to take Japan in divergent directions, served as *the only formal link and convergent point* of all these power centers, which could be simultaneously split from one another or intertwined, while they were divided within themselves. The emperor's effectiveness at any particular time depended upon which of the three power centers had the strongest pull in a three-way political tug-of-war. For the turbulent war years of the 1930s and the first half of the 1940s, it is especially important to reexamine the relationship between the emperor and the military, as many Japanese leftist historians have done, in order to understand the emperor's relations with the aforementioned three power centers. During this period, as Japan's military operations expanded in Asia, it was the emperor alone who received official reports from both government officials and the military. Although the imperial army and navy did not require the central government's approval to carry out military operations, the armed forces did have to obtain a formal imperial sanction from Emperor Hirohito as commander in chief for every major strategic decision. As this study will show, between the emperor and the military (especially the army) lay complex networks of ambivalent loyalties, both personal and organizational. Although military officers had internalized the virtue of unquestioned loyalty to the emperor, they also had the audacity to believe that their expert knowledge made their judgment superior to that of the emperor when he disagreed with their recommendations. The military officers circumvented the emperor's opposition on the grounds that he had been misled by his court advisers and by politicians. By the mid-1930s the emperor became fully cognizant of the army's habitual failure to comply with his wishes: in fact, on a number of occasions the military did not follow the emperor's orders that were formally supported by the supreme command in Tokyo.

It is also important to reexamine the influence of the court advisers who surrounded the emperor in the palace. After the government, military, and court advisers had reached a consensus, the emperor's personal opinion carried little weight, and imperial audiences and conferences would often result in something that was "all show, mere eyewash for the public," as the emperor recalled in his 1946 "Monologue."[21] However, in some circumstances, as when the government and the military disagreed over important national issues such as war and peace, the emperor and his court advisers could collectively tip the power balance one way or the other. In such cases, Emperor Hirohito sought advice from court advisers, such as the *genro*, lord keeper of the privy seal, imperial household minister, grand chamberlain, *jushin*, and senior members of the imperial family.

Because of the important role that court advisers played in the complicated power dynamics, it will be necessary to reexamine the significance of the declining influence of court advisers during the 1930s. The last surviving *genro*, Saionji Kinmochi, became more feeble and less engaged; and a series of assassinations, as well as failed attempts at military coups d'état (notably the February 26 Incident of 1936), eliminated or silenced the moderating influence of the leading court advisers. Leftist historian Fujiwara Akira's seminal study of the court (*kyuchu*) group suggests that the new generation of court advisers with aristocratic backgrounds, who had formed a leadership circle known as the Juichi-kai, began to occupy important political positions and exercise considerable political influence at court. This group included Kido Koichi, Konoe Fumimaro, Harada Kumao, and Matsudaira Yasumasa, among others.[22]

A fresh examination of Emperor Hirohito's fluid place in the middle of the Japanese power triangle partially confirms Robert Butow's enduring conclusions that "the real significance of the role of the Emperor lies in *the influence of the Throne* and not in the authority or personality of its occupant." However, this study modifies Butow's conclusion that "the Emperor was only the instrument, and not the prime mover, of Japan's momentous decision."[23] The question that remains is whether the emperor's personal opinions and actions made any difference in Japan's critical decisions on war and peace. Although the young emperor's personal views and actions are considered here, from the aftermath of the Paris Peace Conference of 1919 to the Sino-Japanese War, the main focus of this book is the role that the emperor played during the period from Japan's decision to go to war with the United States in 1941 through its decision to surrender in August 1945. By examining newly available historical records, as well as reevaluating the well-known sources often cited in existing literature on Emperor Hirohito, we will see that during the war years Hirohito was neither an active absolute monarch who initiated aggressive policies in pursuit of his own interests nor a ceremonial monarch and passive observer who, like a sponge, absorbed what he was told but never did anything about it.

This book provides a realistic reappraisal of Emperor Hirohito as an individual who was, by the accident of his birth, placed in Japan's highest position and who was charged with protecting Japan's national polity (*kokutai*). In carrying out his almost superhuman responsibilities, the emperor had to coordinate his multiple roles as a constitutional monarch, commander in chief, and spiritual leader of Japan. The person who emerges from this study is a more complex historical figure than found in other works on the subject. Hirohito was a politically astute man who possessed the ability to make his own judgments with considerable objectivity. Viewed in a positive light, he was an intelligent, rational, and moderate monarch who had good intentions to fulfill his patriotic duty to preserve Japan's national polity; but viewed in a negative light, the emperor was rigid, conformist, conservative, and reserved and tended to be overly cautious and even timid because he feared the possible negative consequences of his actions. We need to remember that he was a person, not a machine with perfectly consistent behavior. He may have exhibited certain behavioral patterns, but it is difficult to find a clear-cut model to explain the role the emperor played. Throughout the war years, Hirohito struggled to deal with the heavy burden of undefined and ambiguous powers bestowed upon him as a monarch, often juggling contradictory positions and irreconcilable differences among government and military leaders. The biggest question Emperor Showa faced was the fundamental choice between war and peace. He was by no means a pacifist, but he was opposed to the reckless wars that the military leaders advocated. The portrait that emerges from this critical reappraisal of Emperor Hirohito during the most turbulent years in modern Japanese history is that of a lonely monarch who struggled to maintain balance and moderation in an environment marked by feuds between battling factions within the ruling elites and within the military.

In spite of the difficult political environment in which he found himself and the limits to his own authority, available sources suggest that the emperor did occasionally express his personal opinions, through both formal and informal channels. This was especially true during periods of national crisis—for example, after 1928, during the unauthorized activities of the Japanese army in China; after the army's February 1936 coup d'état attempt in Tokyo; throughout the long tortuous period during which Japan's leadership discussed the decision to go to war with the United States; and finally, when Japan's leadership decided to end the war. This book reexamines the emperor's willingness to express himself and asks how and to what extent his personal opinions influenced major state decisions on war and peace in the Pacific. If the emperor was against war with the United States and Great Britain, as numerous sources suggest, did his personal opposition to war make any difference in the course of events in the fall of 1941? If the emperor favored an early end to the war in the Pacific, as evidence shows, how was his personal voice transformed into a state decision? The ultimate question, therefore, concerns the reversal of the American question asked by General Douglas MacArthur and his team at the close of the war: if, as we will see, the emperor could not stop Japan from going to war in the first place, how and why was he able to play a critical role in ending the war through his *seidan*?

※

From the end of the Pacific War until his death in 1989, Emperor Hirohito remained publicly silent about his personal feelings and his responsibility for his country's devastating war ventures. To study his thoughts and actions with regard to the war, historians need to be aware of the limitations of available sources. First of all, one must be mindful that the historical narratives of the role Emperor Hirohito played in the Pacific War were influenced by the Tokyo war crimes trial and by the special postwar domestic and international circumstances surrounding the Japanese imperial house—especially in the context of US-Japanese relations throughout the Cold War. Indeed, SCAP's question on the eve of the Tokyo Trial—if the emperor possessed the power to stop the war on August 15, 1945, why did he permit the war to start in the first place?— itself created a distorted lens through which many historians have been led to examine the beginnings and the conclusion of the Pacific War.

This scholarly bias has, in turn, helped shape the popular memory and image of Hirohito. For instance, today the Japanese public mostly remembers the emperor for his unprecedented radio announcement of August 15, 1945, in which he himself announced his *seidan* that Japan must end the war to save the nation—and all of humanity—from total extinction by the atomic bomb. This continuing myth—that the American atomic bombs on Hiroshima and Nagasaki forced the emperor to issue the *seidan* to surrender—is imprinted on the collective memory of the Japanese people. And in the United States (despite numerous studies that show the contrary), the majority of the American people still accept the official US explanation that the atomic bombs were the means for ending the war swiftly. Thus, Emperor Hirohito's radio announcement became the convergent point for two myths—that is, that the US atomic bomb, as well as Emperor Hirohito, served as peacemakers.[24] Certainly, many historians are astute enough to guard themselves against myths and scholarly bias. However, when it comes to the use of sources, especially the testimonies and memoirs of the emperor's contemporaries, it is not always easy to distinguish between historical records (which show *what actually happened*) from individuals' retrospective recollections (which show how these individuals *want later generations to remember what happened*).

Therefore, besides avoiding the dangerous trap of taking sides in today's highly politicized controversy over the extent of Emperor Hirohito's war responsibility, historians must also deal with the difficulty of interpreting the available historical sources. That is, the emperor himself left very few available primary sources, and a stigma is attached to the reliability of the formal testimonies and memoirs of the people who surrounded Emperor Hirohito. It is well known that the Japanese government and military destroyed many sensitive war-related documents before the Allied occupation began in September 1945. Some Japanese historians and journalists have speculated that prewar and wartime reports submitted to the emperor by government and military leaders, as well as the emperor's own writings, may still be stored somewhere in the palace or in the Imperial Household Agency's archives— if any of these documents survived at all. However, the public has limited access to the archival material held by the Imperial Household Agency and thus has no way of ascertaining exactly what kind of materials pertaining to the emperor's involvement in the war may be held in the agency's archives.

The only written record of Emperor Hirohito's own recollections available to the public, the document in which he addressed himself in the first person, is what came to be known as "The Showa Emperor Monologue" (Showa tenno dokuhakuroku). On the eve of the Tokyo Trial, five times between March 18 and April 8, 1946, the emperor summoned and spoke to his trusted aides about his recollections of the events prior to and during the Pacific War. It is unknown what happened to the official record of the emperor's dictation, entitled "Records of the Emperor's Conversations" (Seidan haichoroku), which was produced by Inada Shuichi, the director of the Imperial Palace Records Bureau. The official annals of Emperor Showa (*Showa tenno jitsuroku*), edited by the Imperial Household Agency and released to the public in 2014, acknowledge that nine volumes of "Records of the Emperor's Conversations" were produced, but these volumes are never quoted in the annals. The agency has not clarified whether "Records of the Emperor's Conversations" has survived to this day or where it is stored.[25] However, another record, written by Terasaki Hidenari, did survive and was published by Terasaki's daughter in 1990.[26] The draft of the first page of the missing "Records of the Emperor's Conversations," discovered along with Vice Grand Chamberlain Kinoshita Michio's diary, suggests that Terasaki's version of the emperor's "Monologue" is considerably abridged but accurately conveys the gist of what the emperor said.[27]

There is no doubt that the emperor's "Monologue" was prepared in anticipation of the Tokyo war crimes trial, but this does not automatically diminish the reliability of the emperor's testimony, as some of his critics have suggested. Those who simply dismiss the "Monologue" as a defensive reaction to the imminent war trials need to carefully review the emperor's personal attitude toward the issue of war responsibility and should look at the circumstances in which he came to dictate his "Monologue." On August 29, 1945, the day after the first of the Allied occupation forces landed on the Atsugi airbase, Kido Koichi, the lord keeper of the privy seal, wrote in his diary that the emperor had told Kido that he (Hirohito) was prepared to assume the nation's responsibility for the war and to abdicate if this could stop Japan's wartime leaders from being handed over to the Allies as war criminals.[28] By the time the emperor began dictating the "Monologue" in mid-March 1946, he had received strong indications from General MacArthur's staff that he would not himself be prosecuted for war crimes. According to the diary of Kinoshita Michio, as early as January 1, 1946 (the day the emperor issued his "declaration of humanity"), the emperor learned from Kinoshita that the SCAP blueprint proposed the preservation of the imperial status of the emperor and his three brothers without granting them real political power.[29]

Apparently, this information came as a great relief to the court, but in early January the emperor was still anxious to know if SCAP wished him to abdicate. On March 20, the second day of the emperor's "Monologue" dictation session, Terasaki Hidenari, who had been working since late January as liaison between the court and SCAP's military secretary, Brigadier General Bonner F. Fellers, brought vital information to the emperor: SCAP had no desire to put him on trial for his war responsibilities or any wish to ask him to abdicate. With this information in hand, the emperor and his aides, including Terasaki, resumed the second of the five dictations that comprised

the "Monologue," which began chronologically with the issues surrounding
the Abe cabinet and the signing of the Tripartite Pact in 1940.[30] Therefore,
it is possible to argue that Emperor Hirohito did not have to worry about
his own fate at the coming war trials while he was dictating the remainder
of the "Monologue."

However, there still remained the possibility that the emperor might have
to testify at the trials, and he was deeply concerned about the fate of those
who had served him and were about to be prosecuted as war criminals. This
timing explains why moderate historians like Masumi regard the emper-
or's "Monologue" positively, calling it "quite candid," while leftist historians
argue that the emperor repeatedly made statements in the "Monologue" that
could incriminate him.[31] The emperor's harshest critics among Japanese leftist historians generally accept the accuracy of the emperor's words in the
"Monologue," because he did not hesitate to state his personal interventions
in governmental and military decision-making processes that might prove
his influence over the course Japan followed before and during the war.

Many chamberlains who served the emperor in the postwar period also
left accounts of the emperor's desire to convey his true feelings about the war
to the public and his agony about not being able to do so. According to the
diary of Irie Sukemasa, who served as chamberlain beginning in 1934 and
became grand chamberlain in 1969, Emperor Hirohito resumed dictating his
recollections of the war to Irie in order to expand "Records of the Emperor's
Conversations," doing so until right before Irie passed away in 1985. Although
the existence of the emperor's dictation to Irie is not officially acknowledged
and it is not available to the public, the fact that Emperor Hirohito continued
to record his recollections about the war indicates that he was conscious
of the historical significance of his role and that he wanted to provide an
enduring record.

Therefore, the "Monologue" can be a valuable primary source if one
carefully checks the accuracy of the emperor's remarks by examining other
historical records. Some of the most useful primary sources consulted here
include diaries of Makino Nobuaki, Kido Koichi, Prince Takamatsu, Nara
Takeji, Honjo Shigeru, Harada Kumao, Takagi Sokichi, Kinoshita Michio, and
Sugiyama Gen; the confidential war diary by the army's war guidance section;
and the memoirs and personal notes by Shigemitsu Mamoru, Togo Shigenori,
Konoe Fumimaro, and several military officers. The sixty-one-volume official
annals of Emperor Showa (*Showa tenno jitsuroku*), released by the Imperial
Household Agency in the fall of 2014, also provided additional information

to understand Emperor Hirohito's daily activities and the timeline and circumstances in which he acted during the turbulent years of Showa.

CHAPTER 1

The Aftermath of the
Paris Peace Conference,
1919—1933

I N 1919, IN THE WAKE OF WORLD WAR I, THE PARIS PEACE CON-
ference was a turning point in world history—or, as historian Margaret
MacMillan calls it, the "six months that changed the world." The conference meant different things to different countries. From the United States'
perspective, it was a battlefield for ideas about a new world order: Ray Stannard Baker, spokesperson for US president Woodrow Wilson, stated that the
peace conference was a contest between the Old Diplomacy of imperialism
and the New Diplomacy of Wilsonian liberal internationalism. According
to historian N. Gordon Levin Jr., the conference was a three-party race,
with European conservative imperialism on the right, socialism and communism on the left, and Wilsonian liberal capitalist internationalism in
the middle. In the colonial world, the "Wilsonian Moment," in the words
of historian Erez Manela, inspired anticolonial nationalists to found a wide
range of organizations bent on self-determination and decolonization. In
the trans-Pacific region, World War I and the subsequent peace at Paris
produced the tipping point that strained relations between the two naval
powers, the United States and Japan. Japanese leaders, who had been studying the realpolitik of the European game of imperialism, were alarmed by the
success of the Bolshevik revolution in Russia and at the same time became
apprehensive about the prospect of a new, Western-centered, Wilsonian
world order. By the war's end, opposing worldviews had emerged between

the Wilson administration and Japan's leadership. While President Wilson was promoting Anglo-American-style internationalism as a universal model, Japan, driven by its sense of national and racial identity, as well as by its sense of vulnerability in the new era of total warfare, was moving toward an anti-Western and particularistic regionalism, with a focus on Asia. The tragic aspect of Japan's regionalism was the military's attempt to pursue an autarkic state at the expense of China and other Asian neighbors.[1]

The problems began in 1919, for the Japanese delegation to Paris was poorly prepared to face the new challenges of the liberal Wilsonian peace program. The Japanese leadership's priority at the peace table was to legitimize the Asia-Pacific footholds that Japan had won from Germany during the war: that is, the German concessions in Shandong, China; and the German islands in the Pacific, north of the equator. However, the Japanese delegation encountered unexpectedly strong opposition from President Wilson, who was determined to protect the Open Door policy in China. The Japanese delegates fought hard to secure the territory Japan had taken from Germany, even at the expense of alienating the governments of the United States and China. Japanese leaders in Tokyo, although they suspected the League of Nations to be largely an attempt by Western powers to dominate the new international order, reluctantly allowed their delegates to join the league for fear of diplomatic isolation. At the same time, both the delegation and the Tokyo leadership were reminded of the harsh reality of Japan's inferior position in the new, Western-dominated world order. Neither the United States nor Japan's ally, Britain, supported Japan's proposal to insert a clause supporting racial equality into the Covenant of the League of Nations. Overall, Japan's experience at Paris in 1919 left most of the Japanese leadership in Tokyo with a negative opinion of the peace conference. However, Japan's chief delegates—the men who were in the forefront of diplomacy at Paris (Genro Saionji Kinmochi, Makino Nobuaki, and Chinda Sutemi), along with Prime Minister Hara Takashi (Kei) in Tokyo—understood that cooperation with the Western powers was essential for Japan's survival. Thus, in post-1919 Japan, there emerged two divergent visions of Japan's role in the world: one held by those who believed in international accommodation; the other held by those who wanted to build a self-sustaining Japanese empire in Asia.

THE YOUNG CROWN PRINCE

Hirohito, the future emperor of Japan, was an eighteen-year-old crown prince at the time of the Paris Peace Conference. During the seven years between 1914 and 1921, while the world underwent tremendous changes (World War I, the Russian Revolution, and the Paris Peace Conference and its aftermath), the crown prince and five classmates, selected by the Imperial Household Ministry, received a secondary-school education at a special academy known as the Togu Gogakumonjo (Academy in the Eastern Palace). Besides subjects commonly taught in most Japanese middle schools in the 1910s, the crown prince also had to take special classes in military science, horsemanship, and, most important of all, in *teiogaku* (learning for the emperor, imperial studies, or imperial ethics), a course of study designed to prepare the crown prince for his future role as emperor of Japan. Crown Prince Hirohito was especially interested in the military and political history of Europe, international politics, and domestic security issues.[2] Of this period in the young prince's life, Kanroji Osanaga (court chamberlain for seventy years, from 1890 to1959), later noted in his memoir, "Since the time he [Hirohito] was a very young man he studied ancient and modern history as well as monarchial history."[3]

How did young Crown Prince Hirohito see Japan's place in the rapidly changing world after the Paris Peace Conference? Although sources on his reaction to international affairs during his formative years are scarce, it is apparent that Hirohito's original views on the new world order, views inspired by the Wilsonian idealism of the Paris Peace Conference, changed dramatically over the next two and a half decades. In 1920, the crown prince optimistically welcomed the new international order, symbolized by the establishment of the League of Nations, and expressed his conviction of the importance of cooperating with the Western powers. However, in 1946, after Japan's devastating defeat in World War II, Emperor Hirohito's ex post facto comments on the impacts of the Versailles system on Japan were conspicuously negative. During the period between the 1919 Paris Peace Conference and Japan's withdrawal from the League of Nations in March 1933, an ominous series of domestic and international emergencies began to challenge and transform the emperor's views.

March 1933 became a significant turning point for Japan because the government's decision to withdraw from the League of Nations signaled Japan's intent to depart from a policy of accommodation with Western powers and to pursue an independent path, especially in East Asia. The events that led to Japan's withdrawal from the League of Nations affected the emperor's youthful, optimistic views of international cooperation with Western powers and made him aware of the harsh realities of achieving international accommodation. By the time of Japan's withdrawal from the League of Nations, even though the emperor had not considered the Versailles-Washington system as an impediment to the advancement of Japan's national interests, he no longer felt that he could insist on international accommodation at the expense of domestic opposition. His primary concern was domestic political stability.

※

In January 1920, after the Japanese government ratified the Treaty of Versailles, in response to the Taisho Emperor's public announcement that peace had been established, Crown Prince Hirohito wrote an essay in his ethics class under the guidance of Sugiura Shigetake (Jugo). What is remarkable about this document is the crown prince's acute awareness of the new international trends in the wake of World War I. He first quoted the Taisho Emperor's words, which had no doubt been drafted by Prime Minister Hara and his cabinet: "Now the world trends have altered dramatically and the state of affairs is rapidly changing." Then the crown prince wrote,

> How did the world trends change? The realm of ideas in the world has become chaotic; radical thoughts are spreading throughout the world; and labor problems are rising. The peoples of the world who saw the miseries after the war are craving for peace and seeking international cooperation. Now we have witnessed the establishment of the League of Nations, and an international labor conference has been held. The world has thus changed. In these circumstances, as the emperor proclaimed, our people must persevere and make efforts to adapt themselves to the changing trends of the time.[4]

The crown prince went on to express his sense of the particular significance of the League of Nations: "I congratulate the establishment of the League of Nations. I will respect the Covenant of the League, promote its spirit, and carry out the important duty to establish eternal peace in the world. What should I do to fulfill this duty? If we show our tolerance as members of the empire, consider each country's well-being and rule with moderation and cooperation [with other powers], and follow international law and world trends, we should be able to attain lasting peace."[5]

These words by Crown Prince Hirohito emphasize international cooperation and sound sympathetic to the ideas of Wilsonian internationalism, but it is important to note that the original Japanese terms he used to express the spirit of international cooperation came from Confucian terms for harmony. This may be partly a result of limited choice, within the Japanese vocabulary, in translating Wilsonian concepts originally expressed in English, but it may also be due to the emphasis placed on Confucianism by his ethics teacher, Sugiura. Evidence of this latter possibility lies in the last section of the essay, in which the crown prince added a typical Confucian warning not to lose the virtues of austerity and frugality: "Now our country is drifting toward arrogance and luxury. Today this is the point that we must pay special attention to."[6]

The other important aspect of the crown prince's essay is that his teachers and advisers seem to have inculcated in him a strong sense of nationalism and patriotism, in the tradition of the Meiji slogan "Fukoku kyohei" (Rich country, strong military). This slogan was a harsh reminder that Japan, as a non-Western late developer, must unite and survive in a hostile international environment controlled by Western imperialist powers. Quoting his father's declaration that "[Japan] must adapt itself to the trend of the time by strengthening its national power," the crown prince wrote, "If [Japan] fails to build a sufficient national defense, it will be unable to defend itself in case of emergency, and in the realm of diplomacy, it will be difficult to assert its national interests and secure them. Japan will not become a wealthy country unless it promotes and grows industries and transportation, and increases labor productivity. If we neglect these, we will not be able to keep up with the Western great powers." Therefore, the crown prince argued that in order to improve the fortunes of his country, the people must wholeheartedly unite and work together—upper and lower classes, military men and civilians, workers and capitalists. He concluded his essay by saying that he who "will be entrusted with an important duty of leading the nation in the future" must keep these points in mind and contribute to the peace and prosperity of the country.[7]

The thinking expressed in Hirohito's essay is similar to that of the three Japanese chief delegates to the Paris Peace Conference: Saionji Kinmochi, Makino Nobuaki, and Chinda Sutemi. The government of Prime Minister Hara, the leading advocate of international accommodation, selected these men to represent Japan at the Paris talks because of their international experience, their familiarity with the way the Western powers operated, and their personal connections with the leaders of the Allied Powers. At that time, these three men were also known within Japan as advocates of cooperation with Britain and the United States (i.e., a pro-Anglo-American faction, or Ei-bei-ha). Perhaps the best way to understand these delegates is to view them as "international accommodationists."[8] That is, although the delegates were patriotic defenders of Japan's national interests, and although they believed in Japan's superiority and its special place in Asia, they also understood the wisdom of the idea of *taisei junnō* (conformity to world trends). The Japanese delegates to Paris, especially Makino Nobuaki, more than once urged the Hara cabinet in Tokyo to take a more conciliatory position on Japanese claims; and in the end, the delegates were instrumental in persuading Tokyo that Japan should join the League of Nations.

This approach to international relations greatly influenced Hirohito, for in the years following the Paris Peace Conference, these three men became the crown prince's closest advisers. For example, Makino Nobuaki became minister of the imperial household in February 1921, and his importance as adviser to the crown prince was crucial after Prime Minister Hara was assassinated by a young ultranationalist on November 4 of the same year. Three weeks after the assassination, on November 25, Crown Prince Hirohito took over his father's duties as regent (*sesshō*) under Makino's political guidance. Makino went on to assume the position of the lord keeper of the privy seal in March 1925, and after Hirohito ascended to the throne on December 25, 1926, Makino continued to serve the young emperor as his closest adviser until December 1935. There is no doubt that Makino played a critical role in defining the emperor's role in Japan's power structure or that he exerted tremendous influence over Hirohito in the early years of his reign, as the emperor came to understand his role as Japan's sovereign and to develop his own views about Japan's role in the world.

Chinda Sutemi, another member of the Paris delegation, also had considerable influence over Hirohito. Chinda was one of the most distinguished diplomats in Japan and had served as Japan's minister to Germany, the United States, and Great Britain. He accompanied the crown prince for six months in 1921, as his chief attendant, during the prince's unprecedented and historic tour in Europe. After returning to Japan, Chinda continued to serve the crown prince in the Eastern Palace, and he later served as Emperor Hirohito's grand chamberlain from 1927 until his (Chinda's) death in 1929.

The nominal but prestigious head of the Paris delegation, Prince Saionji, known as "the last *genro* [elder statesman],"[9] was Japan's most influential court noble and senior politician. He served as the most respected guiding force of the imperial court, as well as holding great influence among party politicians, throughout the 1920s and 1930s.

Throughout the 1930s, Makino and Saionji were seen as committed international accommodationists: they provided a moderating influence on Japanese politics and helped restrain reckless military adventurism on the Asian continent. Because of their views, both men were targets of assassination attempts by army extremists in the May 15 Incident of 1932 and the February 26 Incident of 1936 (which they narrowly escaped). One can safely assume that these two advisers continued to encourage Emperor Hirohito to keep faith in the possibility of international cooperation with Western powers, along the lines that the emperor had expressed in his student essay on the ratification of the Treaty of Versailles.

However, two and a half decades later, shortly after Japan surrendered to the Allied Powers in World War II, Emperor Hirohito made another—very different—comment about the peace made at Paris in 1919. This time, the context was entirely different: in the spring of 1946, the emperor spoke to five of his trusted aides, dictating his recollection of the turbulent years that led to the devastating wars in Asia and the Pacific (presumably as part of his preparation for the coming war crimes trials by the Allied Powers). Contrary to the opinions expressed in his 1920 essay, Emperor Hirohito's 1946 retrospective opinion about the consequence of the Paris Peace Conference was negative. According to two separate records, written by the aides Kinoshita Michio and Terasaki Hidenari, the emperor traced the origins of Japan's wars in Asia and the Pacific to the outcome of the 1919 peace conference.

Terasaki's version of this meeting, now known as "The Showa Emperor Monologue" (Showa tenno dokuhakuroku), starts with words attributed to the emperor: "The long-term cause [of the Greater East Asian War] lay dormant in the terms of the peace treaty after the First World War."[10] According to Kinoshita's more detailed memo, written as part of a draft of "Records of the Emperor's Conversations" (Seidan haichoroku), the emperor stated,

The Western powers rejected the Japanese people's outcries for the principle of racial equality that Japan's delegation demanded at the peace conference after the First World War, and [the Western powers] continued to practice racial discrimination between yellow and white races all over the world. Acts like anti-Japanese immigration legislation in California and the whites-only policy of Australia were enough to outrage the Japanese people, who had considerable potential to develop and grow but were suffering from the extremely limited [geographical] size of the country, from overpopulation, and from a lack of natural resources.[11]

Considering the US-led Washington treaty system created in 1921–22 as an extension of the Versailles treaty system, the emperor deplored the continuation of the Anglo-American powers' policy of containing Japan as a second-rate nation. He said, "In spite of my efforts to cultivate mutual goodwill by visiting Great Britain, immediately after my trip, the Anglo-Japanese alliance was canceled, and the Western powers' pressure to impose arms limitations on Japan continued to increase year by year and month by month. Japan was forced to return the concessions in Shandong." The emperor even blamed the Western powers for supporting China's anti-Japanese education, which he thought exacerbated the problems of the Sino-Japanese relationship. Furthermore, the emperor pointed out the existence of serious internal problems in Japan and suggested that "corrupt political parties had seriously weakened Japan's ability to deal with the adverse international environment surrounding Japan." He said, "The fear spread so widely among the Japanese people that, should Japan be entrusted to the hands of inept party politicians, its future would be in jeopardy."[12]

One can glimpse the emperor's perception of the collective sentiments of the Japanese people when he said, "In the face of a national crisis such as this, the people's sentiments tend to become unsettled." The emperor continued,

Once the military took advantage of the circumstances and rose [to power] against the backdrop of the people's discontent, it became the most difficult of all things to hold it [the military] back, even though some of the young and spirited officers who comprised the core of the military had no scruples about resorting to reckless action. It was difficult because it appeared as though these reckless and violent actions had something to do with patriotic behavior [and as though this behavior was] driven by an intent to save the nation from its own plight.

I was deeply concerned about the consequences of such violent actions and warned the highest military leaders whenever I could, but in the atmosphere of *gekokujō* [overpowering of seniors by juniors], superiors could not restrain subordinates.[13]

Emperor Hirohito sounded sincere in these 1946 recollections when he confessed that the imperial court's influence was not strong enough to stop passionate Japanese militarists from resorting to reckless and violent means, given that these young men were convinced of the righteousness of their cause—that is, in a period when the militarists saw their own patriotic motives to save their country as sincere and when they believed their means were justified. The emperor's statement reflected both his conflicted feelings about the military's aggressive response to the stance of the Western powers in the 1930s, as well as his frustration and regret that the court had been unable to exert a moderating influence over the extremism of the military. But at the same time, in the spring of 1946, the emperor's musings about the legacies of the Paris Peace Conference revealed little sympathy for a Wilsonian vision of a new world order. Rather, his words seemed to echo the resentment and frustration felt by ultranationalists and militarists over the treatment of Japan by Anglo-American powers in the 1920s and the 1930s. One senses that in the emperor's mind there was a logical progression from what happened at Paris in 1919 to Japan's fateful decision to attack Pearl Harbor in 1941. In any case, the emperor's opinions had clearly changed between 1919 and 1941. But how did he arrive at his later position? When did a more pessimistic view of history and indignation over Western powers' treatment of Japan overwhelm his earlier optimistic belief in international accommodationism?

///

After the 1919 Paris Peace Conference, the imperial court and the government in Tokyo faced a series of political crises that could have altered Japan's internal power structure. The decade of the 1920s, when Japan underwent a profound political transformation, was a very difficult period for Crown Prince Hirohito (Emperor Hirohito, after his 1926 accession to the throne). The enormous and unexpected challenges that faced the twenty-six-year-old inexperienced emperor shaped his view of the future of his country. During this period, the emperor had to deal with tremendous political and personal pressure, as he tried to maintain Japan's internal unity and stability through his sometimes conflicting roles as sovereign of the Japanese empire and as *daigensui* (commander in chief) of the Japanese imperial forces. Hirohito became especially sensitive to threats to Japan's internal security and stability, and his domestic concerns no doubt also influenced his perception of an international environment that he believed posed an increasing threat to the security of the Japanese empire.

The first two years after the Paris Peace Conference were especially tumultuous and demanding for the crown prince. Around 1916, his father, Emperor Yoshihito (Emperor Taisho), who had suffered from meningitis in his early childhood, began to lose his struggle for health. By the summer of 1919, the emperor had difficulty with walking and speaking in public. On December 26, 1919, at the opening of the annual session of the Diet (Japanese parliament), Emperor Taisho was no longer capable of reading an address that consisted of five sentences; and over the next two years, his mental and physical condition deteriorated rapidly. Political leaders at the highest level—notably the three surviving *genro*, that is, Yamagata Aritomo, Saionji Kinmochi, and Matsukata Masayoshi (who was serving as lord keeper of the privy seal); Prime Minister Hara; and Imperial Household Minister Makino—were all concerned about a potential crisis. In their view, the incapacitation of the emperor might bring into question the authority and prestige of the throne and the legitimacy of government decisions. As Crown Prince Hirohito began to take over his father's public duties, these high-level leaders agreed to move more quickly toward installing Crown Prince Hirohito as regent.[14]

The idea that the crown prince should visit Europe emerged against this backdrop: that is, Japan's political leaders wanted to establish a regency that could truly command the respect of the Japanese people and other nations. Prime Minister Hara commented in his diary on November 6, 1919, that there was an urgent need for the crown prince to act on behalf of his father, to carry out official duties such as military reviews, and that he (the prime minister) had been seriously thinking that the crown prince should have more experience in political affairs and become more accustomed to meeting with various types of people. Hara initiated the idea that the crown prince's trip to Western countries would serve as an educational opportunity, and Hara approached and secured support from the three *genro*.[15] Hara's intention was not to strengthen imperial rule, per se, but rather to promote a constitutional monarchy. As he wrote in his diary on September 2, 1920: "It is the objective of constitutional government to assume full responsibility so as not to trouble the imperial house." Hara also thought that this method was best for the emperor: "The imperial house will be safe and secure if its members refrain from becoming directly involved in political affairs and engage mainly in charitable work, giving awards and so forth."[16] Lord Privy Seal Matsukata's report to the throne in January 1921, which was designed to overcome the objections of a weary Empress Sadako, explained the rationale behind the proposed trip to the West. The report emphasized the importance of the crown prince's observing Europe and the United States firsthand, in order to broaden his worldview. It argued that the crown prince must learn from the rare opportunity to witness the devastating consequences of "the Great World War," such as "ethnic divisions," "national conflicts," and "popular movements, conflicting ideologies, [and] the rise and fall of nation states."[17]

Crown Prince Hirohito traveled through Europe for six months, from March 3 to September 3, 1921. He stayed mainly in England and France, but he also made visits, of about one week each, to Belgium, the Netherlands, and Italy. Although the original proposal included a visit to the United States, this trip did not materialize, ostensibly because the Japanese Foreign Office was afraid that diplomatic complications over the contemporary issues of Siberian intervention and the Shandong controversy might pose threats to the prince's safety. Prime Minister Hara, who considered this trip the only chance for the crown prince to visit the United States, did not share the diplomats' concern, and he regretted the decision to exclude the United States from the tour.[18]

This trip to Europe turned out to be a life-changing experience for the young crown prince. He celebrated his twentieth birthday near Gibraltar on April 29, 1921, on the naval ship *Katori*, on the voyage to England. In numerous press interviews during the postwar years, whenever asked about the most memorable event in his life, Emperor Hirohito always mentioned his 1921 trip to Europe. He also said he considered his visit to King George V and the British royal family the most valuable lesson of the trip. As the emperor later said, "George V intimately explained to me the British constitutional monarchy as it ought to be. Ever since, it has been always on my mind and I have been constantly thinking about how a monarch under a constitutional monarchy should behave."[19]

If the primary objective of this trip, as far as Prime Minister Hara and the *genro* were concerned, was to educate the crown price about the reality of world politics and about Japan's relations with the Western powers, then it seems the trip was partly successful. Under the guidance of Baron Chinda Sutemi, one of the most experienced diplomats in Japan, Crown Prince Hirohito not only absorbed the lessons of the devastating Great War (fought only three years previously in Europe) but also learned to appreciate the importance of international peace. Looking over the ruins of the Battle of Verdun in France, where more than two million soldiers perished, Hirohito was recorded to have said, "War is such a terrible thing."[20] Upon returning from the trip, he gave Prime Minister Hara a statement to be conveyed to the public. In his statement, the crown prince appeared sincere when he expressed his appreciation for the opportunity to witness the disastrous consequences of a terrible war that was still vivid in Europe. He said that "he deeply felt the need for international peace."[21] Although the crown prince realized that Japan had a unique heritage, he had observed the industrialized societies of Europe and had met with leading political, military, and intellectual leaders: he acknowledged Japan's need to learn more from the West. From this, one may safely conclude that the young crown prince had absorbed the value of international accommodationism from the statesmen—Hara, Makino, and Chinda.

At the personal level, however, what seems to have most impressed Crown Prince Hirohito were the extraordinary circumstances that allowed him to enjoy the experience of "freedom." Comparing himself to a bird in a cage, Hirohito was delighted to be able to read entire newspapers instead of only clippings. He was so thrilled to be able to ride the Paris subway that he brought back the subway ticket to Japan, where he saved it as a memento in his study's desk drawer in the imperial palace.[22] He was also delighted to be able to pay cash when he purchased souvenirs at stores. Among other purchases, at a department store in Paris he bought himself a bust of Napoleon Bonaparte, which he kept in his study, along with busts of Abraham Lincoln and Charles Darwin that he received as gifts at some points in his life.[23]

THE PRINCE REGENT

While Crown Prince Hirohito was traveling through Europe, Emperor Yoshihito's condition continued to deteriorate: it clearly was time to install a regency. Historian Nagai Kazu suggests that sometime between mid-May and mid-June 1921, Genro Yamagata, Prime Minister Hara, and Imperial Household Minister Makino reached an agreement that the crown prince would assume the position of regent when he returned from Europe.[24] However, on November 4, 1921, before the three had agreed on the date the regency would begin, Hara was assassinated by a nineteen-year-old ultranationalist.

This tragedy suddenly removed the nation's most influential leader of party politics, and Japan's historic first "party cabinet" collapsed. There were further repercussions too: eighty-three-year-old Yamagata (who still commanded the respect of the army and dominated the government bureaucracy as "cabinet maker") was deeply shocked by the assassination and died only three months later. As an apparent power vacuum spread rapidly at the highest level of the central authority, Makino had to improvise a mechanism to maintain the prestige of the imperial throne while the court sought recommendations from the surviving *genro* before appointing a new prime minister and his cabinet.

In the middle of this sudden political chaos, Japan still needed a regent. Therefore, having secured approval from both the Privy Council and the Imperial Family Council, twenty-year-old Crown Prince Hirohito became regent of Japan on November 25, 1921. Although the young prince regent was overwhelmed with the burden of his new imperial duties, there is no doubt that he also felt pressure from his own uncertainty and anxiety about the possible growth of political instability and social strife in his country.

The prince regent's duties were limited to performing ceremonial roles and signing state papers on behalf of his father. As regent, Hirohito understood that his role was to rubber-stamp the government's decisions, but through this experience he soon realized that the very process of the throne's automatic ratification of governmental decisions resulted in the transformation of these political decisions into sacred national decisions. In an unexpected way, the prince regent lived a robot-like existence in which he "reigned" without actually ruling, and during this period there is little record of involvement by the prince regent in major decisions that affected domestic and foreign policy. For example, Hirohito had little say in decisions about the Washington Conference (1921–22), a meeting that had a far-reaching impact on trans-Pacific relations in the interwar years. The prince regent thought his earlier visit to England had helped strengthen the Anglo-Japanese alliance, and he was obviously disappointed when the alliance was canceled and replaced by a loose security arrangement under the Four Power Pact. When the Prince of Wales (Edward VIII) visited Japan in the spring of 1922, Hirohito reportedly told him that "even though the bilateral alliance is replaced by the new broader arrangement of the Washington Conference, the historic friendship between the two empires will never change."[25]

The prince regent continued to worry about Japan's internal stability and well-being. The Great Kanto Earthquake of September 1, 1923, destroyed much of Tokyo and the surrounding Kanto region, killed over 100,000 people, and made over 2 million people homeless. Social unrest ensued, notably with attacks on Koreans, communists, and socialists. The people's suffering was so acute that the prince regent offered to postpone his own wedding.[26] Two months later, on December 27, 1923, the prince regent himself became the target of an assassination attempt by a young anarchist, Nanba Daisuke. While Hirohito was on his way to address the opening session of the House of Peers, Nanba fired a shot at the regent's carriage. The shot missed him but injured his grand chamberlain. Although Hirohito remained calm, and he impressed Makino and others by carrying out his duties at the Diet as though nothing had happened, a disbelieving Makino wrote in his diary that there had been "astonishing changes" in the thoughts of a small group of (Japanese) people with regard to the concept of *kokutai* (national polity).[27] Regent Hirohito conveyed similar sentiments about the attempted assassination to one of his chamberlains: "It is truly regrettable. I thought that the relationship between His Majesty and his subjects was a monarch-subject relationship in principle, but in sentiment a father-child relationship. I have always tried to be mindful of mutual affection. But witnessing today's incident, and learning that the perpetrator was a subject of His Majesty [*sekishi*], I am unbearably saddened. I want my thoughts to be thoroughly understood."[28] These words convey the young prince regent's bafflement about the incident and his frustration with the inability of the political system to preserve security and stability within Japan.

EMPEROR HIROHITO (EMPEROR SHOWA)

After Emperor Taisho died, Crown Prince Hirohito succeeded to the throne on December 25, 1926, with "Showa" as the name of his reign era. The transition was fairly smooth, with Makino Nobuaki continuing his duties as lord keeper of the privy seal, Chinda Sutemi as grand chamberlain, and Ichiki Kitokuro as imperial household minister. In addition, the last surviving *genro*, Saionji, continued to provide advice for his emperor.

Hirohito soon found himself in an almost impossible situation as he became more aware of the contradictions inherent in his new role as emperor. Under the Meiji Constitution, the sovereign in theory possessed the supreme power to sanction state decisions. However, for the five years he had been serving as regent, Hirohito consciously avoided questioning or influencing government decisions because he was acting on behalf of his father. After he became emperor, he realized that there was ambiguity and flexibility in the Japanese political system—unlike the more formally and legally restrained British constitutional monarchy that he admired as a model. In the Japanese system, Hirohito saw that a more flexible legal structure allowed the emperor to exercise his influence by using his ability to question, agree, or disagree with the government's decisions (at least under certain circumstances). As Nagai Kazu and many other Japanese historians have pointed out, as long as the Meiji Constitution defined the emperor as the ultimate entity sanctioning state decisions, nothing could prevent the emperor from possessing a degree of political will, from exercising his own judgment, or from asking indirect and subtle questions to make sure that the decisions he made as emperor were the most appropriate ones.[29] The ambiguity of the situation and the dilemma Emperor Hirohito faced had been created by the Meiji oligarchs (*genro*), who had invented a constitution that produced a hybrid between a constitutional monarchy and an absolute monarchy. This political form gave the *genro* room to maneuver behind the scenes, beyond the reach of the constitution, and to steer the country in the direction they wanted by commanding both political and military authorities. But other than Genro Saionji, by the late 1920s none of these former Meiji leaders were there to help the young emperor, and no political or military leaders could attain the level of power and prestige that the *genro* who led the Meiji Restoration could enjoy.

The new emperor also faced an extraordinary challenge in the realm of military affairs. Under the Meiji Constitution, he, as *daigensui*, had supreme command of the army and the navy: the emperor held the authority to give final approval to military orders at the highest level. During the Taisho Emperor's reign, the emperor had practically rubber-stamped all government decisions recommended by his prime ministers and cabinet officials. At the same time, this key group of officials built consensus with party politicians, government bureaucrats, and the *genro* who had tremendous influence over military organizations. As a result, the Taisho Emperor's civilian prime ministers and cabinet officials had prevailed over the military branches of government. Even during World War I, although the military held the prerogative of supreme military command, it did not challenge national decisions reached by the Advisory Council on Foreign Relations (Gaiko Chosakai), which served as the highest advisory organ to the government and was placed directly under the Taisho Emperor's command during the period of emergency from June 1917 to September 1922.

However, by the time young Emperor Hirohito became commander in chief, the balance of power between civilian and military authorities was fluctuating, at the mercy of threatening domestic conditions and a foreboding international environment. After about six months of mourning for his father, as the new emperor embarked on a demanding schedule of military ceremonies and inspections in the latter half of 1927 and through 1928,[30] he had to quickly gauge what it really meant to be commander in chief.

During this period, the closest military adviser to Emperor Hirohito was General Nara Takeji, who served as his chief military aide-de-camp from 1922 to 1933. General Nara was considered one of the army's leading experts on the West. The general had accompanied Makino and Chinda, as part of the Japanese delegation, to the 1919 Paris Peace Conference. He had also joined with Chinda to accompany Crown Prince Hirohito on the 1921 royal visit to Europe. Therefore, in the eyes of the civilian court advisers—who were mostly international accommodationists like Makino, Saionji, and Chinda—General Nara was a most appropriate military adviser for the young emperor.

POLITICAL AND MILITARY CRISES (1928–1933)

The series of crises in Manchuria that began in 1928 and ended with Japan's 1933 decision to withdraw from the League of Nations posed great challenges for Emperor Hirohito; and the events of this period led to important changes in his point of view about Japan's international role. Nevertheless, historians can cite numerous sources to demonstrate that, throughout the 1930s, the emperor was still personally inclined toward his earlier belief in international accommodationism. Many historians have pointed out Hirohito's growing distrust of the Japanese army in the 1930s and during the Pacific War. The emperor was a patriotic monarch who was determined to preserve the kokutai (national polity) that centered on the imperial institution and protected his country's national interests abroad, especially on the Asian continent. The emperor was personally against the aggressive and illegal use of force against China and other unfriendly countries, and he often expressed his doubts and frustration about reckless military actions. However, the emperor's opposition to such military actions came not from pacifist convictions but from his concern about possible repercussions from Western powers. This was a position that the emperor's close advisers (Makino, Saionji, Chinda, and Nara) convinced him to embrace as his own.

However, in the early years of his reign, Emperor Hirohito did not manifest a single, consistent position in his relations with the government and the military. This suggests that the young emperor was still searching for his proper role as sovereign and commander in chief, that is, for a role that would give him room for action in both state and military affairs. This turned out to be an impossible task, for by this time Japanese state and military affairs were inextricably intertwined, but with the leaders of the two power centers increasingly divided, both sides competing for the emperor's support.

The assassination of the Manchurian warlord Zhang Zuolin in 1928 was the first major challenge faced by the young emperor. The emperor disagreed with Prime Minister Tanaka Giichi's handling of the perpetrators of the assassination. The prime minister had initially told the emperor that the army should formally prosecute the ringleader, Colonel Komoto Daisaku, and his co-conspirators in Japan's Kwantung Army; but later the prime minister reported to the emperor that the government had reversed its position on formal prosecution and was going to treat the matter as an internal army administrative issue. The emperor could not ignore the inconsistency of the prime minister's contradictory reports, and he was unwilling to sanction governmental decisions, made in the emperor's name, that lacked a persuasive rationale. According to Terasaki Hidenari, many years later, in 1946, the emperor recalled that in 1928 he had told the prime minister something along the lines of the following: "Is this not different from what you said before? How about submitting your resignation?"[31] Historians are still debating whether the emperor actually spoke these words directly to Prime Minister Tanaka and why he would have done so. Recent studies by Japanese scholars suggest that the emperor simply refused to hear Tanaka's excuses during an audience and that the emperor later clarified his desire for Tanaka's resignation via Grand Chamberlain Suzuki Kantaro.[32] However, most historians can at least agree that the emperor and his court advisers (especially the lord keeper of the privy seal, Makino Nobuaki) had been unhappy about Tanaka's tendency to slight the imperial court since assuming the premiership. The consensus is that for the emperor and his advisers, the prime minister's inconsistent handling of the assassination prosecution was just the last straw. In other words, many historians believe that, after consulting with his court advisers, the emperor *did* express his desire for the prime minister's resignation, which resulted in the collapse of the Tanaka cabinet.

The resignation of Prime Minister Tanaka in the wake of Zhang Zuolin's assassination deeply affected the young emperor's thoughts about his own position in the existing power structure under the Meiji Constitution. In retrospect, according to the emperor's aide, Terasaki Hidenari, Hirohito regretted his "youthful" indiscretion in becoming too involved with governmental details. According to another aide, Kinoshita Michio, the emperor later confessed that the episode of Tanaka's resignation became the "bitter experience" that convinced him of the following: "In a true constitutional monarchy, when the highest authorities of state [political] affairs and supreme [military] command reach a unanimous decision and report it to the throne, I believe that the monarch's proper course of action is to sanction that decision even if he personally does not agree with it. If the monarch sanctions what he favors and rejects what he does not favor, he may be still nominally a constitutional monarch, but in practice he is acting like an absolute monarch."[33]

The strong words used by the young emperor to criticize Prime Minister Tanaka in 1928 demonstrated Hirohito's attempt to express support for a rational military policy based on international accommodationism and international law. However, this action created an apparent violation of the emperor's neutral role under Japan's constitution in dealing with policies decided by the prime minister and his cabinet. Emperor Hirohito's 1946 recollection shows that he held conflicting views about his own ambiguous and paradoxical role under the Meiji Constitution: he saw himself as a constitutional monarch, bound by law, yet he believed he served Japan as an infallible divine monarch. In other words, Hirohito found himself in the impossible position of simultaneously serving Japan as a constitutional monarch, with only nominal power, and reigning over his country as an absolute, imperial ruler. He seemed to be looking for an acceptable compromise or a balance, vacillating between the two extremes.

In his 1946 recollections, the emperor suggested that, throughout the 1930s and into the first half of the 1940s, he retreated to a position of what historian Stephen Large calls "self-induced neutrality." Hirohito took this position in the name of the constitutional monarchy, but in the end it was this position that ironically contributed to "the weakening of resistance to the military."[34] In this discussion, it is important to ask why, as the 1930s progressed, the emperor felt he must retreat toward such a self-induced neutrality, for he already knew the limitations of acting as a mere rubber stamp from his service as prince regent on behalf of his father.

In contrast, during the first years of his reign, Emperor Hirohito—with encouragement of court advisers eager to restore the prestige of the imperial court in the decision-making process—at times consciously tried to transform himself into a more activist emperor, one who could think rationally and sanction state decisions by exercising his own will. Although his actions were much more constrained in his later reign, the emperor may have been more activist than Large suggests: Hirohito never completely stopped trying to influence state and military affairs whenever he deemed it necessary. Nevertheless, the emperor *did* change his position over time. In order to understand the reasons behind this complex change of position—that is, movement toward a self-induced neutrality and an almost automatic acceptance of the government's recommendations—it is necessary to examine the precarious political circumstances in which he found himself. During the early 1930s, Emperor Hirohito had to defend his throne during a tumultuous period of violence and instability, both at home and abroad.

Historian Thomas Burkman suggests that the Manchurian Incident of 1931 and Japan's subsequent decision to withdraw from the League of Nations in 1933 became the "acid test" of the willingness of Lord Privy Seal Makino, Genro Saionji, and other leading Japanese international accommodationists to cooperate with the Western powers.[35] Burkman aptly argues that proponents of international accommodation could not support the League of Nations at the expense of Japan's vital national interests in Manchuria and preeminent position as a regional power in East Asia. By 1933, these accommodationists thought (with many other Japanese) that the League of Nations was supposed to be an embodiment of a new and universal world order but was, in reality, an organization that preserved a status quo dominated by the Western great powers, at the expense of Japan's aspirations in East Asia.[36] This group of officials believed that they had to choose between their commitment to international cooperation through the League of Nations and to Japan's independent pursuit of its own regional interests, especially in Manchuria. Because of this, Makino, Saionji, and other international accommodationists chose, however reluctantly, the latter course of action.

The young emperor was persuaded to accept the government's decision, but this did not necessarily mean that his trust in international cooperation was wavering. The emperor and his close advisers opposed the unauthorized military expansion initiated by the Japanese Kwantung Army in Manchuria in September 1931, and the emperor was personally reluctant to approve Japan's withdrawal from the League of Nations. To understand his thought processes, it is important to reexamine the circumstances in which the young emperor handled the first major international crises that occurred under his reign.

THE MANCHURIAN INCIDENT

Japanese leftist historians, particularly Fujiwara Akira and Yamada Akira, raise an important question about the role the emperor could have played as *daigensui* after it became clear that the government in Tokyo under Prime Minister Wakatsuki Reijiro was unable to control the Kwantung Army in Manchuria. These historians suggest that the Manchurian Incident was the first test of the young emperor as *daigensui* and that he could have exercised his influence more effectively to make sure the army followed the Wakatsuki cabinet's decision and bring the Kwantung Army under the firm control of Tokyo.

The first problem that demanded the emperor's immediate attention was how to respond to the unauthorized incursion into Manchuria by the Japanese army stationed in Korea. Between September 19 and 22, 1931, the emperor repeatedly expressed his support for the Wakatsuki cabinet's position that military conflicts in Manchuria should not expand any further.[37] However, without the cabinet's approval, and without imperial sanction to move Japanese troops in Korea, the local commander in Korea, presumably with the tacit understanding of army headquarters in Tokyo, allowed one division to cross the Sino-Korea border and enter Manchuria. On September 22, when Prime Minister Wakatsuki and his cabinet learned that Japanese troops in Korea had already crossed the border, the cabinet acknowledged the army's unauthorized action after the fact and appropriated the necessary funds. Fujiwara Akira points out that if the government in Tokyo had really wanted to contain the military conflict with China, this initial unauthorized troop movement could have provided the emperor with the opportunity to question, and possibly forestall, the army's further independent actions.[38]

Was this really a lost opportunity for the emperor? Could he have stopped a conspiracy of the Kwantung Army to take over Manchuria? Historical records indicate that neither the Wakatsuki cabinet nor key court advisers intended to rely on the emperor to restrain the army. They believed that they should bypass the emperor and that Prime Minister Wakatsuki and his cabinet should handle the crisis. However, the prime minister needed support from Genro Saionji and Lord Keeper of the Privy Seal Makino to overcome constant pressure from the war minister and the army chief of staff, both of whom supported sending military reinforcements to Manchuria.

As early as September 19, when the prime minister heard about the possible unauthorized transfer of Japanese troops from Korea to Manchuria, he contacted Genro Saionji's private secretary, Harada Kumano, to seek the *genro*'s advice. At that time, the prime minister stated clearly that the forces in Korea should not be moved without the emperor's permission, which in reality meant with the Wakatsuki cabinet's approval.[39] Saionji, who realized the seriousness of this imminent, independent action by the army, ordered Harada to convey his advice to the court. According to Harada, Saionji told him, "In case the army minister or the chief of the General Staff reports to the throne that the troops have already moved without imperial sanction, His Majesty must never give his sanction to that move. He ought not to keep silence either. He should say that he would think about it and withhold his approval. Since he eventually has to dispose the matter somehow, you need to caution him about that point as well."[40] On the evening of September 21, Harada called Kido Koichi, who was then working as the chief secretary of the lord keeper of the privy seal, Makino, and passed on the *genro*'s message. Kido, in turn, communicated this message to Makino in a visit to Makino's residence that same evening. Although Makino's diary does not mention the *genro*'s warning, as conveyed by Kido, Makino did record the grave concerns expressed by Finance Minister Inoue Junnosuke that same evening regarding the war minister's inability to control his subordinate officers. From such evidence, it is clear that Makino was determined to support the Wakatsuki cabinet's policy of nonexpansion of military operations in Manchuria;[41] and it is probable that Makino conveyed Genro Saionji's warnings about the troops in Korea when he had an audience with the emperor on the morning of September 22.

At about same time, on September 21, General Nara, the emperor's chief aide-de-camp, who had been overly optimistic about the intentions of the Army General Staff, was stunned to hear news of the unauthorized actions by Japanese troops. The following day (September 22), when the chief of the General Staff, who had failed to obtain the prime minister's approval for sending reinforcements to Manchuria, came to the palace to directly request the emperor's sanction, Nara advised against petitioning the emperor, on the grounds that the emperor would not ratify any military action without the cabinet's approval. In other words, although Nara realized the army in Korea and Manchuria had violated the chain of command, he expected the Wakatsuki cabinet to deal with the crisis, rather than the emperor. As military historian Yamada Akira points out, Nara underestimated the Kwantung Army officers' determination to solidify Japan's presence in Manchuria, even at the risk of military insubordination.[42] Treating the unauthorized action by troops in Korea as an isolated case, Nara simply expected that the Wakatsuki government and Army General Staff would help stabilize the situation in Manchuria. Nara planned to deal with the Korean army's insubordination after the Manchurian Incident had been settled. Therefore, when the emperor, who presumably had received the warning from Genro Saionji through Makino about the Korean army's unauthorized action in Korea, asked Nara whether "he [the general] had cautioned the chief of the General Staff not to expand military actions," Nara told the emperor that he had already warned the chief of the General Staff and that the chief had been trying to comply with the Wakatsuki cabinet's decision. Nara, however, admitted the regrettable fact that there were "not a few cases that got out of control" under the initiative of the local military commanders.[43]

In the end, Prime Minister Wakatsuki and his cabinet reluctantly accepted the army's fait accompli in Korea and agreed to provide necessary funding. The prime minister reported the cabinet's decision to the emperor during the afternoon of September 22. Therefore the emperor did not have a chance to follow Saionji's advice to refrain from sanctioning the military action in Manchuria. Instead, Emperor Hirohito accepted the Wakatsuki cabinet decision and approved the transfer of Japanese troops from Korean to Manchuria after the fact. The emperor simply told the chief of the General Staff to "be more careful in the future."[44]

Influenced by General Nara's misguided optimism, the emperor seemed to expect that Tokyo would be able to contain the military conflict between the Japanese and Chinese forces in Manchuria. At the same time, there was no indication that other key court advisers—Saionji, Makino (or their respective secretaries, Harada and Kido)—felt much sense of urgency about acting together and working with the Wakatsuki cabinet to set the stage for the emperor's intervention in the unauthorized military actions in Korea and Manchuria. In fact, during an afternoon meeting on September 22, junior court advisers—including Konoe Fumimaro, Okabe Nagaakira, Harada, and Kido—were more concerned by reports that army officers were resentful because court advisers were advising the emperor against the military expansion in Manchuria. To avoid further resentment on the part of the army, the junior advisers agreed that the emperor should refrain from making any formal statement about the incident. They also discouraged Genro Saionji from coming to Tokyo to have an audience with the emperor, for they feared that a visit by the *genro* might further anger militant army officers.[45]

However, as the Kwantung Army's operations continued to expand in Manchuria—and especially after the army's bombing of Jinzhou on October 4—the emperor began to make his own inquiries. For example, he asked General Nara on October 6 if there was any way to restrict the military's actions. According to Nara's October 8 diary entry, the emperor learned from the Foreign Ministry's liaison official (Shiratori Toshio) that the Foreign Office opposed the army's idea of creating an independent Manchurian state. When he learned this, the emperor told Nara that he considered the army's position "insupportable," and he asked the general to warn the Army General Staff of the emperor's opposition.[46] There is evidence that the emperor was reluctant to support the creation of an independent state of Manchukuo because he was afraid that such aggressive Japanese actions might invite hostilities from the British and Americans.[47]

Throughout the 1930s, the emperor continued to warn military officials, in vain, that they should not take reckless and aggressive action in China; he believed that international accommodation was in Japan's best interest, and he was genuinely afraid of confrontation with Anglo-American powers and the Soviet Union. During this period, when Japan's perceived national interests collided with the rest of the world, the emperor faced a wrenching dilemma. He was torn, on the one hand, between his belief that international accommodation was the correct path and, on the other, his responsibility as sovereign to maintain internal unity and order and to champion Japan's national interests abroad, especially when Japan's national survival seemed at stake in the midst of worldwide economic depression.

Yet, one still wonders why the emperor failed to intervene more forcefully to curb the Kwantung Army's reckless actions in Manchuria and northern China, or why he did not insist on Japan's adherence to the League of Nations. Indeed one may ask if he thought that these options were even in the interests of his country.

THREATS OF ASSASSINATION AND MILITARY COUP

One important aspect of the emperor's reluctance to assert his will (hence his "self-induced neutrality") lay in his fear of a breakdown of the constitutional monarchy and the domestic chaos that would be caused by a military coup. The emperor's critics dismiss his fear of military coup and attempted assassination as merely an excuse for condoning the military's aggressive behavior. However, it is known that Hirohito was genuinely fearful of assassins: from the outset of his reign, Emperor Showa had been plagued by a series of assassinations that removed some of Japan's most influential and moderate political leaders, such as Prime Minister Hara in 1921. At the time of the Manchurian Incident in September 1931, the fatal shooting of Prime Minister Hamaguchi Osachi (Yuko) in 1930—the man who had authorized Japan's signing of the London Naval Treaty despite the military's objections— was still fresh in the nation's memory.

It is also likely that the disquieting news about potential military coups in 1931 had prevented the emperor and his court advisers from initially taking a firm stance against the Kwantung Army's actions in Manchuria. On the eve of the September 18 Manchurian Incident, Harada Kumao (Genro Saionji's secretary) and Kido Koichi learned the details of an earlier failed coup attempt on March 20, 1931 by a group of ultranationalists (an event known as the March Incident). The plotters had tried to carry out the coup with General Ugaki Kazushige as their leader, but the attempt was suppressed at the last minute by Ugaki's own order.[48] Although it is not clear how many details of the incident reached the emperor, Lord Privy Seal Makino did warn the emperor about potential problems of military discipline on September 8. Following this, the emperor summoned the navy minister on the tenth and the war minister on the eleventh of the same month to ask whether they were aware of any breach of military discipline. War Minister Minami Jiro, in his efforts to avoid the emperor's criticism and his probing questions, readily admitted that some young army officers had complained of the weak-kneed diplomacy of their government. But at the same time, Minami confirmed his own firm commitment to enforcing discipline and order in the army.[49]

After the September 18 incident in Manchuria, Lord Privy Seal Makino and his chief secretary, Kido, received repeated warnings about another scheme for a military coup d'état, which did take place on October 17 (the so-called October Incident). On September 22, Kido visited the residence of Harada Kumao, and they came to a mutual understanding that Genro Saionji should stay out of Tokyo so as not to arouse more military hostility toward the court. The two men were very concerned about the military's criticism that court advisers were dissuading the emperor from supporting expanded military operations in Manchuria. So urgent did the threat appear, that on October 1 Kido again visited Harada's house, where he met with Konoe Fumimaro and Shiratori Toshio (from the Foreign Office). They discussed the imminent danger of a military coup by a nucleus of army officers. Kido noted in his diary, "This is truly a national crisis."[50] This concern was widespread in the Japanese government: over the next two weeks, Prime Minister Wakatsuki, Imperial Household Minister Ichiki, Lord Privy Seal Makino, and General Nara were all concerned about the possibility that the Wakatsuki cabinet's reluctance to endorse the Kwantung Army's action in Manchuria might encourage the army's radical elements at home to take violent measures.[51]

It is quite possible that rumors of military insurgency reached the emperor's ears before the October 17 Incident, but in any event, on the nineteenth of the month, General Nara reported to the throne that a military coup had been averted by the arrest of ten army officers on the night of the sixteenth. Nevertheless, the emperor continued to worry about insubordination within the army. For example, when War Minister Minami had an audience with the emperor to discuss the October Incident, the emperor asked the minister "whether the situation in Manchuria would be all right." The war minister assured the emperor that rumors of the Kwantung Army's taking independent, insubordinate action were unfounded.[52] However, the war minister's assurance did not ease the emperor's worry, especially after the Council of the League of Nations voted on October 24 to demand the immediate withdrawal of Japanese and Chinese troops from the contested area in Manchuria. The emperor was so concerned about the crisis and the threat of a military coup that he asked Lord Privy Seal Makino if he should summon the ministers of the army and the navy together to discuss the situation. The emperor wanted to remind his top military officials of the seriousness of the crisis and to ask them whether Japan was prepared to deal with possibly negative consequences—ranging from international economic sanctions to possible war with the Western great powers.[53]

The situation continued to deteriorate, and Genro Saionji's son, Hachiro, had to visit his father in Shizuoka to convey the message that the lord keeper of the privy seal wanted the *genro* to come to Tokyo and offer advice to the emperor.[54] Genro Saionji traveled to Tokyo for an audience with the emperor on November 2. The emperor expressed his fear that Japan's activities in Manchuria might cause the League of Nations to impose economic sanctions against Japan, and he asked the *genro* if he should call a meeting of the ministers. Saionji's response was revealing, both in his view of the emperor's role and in the way he guided the young emperor. Saionji advised the emperor against holding a formal meeting with the ministers, saying that it would not do any good if they failed to reach an agreement among themselves. Instead, he advised the emperor to have an informal meeting with Foreign

Minister Shidehara Kijuro. Saionji reminded the emperor that in order to keep Japan from making mistakes, the two most important responsibilities of the emperor were, first, to protect the spirit of the Meiji Constitution and, second, to observe international law. The emperor concurred.

What the emperor did *not* know was that Saionji had confidentially asked his own secretary, Harada, to tell the foreign minister that "although he [Saionji] is not suggesting that [the foreign minister] should lie to His Majesty, [the minister] should informally talk to him in a way that would be agreeable to him so that he will not have to worry so much."[55] Saionji was thus trying to protect the emperor and the court from the military's criticisms by keeping the court out of the fray—in other words, by encouraging the emperor to take a position that was less intrusive into military affairs and more neutral concerning the controversies in Manchuria.

Whatever the emperor's inner thoughts might have been, his actions toward subsequent events in Manchuria were mixed and ambivalent. If we consider his actions in a positive light, he seemed to be seeking a middle way, trying to balance the army's aggressive, expansionist actions in Manchuria against the civilian government's efforts to comply with League of Nations' resolutions and to contain the military conflict. In a negative light, however, the emperor's middle way did not necessarily help the cause of moderation, for his position worked to the advantage of the one side (the military) that resorted to the use of force and violence.

By this time, the emperor was well aware of the difficulties he faced. Behind closed doors at the imperial palace, the anxious emperor observed, "Political disturbance and public anxiety seem to be affecting various quarters," and he needed advice from Makino and Saionji. In the meantime, the Wakatsuki cabinet, which had been unable to control the Kwantung Army's actions in Manchuria, tendered its resignation, and Inukai Tsuyoshi, the president of the opposition party (Seiyukai), who was known for his constitutionalism, succeeded to the premiership on December 13, 1931. On the previous day, the emperor had asked Saionji to convey a message to the new prime minister: "The current military's insubordination and violence—namely, the fact that the military interferes with domestic politics and diplomacy and insists on having its own way to this extent, is truly a grave situation for the nation. I cannot stop thinking about it. Keep my concerns on your mind, and explain it to Inukai. I will summon him afterward."[56]

Throughout 1932, the emperor's seemingly contradictory balancing act continued. On the one hand, he issued an imperial edict on January 8, in which he declared that the Kwantung Army's military actions in Manchuria were an "act of self-defense" and praised the army's brave efforts. In this edict, he expressed his hope that the military would build the foundation for peace through perseverance and prudence.[57] This no doubt encouraged the Kwantung Army to justify its military operations in Manchuria as patriotic acts. On the other hand, the emperor was determined not to spread the armed conflict beyond Manchuria. When hostilities broke out between Chinese nationalists and Japanese soldiers in Shanghai, the emperor resorted to an unusual measure: he gave a direct order to the commander of the expeditionary force to Shanghai, General Shirakawa Yoshinori, during his audience with the general on February 25. The emperor told the general to "respect the treaties, cooperate with the great powers, and settle the conflict immediately."[58] Obviously, he did not hesitate to use his personal influence when he held strong convictions and circumstances allowed him to take action.

Curiously, the emperor and the court remained silent when the Kwantung Army and Japan's puppet ruler (the last Qing [Manchu] dynasty emperor, Pu Yi) declared the independent state of Manchukuo on March 1, 1932. One could explain part of the emperor's reluctance to challenge the fait accompli in Manchuria in the context of his constant fear of violence in Tokyo at that time. For instance, on January 8, 1932, when the US government notified Tokyo that it would not recognize any new situation created in Manchuria by the use of force, in violation of existing treaties, the emperor, by coincidence, became the target of an assassination attempt by a Korean nationalist (the Sakuradamon Incident). An explosion missed the emperor, and Makino recorded in his diary that the emperor was calm and appeared more concerned about the Manchurian issue than his own safety. Makino added that when he realized how deeply the Manchurian problem was troubling the emperor, he felt overwhelmed. Over the next few days, the emperor and his advisers were distracted from the safety issue by the question of whether they should accept the letter of resignation submitted by Prime Minister Inukai (the person who would customarily be expected to take responsibility for dealing with any attempt to assassinate the emperor). However, Emperor Hirohito asked Inukai to stay on and Inukai complied.[59]

Eventually, Prime Minister Inukai himself fell a victim to the May 15 Incident of 1932, in which a group of young naval officers, army cadets, and civilian ultranationalists broke into the prime minister's residence and killed him. There had been warnings about his safety, because his secret attempt to negotiate directly with Chiang Kai-shek for a peaceful solution of the

Manchurian conflicts angered the military. The conspirators also attacked a number of places, including the residence of the lord keeper of the privy seal, the building of the Bank of Japan, the headquarters of the Seiyukai, and the metropolitan police headquarters. Before this violence erupted in May, two prominent leaders had already been assassinated by members of the civilian ultranationalist group Ketsumei-dan (Blood League): Inoue Junnosuke (former finance minister) on February 9 and Dan Takuma (managing director of the Mitsubishi partnership) on March 5.

In addition to the emperor's well-founded fear of domestic upheaval and military coup, historian Yamada Akira offers another possible explanation for the emperor's acquiescence to the establishment of Manchukuo. According to Yamada, there are strong indications that the emperor believed that if Japan limited its hegemonic expansion only to Manchuria, the Anglo-American powers might tacitly approve Japan's actions. Yamada quotes from the emperor's 1946 "Monologue" as evidence: "There were no very serious consequences when the incident broke out in Manchuria because it was countryside [i.e., not metropolitan centers]. But if an incident had happened in Tianjin or Beijing, I was afraid that the interference of the Anglo-American powers would surely escalate and might result in a clash with us." One cannot overemphasize the importance that the emperor placed on the attitudes and possible reaction of the Anglo-American powers. As Yamada points out, in January 1933 the Japanese army showed its intent to move to Rehe (Jehol), an area located north of the Great Wall, in a corridor between Manchuria and Hebei. At this time, the emperor was so afraid of antagonizing the Anglo-American powers and the League of Nations that he resorted to unprecedented firm action to curb the expeditionary force. The emperor proposed to Lord Privy Seal Makino and Grand Chamberlain Suzuki Kantaro that he should convene an imperial conference in order to have a tighter grip over the expeditionary forces. However, Genro Saionji advised against holding an imperial conference, on the grounds that imperial prestige would be in jeopardy if the decisions reached by such a conference were not carried out by the military.[60]

In the first few years of the 1930s, the emperor's growing fears about the League of Nations' actions became reality. The Lytton Commission, which had been sent by the league to investigate the situation in Manchuria in February 1932, produced its report half a year later. The commission concluded that the Japanese military actions in September 1931 "cannot be regarded as measures of legitimate self-defense" and that the birth of Manchukuo "was only made possible by the presence of Japanese troops." The Japanese government's firm determination to challenge the report antagonized the Council of the League of Nations, and Japan's case was further weakened by its own army's actions in Manchuria. The Kwantung Army began to send troops to Rehe (Jehol) on February 23, 1933; the following day, on the basis of the Lytton report, the League of Nations Assembly voted to accept the resolution to condemn Japan's actions in Manchuria. The Japanese delegation cast the only opposition vote and walked out of the assembly.[61]

The emperor was greatly troubled by this decision. According to Makino's diary, the emperor had repeatedly expressed his reservations about Japan's withdrawal from the League of Nations. As late as March 8, 1933, even after the prime minister and his cabinet had already reached a decision to pull out of the league, the emperor asked Makino if the government could reconsider that decision. Makino had to tell the emperor that it was too late, though Makino himself was troubled by the government's decision. He added in his diary, "We have no choice but to leave it to future historians to judge our actions."[62]

Another diary entry, written by the emperor's younger brother, Prince Takamatsu (Takamatsumiya Nobuhito), on June 10, 1933, provides additional, more intimate observations about the emperor's state of mind:

His Majesty's worries are indeed tremendous. What is the army doing? The command from the center does not work. The credibility of the nation continues to be steadily destroyed. Even if the withdrawal from the League of Nations was unavoidable, it is unbearable [for Emperor Hirohito] to abandon [the treaty] the late emperor had concluded. He [Hirohito] does not know how to apologize to the imperial ancestors if he allows Japan to be injured in the midst of internal and external turmoil. In this way, the emperor's concerns are not limited to current and future interests alone. I hear that in the past several months, he has lost nearly two *kan* [16.5 pounds], although I thought he looked better and more invigorated than usual. Certainly, troubles are the best training and mental challenges add to the advancement of imperial learning. However, I regret to hear that his worries have reduced his appetite, and I believe that he should have more courage on such an occasion.[63]

To us, looking back over the decades, the emperor seems to have been grop-ing in the dark, trying both to transcend his paradoxical role as a nominal, symbolic monarch and to serve as an absolute and infallible monarch. In this context, let us revisit the emperor's 1946 comments on constitutional mon-archy. Why did he make the following statement? "In a true constitutional monarchy, when the highest authorities of state affairs and supreme [military] command reach a unanimous decision and report it to the throne, I believe that the monarch's proper course of action is to sanction that decision even if he personally does not agree with it. If the monarch sanctions what he favors and rejects what he does not favor, he may be still nominally a constitutional monarch, but in practice he is acting like an absolute monarch."[64]

One possible explanation for the emperor's inconsistent actions during the 1920s and early 1930s may lie in his struggle to maintain the authority of the throne, which he was expected to sustain. He had to reconcile his theoretical, undefined power under the Meiji Constitution with his well-founded fear of military insubordination and internal disorder. To do this, the emperor found a solution in the name of constitutional monarchy. It is possible to argue that during the first trying years of his reign (beginning with the problems of the Manchurian Incident and extending to Japan's departure from the League of Nations), the emperor's personal conviction in interna-tional accommodation with the Western powers became a casualty of his struggle for domestic political survival as a constitutional monarch, at least as he wanted to define his role.

Historian Peter Wetzler makes a noteworthy point about this period: "Hirohito advocated British constitutional norms not only as a model for governing but, more important, to preserve, protect, and legitimize in mod-ern terms the imperial line and the supreme position of his house in Japanese society." Wetzler suggests that this line of thinking allowed the emperor to both participate in prewar military policymaking and claim his nonpartici-pation in the process. Wetzler says, "Hirohito could simultaneously explain himself and justify his actions, or lack of actions, in terms of Western consti-tutional monarchy."[65] It would be difficult to prove exactly how many of the emperor's thoughts and actions in the early 1930s were driven by his desire to practice a British-style constitutional monarchy, how many were driven by fear of Japan's internal violence and instability, and how many were motivated by his desire to protect the imperial line (as Wetzler suggests).

The real tragedy for the nation of Japan was that the general Japanese public was unaware of the emperor's personal opposition to the actions of the

"Emperor's Army" in Manchuria and his serious reservations about his government's decision to withdraw from the League of Nations.[66] The Japanese people, who had been taught to act as the emperor's loyal subjects, accepted Hirohito's public endorsement of the military action, supported the Kwantung Army's incursions in Manchuria, and backed the Japanese government's assertive policy against the League of Nations. Ordinary Japanese were not aware of the shrewd way the military had exploited the formal imperial will (as distinguished from the emperor's own personal desires) to further fuel a general sense of pride and patriotism. In retrospect, Japanese historian Irokawa Daikichi comments, "If, as Hirohito later stated, he had desired to be a constitutional, peace-loving monarch at that time, he should have taken a stand by 1933, when the aggression was beginning in earnest. Soon after, it became extremely difficult to take any action against the militarists."[67] But, in reality, would it have been possible for the young emperor to stand firm against the military establishment and to assert his personal opinion as the "imperial will" for the Japanese nation? Whatever the answer, history shows that Emperor Hirohito's ordeals had just begun.

CHAPTER 2

Crises at Home and Abroad

From the February 26 Incident to
the Sino-Japanese War

M ANY LEFTIST CRITICS OF JAPAN'S MILITARY ACTIVITIES IN
Asia and the Pacific see the period from September 1931 (when the
Manchurian Incident occurred) to August 1945 (when Japan surrendered to
the Allied Powers) as a continuous fifteen-year war.[1] In retrospect, it is difficult to deny that a causal relationship existed between the individual links
of a fifteen-year-long chain of events. For example, the Manchurian Incident
allowed the Japanese military to carry out a large-scale invasion of Chinese
territory, and the ensuing Sino-Japanese disputes escalated into open hostilities in China. Although it is beyond the scope of this book to reexamine
the multitude of forces that propelled Japan down the road to Pearl Harbor,
a causal chain is evident. Japan's decision to expand the Marco Polo Bridge
Incident of July 7, 1937, in which Japanese and Chinese soldiers clashed, into
a full-fledged war with China (though falling short of a declaration of war)
was the major turning point that ultimately led to Japan's war with the United
States and the European Allied Powers in late 1941. There is no doubt that
in the mid-1930s Japanese leaders—who made decisions on war and peace
without the advantage of hindsight—badly miscalculated the situations at
home and abroad and thus became the prisoners of their own actions.

In the first half of the 1930s, Emperor Hirohito was personally against the
army's aggressive policy to use force in Manchuria, and he was reluctant to
approve the government's decision to leave the League of Nations and pursue

an independent and assertive foreign policy. In the latter half of the 1930s, the emperor supported neither the expansion of Japan's military operations in China nor confrontations with Western powers. Yet the Japanese government still chose to expand Japan's military operations first within China and then into Southeast Asia. Why, then, did the emperor allow the Japanese government and military to expand relatively local Sino-Japanese conflicts into full-fledged hostilities with many adversaries across Asia?

In order to understand the reasons behind Emperor Hirohito's actions as well as his inactions, it is important to examine the considerable changes that occurred in the triangular power relations of government, military, and imperial court during the latter half of the 1930s. The emperor's perception of his country's troubled internal conditions deeply affected his attitude toward Japan's policy toward China and the Western powers. The Kwantung Army continued to drag the Japanese government toward taking forcible measures to extract recognition from the Chinese Nationalist government for the state of Manchukuo, while the Japanese government turned its back on the arms-limitation efforts of the 1935 Second London Naval Conference. Certainly the emperor was nervous about the negative impacts these actions might have upon Tokyo's relations with the Anglo-American powers. But what worried him most was that the Japanese military, especially army officers, were eager to accomplish expansionist goals in China by changing the dynamics of political power within Japan by means of violence, even though this method verged on military insubordination. The February 26 Incident of 1936 and the Marco Polo Bridge Incident of 1937 became convergent points for ultranationalist assaults on political moderates and international accommodationists in Japan and efforts of hardline Japanese military officers to enact a military solution in China. These two points of crisis (at home and in China) significantly undermined the influence of moderate groups over Japan's government and military; and this paralyzed the emperor's and the court's ability to put a brake on forceful measures advocated by militant extremists. In retrospect, one may wonder why the emperor, who was situated in the most advantageous position to receive accurate data and to make balanced and prudent judgments, was unable or unwilling to exercise his influence when Japan was facing these crises at home and abroad.

ABROGATION OF THE NAVAL LIMITATION TREATY

After its withdrawal from the League of Nations in 1933, Japan's refusal to participate in the Second London Naval Conference of 1935 became another event that suggested the willingness of the Japanese military to assert its own interests at the risk of alienating the Western powers. By 1934 the Japanese navy, which had been traditionally more conciliatory toward Anglo-American powers, increasingly turned against the existing policy of accommodation and moved toward abrogation of the Washington Naval Limitation Treaty of 1922 (Five Power Pact), which kept Japan's naval tonnage inferior to that of the United States and Great Britain. Some of the highest-ranking leaders of the Japanese navy took an increasingly hard line on the need for naval parity with the United States and Great Britain. Although the emperor appeared to have no objection to Japan's insistence on such parity, he personally did not support the breakup of the naval conference or the abrogation of the treaty. In August 1934, Admiral Okada Keisuke, who had just assumed the premiership the previous month, reported to the emperor that his cabinet would insist on naval parity at the preliminary international meeting (to plan the upcoming Second London Naval Conference, scheduled for 1935) and that the navy desired an eventual cancelation of the Washington treaty. The emperor replied that "because of the military's demands there may be no other way but to settle the matter as you suggested, but in the event that Japan must abrogate the Washington treaty, we should do so without antagonizing the great powers." Okada told the emperor that he expected a great deal of difficulty at the coming London conference, and the emperor said, "Even if the conference fails, you must think carefully not to make Japan a villain."[2] The emperor again warned the prime minister on September 6 that Rear Admiral Yamamoto Isoroku must do his best to reach an agreement at the preliminary negotiations.

The diary of General Honjo Shigeru, who served as chief military aide-de-camp from April 1933 to March 1936, offers valuable records of the emperor's exchanges with Prince Fushimi, his own uncle, who was then serving as the chief of the Naval General Staff. When the two met on September 8, 1934, the emperor expressed apprehension about the navy's insistence on parity with the United States and asked, "What is the logic behind the argument that the successful conclusion of a treaty for naval parity will necessitate naval buildup to achieve parity, while a failure to conclude such a treaty will leave the naval gap as it is? Or, are we to insist on naval parity at all cost and denounce the naval inequity with the United States under any circumstance?" Prince Fushimi's explanations failed to persuade the emperor, and Honjo wrote that the emperor thought the hardline officers in the army and the navy were jointly pressuring the government to take a tough stand. According to Honjo, "The emperor was afraid that the navy command was about to sacrifice the critical international issue [of naval limitation] in order to maintain control over the lower-ranking officers."[3] Apparently, the emperor was worried about the increasing tendency of insubordination among junior officers within the navy, and he suspected that the navy's leadership was trying to pacify the mid- and lower-ranking hard-liners by abandoning the Washington naval limitation arrangements.

The emperor continued to question the navy's hard-line position on abrogating the naval limitation treaty. On September 11 he asked the navy minister whether some sort of gentlemen's agreement could be worked out in the event that a treaty for naval parity was not possible. The navy minister argued that, judging from past experiences, such an alternate agreement with the United States would not be effective. The emperor also asked if the navy would move toward an increase in naval tonnage (in excess of the treaty) regardless of the outcome of the treaty negotiations. The navy minister replied that he would do his best not to allow naval expansion.[4] On October 24, the emperor asked Prince Fushimi if failure to renew the naval treaty might lead to a naval buildup that would significantly increase the economic burden on the Japanese people. The prince denied that possibility.[5]

Like the Kwantung Army in Manchuria, the hard-liners in the navy, along with the emperor's uncle, Prince Fushimi as the chief of the Naval General Staff, eventually prevailed over the cautious and reluctant emperor: the Japanese government decided to withdraw from the Washington Naval Limitation Treaty and declined to participate in the Second London Naval Conference in 1935. This freed Japan from treaty obligations to maintain its inferior ratio of naval tonnage compared to the United States and Great Britain and to preserve the defense status quo in Asia and the Pacific, which included Japan's nonfortification pledges.

On October 31, 1934, Prince Fushimi and Prince Kanin (another uncle of the emperor, this one serving as the chief of the Army General Staff) jointly met with the emperor. They reported the final decision of the Supreme Military Council (Gensui Kaigi) in favor of Japan's abrogation of the naval limitation treaty. At this point, the emperor, on his own initiative, told both chiefs of staff, "Since the issue is so serious, make the responsible authorities deliberate it more carefully. The military must be warned that it should not insist merely on what it wants and refuse to cooperate."[6] The emperor's strong words criticizing the military appeared to surprise Princes Kanin and Fushimi; Prime Minister Okada later asked the court not to include these specific words in the emperor's order, because Okada's government was afraid of the military's angry reaction.

The emperor's uneasiness about the role of the military increased throughout 1935, as the Japanese leadership continued to lean further to the right and as the military's influence over the decision-making process for Japan's foreign and domestic policies became more and more apparent. In late 1934, the Kwantung Army tightened its control over Manchukuo by ensuring that military officers held a monopoly of power within the Tokyo bureaucracy in charge of Manchurian affairs. The emperor, who preferred civilian control over Japan's foreign policy toward Manchuria, felt compelled to ask Prime Minister Okada, "Is it [this monopolization of power by the military] allowed to be this way?" In his postwar memoir (published in 1950), Admiral Okada wrote, "In my mind, I never thought that it should have been allowed, but I was distressed and at a loss, not knowing how to say so [to the emperor]. Thinking back on the way the army pushed step by step and extended its interference into domestic politics, I have to admit that I was weak then and regret it now."[7]

THE CONTROVERSY OVER THE "EMPEROR ORGAN THEORY"

There is no doubt that, against the backdrop of the rise of militarism in the mid-1930s, the February 26 Incident of 1936 became the springboard that allowed the army to dominate the Japanese government. Few moderates were left in the leading political parties—especially in the case of the Seiyukai and Minseito Parties, and the parties were badly divided and ineffective. Some were willing to go along with the military solution to Japan's problems advocated by militarists and ultranationalists; others opposed extreme militarist solutions but had lost control over their more militant opponents and were paralyzed by fear of being assassinated in a military coup. As we will see in this chapter, only the high-ranking senior military officers in the army, who were generally identified with the control faction (*toseiha*), were able to put an end to this unprecedented coup attempt in February 1936, and it was these senior officers alone who were able to maintain unity and order within the military and preserve political and social stability throughout the Japanese empire. The February 26 Incident emotionally affected Emperor Hirohito deeply, influenced his thinking, and necessitated his playing a role in the incident. The emperor's reactions to the 1935 controversy over the so-called emperor organ theory (*tenno kikan-setsu*, in which the emperor is considered an organ of government), which preceded the February 26 Incident, along with his reaction to the incident itself, reflect his concerns and priorities.

First, let us look at the dispute over the emperor organ theory between factions on the right, who believed in a divine imperial sovereignty, and moderates, who supported a constitutional monarchy. Emperor Hirohito had a keen interest in and appreciation of history. Admiral Suzuki Kantaro, who served as grand chamberlain from 1929 until 1936 (when he was badly injured by multiple gunshots during the February 26 Incident), later noted that the emperor had an uncommon insight into history and geography. Suzuki recalled that, before the emperor organ theory had generated a national controversy, the emperor had already foreseen the problematic implications of this theory when he read a newspaper article about it. Comparing the situation to ideological conflicts in early modern Europe, the emperor had said, "It will become a troublesome issue in the near future."[8] As the emperor feared, throughout 1935 the emperor organ theory became the target of criticism by ultranationalists, which further precipitated Japan's move toward the political right, thus paving the way for the February 26 Incident.

Scholars and politicians who supported the emperor organ theory were advocates of constitutional monarchy under the Meiji Constitution. They contended that sovereign power rested with the state and that the emperor was the highest organ within the state under the constitution. On the other hand, civilian and military ultranationalist groups who believed in the divine origins of the imperial institution as the foundation of Japan's national polity (*kokutai*) argued that sovereignty rested with the emperor. They also promoted a spiritual argument that the emperor transcended the modern notion of state (*kokka*). In early 1935, under the slogan "Kokutai yogo, kikan-setsu bokumetsu" (Defend the *kokutai*, destroy the [emperor] organ theory), the ultranationalists organized a coalition to publicly denounce Professor Minobe Tatsukichi, the leading advocate of the emperor organ theory, and they demanded his resignation from public positions at the Imperial University of Tokyo and at the House of Peers. The ultranationalists also targeted Ichiki Kitokuro, the president of the Privy Council, who also served as imperial household minister from 1925 to 1933, because he was Professor

Minobe's mentor at the University of Tokyo. Considering Ichiki to be the leading advocate of the organ theory among the emperor's close advisers, on March 23, 1935, an extremist broke into Ichiki's house with a Japanese sword on the day of the funeral for Ichiki's wife.[9] Besides a public campaign to discredit supporters of the emperor organ theory, the ultimate political goal of the theory's critics was to oust Prime Minister Okada and his cabinet and destroy the influence of Genro Saionji and senior statesmen (*jushin*) like Makino Nobuaki, who had been guiding the emperor to act as a constitutional monarch.[10] It was no coincidence that those who attacked the organ theory also supported an aggressive expansionist policy with the use of force in China and considered moderates in the court and the Okada cabinet to be obstacles.

The Okada cabinet tried to weather the assaults from the right by taking a middle course. On the one hand, the Japanese government banned the sale of Professor Minobe's publications on April 9, and Prime Minister Okada publicly denounced the emperor organ theory on August 3. On the other hand, the government maintained the traditional interpretation of constitutional monarchy under the Meiji Constitution by promoting its own version of the *kokutai* clarification campaign, in which the government pledged its commitment to protecting Japan's *kokutai*. However, there was an irreconcilable ideological gap between the ultranationalists, who denied constitutional monarchy and placed the emperor beyond the authority of the state, and the Okada cabinet, which tried to interpret the emperor's power within the framework of the state as defined by the constitution. During the summer, it became increasingly difficult for the Okada cabinet to control extremist attacks against supporters of the emperor organ theory. The effectiveness of the officers serving in the War Ministry was affected by factional rivalry within the army—between the "imperial way faction" (*kodoha*) that collaborated with civilian ultranationalist groups to attack the emperor organ theory, and the "control faction" (*toseiha*) that began to suppress the extremist activities of the imperial way faction. In this political environment, Prime Minister Okada failed to gain support from the control faction to quiet the organ theory debate.

On August 12, General Nagata Tetsuzan, chief of the Military Affairs Bureau of the War Ministry and a leading figure of the control faction, was assassinated in his office by Lieutenant Colonel Aizawa Saburo of the imperial way faction. The immediate reason for Aizawa's action was the government's replacement of General Mazaki Jinzaburo, the inspector general of military education and the leader of the imperial way faction, with the more moderate General Watanabe Jotaro, who was closer to Genro Saionji and the moderate court advisers. Nagata's assassination also revealed the serious problem of military discipline within the army. Unlike past political assassinations, in which the victims were civilians, General Nagata was one of the highest-ranking army officers on active duty. After this incident, the army leadership, while accelerating its efforts to quiet the radical movements within the active duty army and the military reserve associations, pressured the Okada cabinet to issue another public statement in mid-October in order to clearly denounce the emperor organ theory.[11]

The most curious—and even ironic—aspect of the 1935 controversy over the emperor organ theory was that the whole debate took place without input from Emperor Hirohito, as though what he thought about the controversy was irrelevant. As the controversy intensified throughout the summer and fall of 1935, the emperor remained publicly silent, primarily because his advisers, especially his military advisers, urged him to remain neutral. However, as shown in the diary of Chief Aide-de-Camp Honjo, in the early stage of the controversy, the emperor, feeling trapped between the two sides, did not hesitate to express his sympathy for the emperor organ theory that rationalized the constitutional monarchy. On March 11, 1935, Honjo wrote in his diary that, when the emperor saw the war minister's critical statements in the Diet against the organ theory (and in defense of divine imperial sovereignty), the emperor summoned the general and told him that "although there might be a difference in status between the two of us [Honjo and the emperor], he [the emperor] did not believe physically there was any difference whatsoever. In light of this he found it highly upsetting both mentally and physically that in order to attack the organ theory he was being turned into an entity without any freedom whatsoever."[12] Later on the same day, Hirohito summoned Honjo and defended Ichiki, the president of the Privy Council, who had been the target of the military's criticisms. The emperor trusted Ichiki's loyalty and praised Ichiki's prudent position regarding the role of the imperial family.[13]

As the military and rightist attacks on the emperor organ theory escalated, the emperor increased his personal comments, expressing his preference for the organ theory over the principle of imperial sovereignty to both Prime Minister Okada and Grand Chamberlain Suzuki.[14] On March 28, 1935, the emperor told Honjo, "If we pursue the logics of the theory of imperial sovereignty and the emperor organ theory, they seem to amount to the same thing: but in international relations, in such matters as labor treaties, loans, and the like, it seems more convenient to follow the organ theory." Honjo defended the military's official position, saying, "The military worships His Majesty as *arahitogami* [divinity incarnate], and if His Majesty were to be treated just like any other person in accordance with the organ theory, it would create grave difficulties in military education and the supreme command." The following day, March 29, the emperor again summoned Honjo and asked if the army "was not pressuring the prime minister to resolve the question of the organ theory." Then the emperor expressed his opinion that "Article IV of the Meiji Constitution, stipulating that 'the emperor is the head of the state,' is based on the organ theory." Hirohito said, "If the organ theory were to be revised, the Constitution would have to be revised as well." The emperor pointed out that Ito Hirobumi's commentaries on the Meiji Constitution stated that "the emperor *reigns* [*ringyo*] over the state."[15]

The emperor paid special attention to the directive issued by the inspector general of military education, General Mazaki Jinzaburo, whose followers would eventually carry out the military mutiny of February 26, 1936. Pointing out General Mazaki's argument that the emperor was the locus (*shutai*) of state governance, Hirohito told Honjo, "To hold that sovereignty resides not in the state but in the monarch is to court charges of despotism." He added with frustration, and almost with sorrow, "I, too, would gladly adopt the theory of imperial sovereignty if it did not lead to the bane of despotism, if it did not result in disapproval by foreign nations, and if it did not conflict with our national polity and history. Unfortunately, I have yet to encounter an explanation of this theory that is worthy of respect."[16]

The emperor also saw the contradiction, and even the audacity, of the military's advocacy of imperial sovereignty. Hirohito thought that the military was using the emperor as an organ of state in order to carry out its own purposes, while at the same time publicly attacking the emperor organ theory, and he often complained to General Honjo about the army's tendency to ignore his wishes. On April 19, 1935, he told Honjo, "When the Manchurian Incident broke out, military officers came to the office of the imperial aide-de-camp, making all sorts of demands. . . . The army would not provide me with the information I sought from the cabinet. As a result I had to find out the cabinet's intentions by other informal means. Why does the army prevent me from gaining information that I require for my own reference?"[17] On April 25, upon learning of the military reserve association's pamphlet attacking the emperor organ theory, Hirohito expressed his opinion that the association "was going too far." He told Honjo, "For the military, while [it is] attacking the organ theory, to do something like this, which goes against my own wishes, is, in effect, to treat me as an organ in accordance with the principles of the organ theory."[18]

Honjo's diary reflected the emperor's general inclination to find a moderate and harmonious resolution to the controversy between the right-wingers, who believed in divine imperial sovereignty, and the moderates, who supported constitutional monarchy. Honjo wrote, "His Majesty responded that if matters of faith and beliefs were used to suppress scientific theories, then world progress will be hindered. Theories such as evolution would have to be overturned. Of course, he said, he realized that faith and beliefs were important. Beliefs and science must move forward side by side."[19] Perhaps this was the only way for the rational-minded man who occupied the chair of a sacred throne to cope with a contradictory reality. General Honjo conveyed to General Mazaki the emperor's desire for military and civilian authorities to move forward on this issue side by side. Honjo also warned Mazaki about the emperor's concerns that the army might have gone too far in its criticism of the organ theory.[20]

In late May, however, sensing that the court's favorable attitude toward the emperor organ theory might confuse soldiers of all ranks, the emperor's military advisers recommended that the emperor should stay out of the organ theory controversy. On May 18, 1935, Honjo wrote in his diary, "A certain individual told me that the imperial court wished to contain the spread of the organ theory controversy and that this information had reached the military authorities and was causing the army's attitude to become indecisive." Conveying this information to the emperor, Honjo told Hirohito that he had warned this individual that "His Majesty does not discuss the pros and cons of such controversies, and he stands above such debates." By telling this to the emperor, Honjo was actually trying to advise Hirohito not to take sides in the organ theory controversy. On May 22, the emperor summoned his naval aide-de-camp, Rear Admiral Idemitsu Manbei, to find out about the navy's position on the organ theory. He asked Idemitsu, "Don't you think the army is contradicting itself by advocating the theory of imperial sovereignty against my wishes?"[21] According to Honjo's diary, Idemitsu, too, advised the emperor to rise above the controversy. He told the emperor, "His Majesty would be confusing basic and secondary issues if he were to conclude that because the army does not agree with his views on specific issues it is acting contrary to the theory of imperial sovereignty, or if he makes the issue a question of fundamental interpretations of the *kokutai*. His Majesty should observe the debates of his subjects in a detached fashion from a higher vantage point, and maintain a broad perspective that transcends these discussions."[22] After this, the emperor followed his military aides' advice and refrained from expressing his own opinion on the organ theory.[23]

However, the emperor did not remain quiet about another problem that the Japanese army had caused in Tianjin (Tientsin), China. Some hostile Chinese actions were used by Japanese garrisons in northern China as a pretext to demand the suppression of anti-Japanese activities in the region. As the Kwantung Army's involvement appeared imminent and the Japanese local commanders in Tianjin increased diplomatic pressure on the Chinese government in Nanjing, tensions were mounting. Honjo recorded on July 10 that the emperor was "gravely concerned" about the situation in China and he asked questions "almost daily." The emperor feared that Japan might be accused of having "a dual foreign policy" between military and civilian authorities. He was especially worried about adverse reactions by European powers and the United States.[24]

On July 13, the emperor warned Prime Minister Okada that the cabinet must not be "led around by the nose" by the military forces stationed in China. The emperor also summoned General Honjo and asked that he find ways to keep in touch with the army while the emperor was staying in Hayama. He told Honjo, "The army ought to be very careful in appointing appropriate officers to overseas posts and [should] make sure that their actions will not deviate from the intentions of the central authorities."[25] However, there was little indication that the emperor's warning to the military made any difference in the behavior of the Japanese forces stationed in northern China.

Although Emperor Hirohito expressed his displeasure with General Mazaki and his followers for their stance against the emperor organ theory, the army's decision to remove Mazaki from the position of inspector general of military education was not initiated by the emperor. In fact, Hirohito wondered if Mazaki's transfer might cause disturbances in the army and decrease the army's ability to maintain military discipline. However, the war minister denied such a possibility. Unfortunately, Mazaki's removal from office prompted one of his followers, Lieutenant Colonel Aizawa, to assassinate Mazaki's rival, General Nagata Tetsuzan (who was then serving as chief of the Bureau of Military Affairs). The assassination of General Nagata shocked the emperor. He told Honjo, "It is truly regrettable that the army had an outbreak of such an extraordinary incident."[26]

Throughout the rest of 1935, Hirohito continued to worry about the army's inability to keep its extremists under control. On September 26, he told the army chief of staff, Prince Kanin, to warn the war minister of the following: "There is widespread tendency of *gekokujo* [overpowering the higher ranks by the lower ranks] in all areas. The military, especially the army, seems to be getting aggressive in its demands in current affairs. The minister should certainly try to accommodate his subordinates' wishes, but if he were to be led around by the nose by the subordinates, it would only increase the harm of the practice of *gekokujo*. Especially in Chinese affairs, [the war minister] must reprimand any unauthorized actions by the outpost officers." The emperor also told General Honjo to take note of these factors and do whatever was necessary. Honjo wrote in his diary that he was struck with awe by the emperor's strong words. Another aide-de-camp also overheard the emperor mutter to himself, "The recent weather is erratic, but so are political affairs."[27]

Hirohito could not overlook the army's increasing interference in the government, especially its efforts to remove all sympathizers of the emperor organ theory from the Okada cabinet. The army's main target was Kanamori Tokujiro, chief of the Cabinet Legislative Bureau. General Honjo recorded his impressions of the emperor's anxieties on December 18:

His Majesty observed that earlier, when the government was compelled to issue a second statement on the "clarification of national polity," the military had stated that it would not interfere in matters of personnel. For the military to raise objections to Kanamori now would, he feared, affect Ichiki's status. If the military changes its position periodically in this manner, one cannot be certain about its reliability. Unless a clearly defined limit is placed on all matters, is it not likely that if ever the tide of fascism rises in Japan the military would support the movement?[28]

In December 1935, in an atmosphere of increasing uneasiness about the military's criticisms of the emperor organ theory and the army's reckless actions overseas, the emperor lost the service of his most trusted and closest senior adviser. Lord Keeper of the Privy Seal Makino Nobuaki submitted his resignation on December 20. Makino had felt a sense of growing crisis ever since the Manchurian Incident. He had to not only deal with the recklessly aggressive behavior of his own country's army in China and subsequent friction with the Western powers but also with the increase of military interference in political processes at home. The ultranationalists in the military, notably those in the army's imperial way faction, pressured (and even threatened) Makino to induce him to cooperate. Makino's refusal pushed the extremists, including General Mazaki, to conspire to eliminate the entire group of moderate senior court advisers. The emperor organ theory controversy thus became a turning point in this power struggle, because civilians of the rightist political parties joined with the military in attacking these moderate senior advisers who defended constitutional monarchism. Makino consistently explained his decision to resign as due to his excessively long tenure as lord keeper of the privy seal and his poor health. On November 15, 1935, Makino told Kido Koichi, "My health has been deteriorating recently and I have no energy." He explained that he wanted to resign because he had no confidence in his ability to perform his official duties. Two days later Makino described his condition to Kido as an "old man's nervous breakdown."[29] Historian Chadani Seiichi suggests that Makino was mentally exhausted for a number of reasons. Chadani argues that Makino's efforts to strengthen the court's ability to resist the ultranationalists were frustrated by growing disagreements among the senior court advisers, especially the disagreements between himself and Genro Saionji, who continued to advise the emperor to stand by and watch while army extremists radicalized politics at home and pursued an unauthorized and aggressive policy in China.[30]

To add to the upheaval at court, Ichiki Kitokuro, president of the Privy Council and Makino's closest ally, who had been targeted by the military in the debate over the emperor organ theory, also expressed his desire to resign in early December. The emperor was at a loss as to how to handle this departure and was reluctant to grant permission. (Ichiki eventually resigned from his post in March 1936.) In this atmosphere, Makino felt isolated and powerless to reverse the tide. He confessed to his family that the situation was deteriorating.[31]

Makino's resignation created a power vacuum within the court and weakened the emperor's influence vis-à-vis the government and military. Moreover, the emperor personally felt a great loss. In 1921, when Makino became the minister of imperial household at the age of sixty, Hirohito was a twenty-year-old crown prince who was about to assume regency on behalf of his sick father, Emperor Taisho. As the lord keeper of the privy seal, Makino had served as Hirohito's mentor and father figure since 1925. According to Chamberlain Irie Sukemasa, on December 26, 1935, after accepting Makino's resignation, "the emperor cried out loud."[32]

The emperor, as well as Makino and others who were serving the court, sensed the dangerous possibility that the army might take violent action, given the continued radicalization of the army's imperial way faction. Chief Aide-de Camp Honjo, for instance, was aware of a rumored plan for a coup by said faction in the army's First Division; and Honjo frequently warned his son-in-law, Yamaguchi Ichitaro, a company commander in the First Division, to be cautious.[33] In the meantime, the trial of Lieutenant Colonel Aizawa, who had assassinated General Nagata (the leading figure of the control faction), was carried out under the jurisdiction of the First Division. The officers of the imperial way faction used the trial as a public campaign to denounce their opponents in the control faction.[34] On February 25, 1936, General Mazaki testified at Aizawa's trial. At this juncture, the orders to transfer the First Division to Manchuria triggered an uprising in Tokyo—the largest-scale military mutiny in Tokyo during the reign of Emperor Showa.[35]

THE FEBRUARY 26 INCIDENT

At 5:00 AM on February 26, 1936, under the leadership of officers from the imperial way faction, over fourteen hundred soldiers occupied the heart of downtown Tokyo. The men, who came mostly from the First Division (with some from the Third Infantry Regiment of the Imperial Guard), took over the official residence of the war minister, the buildings of the War Ministry and the Army General Staff, and the metropolitan police headquarters, which was located directly across from the imperial palace. Rebel troops denounced Genro Saionji, senior statesmen, the control faction of the military, party politicians, and government bureaucrats for undermining Japan's national polity; the troops proceeded to methodically assassinate key leaders surrounding the emperor. However, the rebels' call for a Showa Restoration with military stewardship did not include concrete plans for a new government; therefore, the success of the military coup depended on the willingness of the highest-level army leaders to support the coup attempt. Consequently, these troops demanded that War Minister Kawashima Yoshiyuki take over the government on behalf of the emperor and that General Kawashima appoint General Araki Sadao as commander of the Kwantung Army, which was expected to deal with the threat of the Soviet Union.

While these activities took place, some two hundred soldiers surrounded the home of the new lord keeper of the privy seal, Admiral Saito Makoto, who had just succeeded Makino two months previously. Saito was shot and died instantly under a hail of bullets. In addition, another group of two hundred soldiers broke into the residence of General Watanabe Jotaro of the control faction (Watanabe had replaced General Mazaki as inspector general of military education), and they quickly killed the general. Finance Minister Takahashi Korekiyo, Japan's foremost financial expert and outspoken moderate of the Seiyukai, was also shot and killed instantly in his residence.

Three other units (each comprising two to three hundred men) were sent to assassinate three other key figures closely associated with the emperor, but these targets managed to survive the assaults. The grand chamberlain, Admiral Suzuki Kantaro, was shot four times in the head, chest, shoulder, and groin, but he narrowly escaped death through the brave efforts of his wife, who pleaded with the rebel officers to spare her husband from another stab to the neck, which would have killed him.[36] Prime Minister Okada Keisuke also dramatically escaped the assassins' bullets. Okada's brother-in-law, Colonel Matsuo Denzo, who was serving as Okada's secretary and bodyguard, had some physical resemblance to Okada. A band of rebel soldiers mistook Matsuo for the prime minister, killed Matsuo, and believed that their mission had been accomplished. The prime minister hid in a closet in a maid's room for two days before he successfully escaped from his residence with the assistance of his aides and military police (*kenpeitai*) in the middle of his own purported funeral service, with Matsuo's body in the coffin and under tight surveillance by rebel soldiers. The survival of these two senior statesmen—Okada and Suzuki—is especially noteworthy because both of them were to play critical roles a decade later, in the summer of 1945, when Japan was on the verge of committing national suicide.

As part of the February 26 Incident, a band of soldiers was sent to assassinate Makino Nobuaki in Yugawara, a hot spring in the mountains south of Tokyo. The rebel soldiers killed a police guard and set fire to the building in which Makino was staying, but Makino managed to escape. Genro Saionji was also on the original list of targets, but he was spared because of disagreement among rebel officers.

"So they have finally done it." These were the first words Chamberlain Kanroji heard from the emperor on the morning of February 26, when Kanroji rushed to awaken Hirohito and report that soldiers had killed Lord Keeper of the Privy Seal Saito and had critically wounded Grand Chamberlain Suzuki.

"Then, after a pause," recalled Kanroji, "[the emperor] said, as if to himself, 'It's all due to a [personal] failing in myself.'" The emperor's emotional reaction to the news of the incident was so intense that Kanroji wrote, "I would like to add that never have I seen the emperor, a peaceful man who rarely loses his temper, as angry as he was when he learned of the assassinations."[37] From the outset, the emperor called the soldiers who took part in this action "rebel troops" (*hanran-gun*),[38] and he acted decisively to stop the mutiny. By the time General Honjo came to see him around 6:00 AM, the resolute emperor, who had already changed into the uniform of commander in chief (*daigensui*), told Honjo, "Put an end to the incident immediately. Turn this misfortune to good account."[39] When War Minister Kawashima arrived in the palace around 9:00 AM with the rebel troops' manifesto, the emperor ordered the war minister to swiftly suppress the mutiny. Without the prime minister, the lord keeper of the privy seal, and the grand chamberlain at his side, the emperor had to rely on his chief aide-de-camp, General Honjo. The emperor asked Honjo to report back on the course of events every twenty or thirty minutes, fourteen times during that day, and repeatedly demanded that the rebellion be subdued immediately.[40]

On the second day of the mutiny, February 27, although the commander in charge of enforcing martial law was authorized to disarm the mutineers by force, he was still trying to persuade the rebels to put down their arms and return to their barracks. Increasingly impatient with the army's handling of the situation, the emperor told General Honjo, "I will personally lead the Imperial Guard Division and subdue them [the rebels]." Mortified, Honjo advised the emperor that such extreme measures were unnecessary. Because the emperor frequently referred to the rebel troops as *boto* (insurgents), Honjo begged him to soften his wording, saying that although the officers had violated orders from the supreme command and had moved troops without the emperor's permission, the officers were motivated by love of their country. The emperor later asked, "How can we not condemn the spirit of these criminally brutal officers who killed my most senior right-hand men?" On another occasion he remarked, "To kill the senior statesmen whom I trusted the most is like strangling my neck slowly with silk floss."[41]

Hirohito had no sympathy for either the actions of the rebel troops or the reasoning behind their actions. He never supported the proposal of the imperial way faction that Japan's emperor should rule the state as an absolute monarch with the support of military stewards. The radical ideas publicized by authors such as Kita Ikki (whose ideology paradoxically combined nationalist socialism with a concept of a welfare state) had nothing in common with the elitist world in which the emperor lived. There is no evidence that the emperor ever understood why Kita's followers—who included some young officers and also soldiers who came from the poor peasant class in the countryside—were drawn to his ideas or why these followers were driven to advocate a military coup. Hirohito's persistent desire to restore military discipline came from his eagerness to maintain political stability and national unity, which in his mind were essential for the survival of Japan as a nation.

However, it should be noted that Honjo's diary entry of February 28 offers an additional explanation for the emperor's eagerness to subdue the rebel troops as quickly as possible. Hirohito was afraid that the prolongation of the incident might undermine Japan's image in the world. He told Honjo, "The war ministry and the general staff headquarters in the imperial capital have been occupied by rebels for the past three days and are still under their control. This situation will give the impression to the foreign powers that the Japanese military is impotent."[42] Honjo also noted that the emperor was seriously concerned about the impact of the February 26 Incident on Japan's international monetary transactions and its negative effects on Japan's domestic economy. Hirohito later recalled that it was the finance minister's warning about the potential of economic panic that prompted the emperor to take decisive action.[43]

The basic dilemma facing the emperor was that he had to depend on an army establishment he did not fully trust in order to suppress the insubordination of more objectionable, more extremist groups within the army. By February 29, army authorities had persuaded rebel soldiers to return to their barracks, and the officers who led the munity either committed suicide or were arrested and eventually punished.

There is no doubt that the February 26 Incident was a critical moment for Emperor Hirohito as he reconsidered his own role within the triangular power relationship that governed Japan. Although the military coup failed, the incident considerably weakened the influence of more moderate court advisers and civilian officials. At the same time, the February 26 Incident allowed the control faction of the army to solidify its power base in the government, as well as at court. The way the army responded to the emperor, in the wake of settlement of the mutiny, clearly demonstrated this. Because the attempted coup had caused so much anguish to the emperor, General Honjo and officers from the Office of the Aide-de-Camp believed that the emperor should issue a statement censuring the war minister. Following the advice of Ichiki (president of the Privy Council), Honjo first asked the emperor to formulate a statement in his own words, offering assistance if any modification was necessary. Although the emperor worried about the possibility that his own severe censure of the army might make the new lord keeper of the privy seal an object of resentment again, on March 4 Hirohito frankly told Honjo, "So far as I am concerned, the senior statesmen and generals whom I have trusted the most as my hands and feet have been killed. . . . Their actions have violated the constitution, gone against Emperor Meiji's Rescript to Soldiers and Sailors, blackened the national polity, and defiled its purity. I am gravely concerned about all this. At this time the army should be cleansed thoroughly, and steps should be taken to prevent such a disgraceful incident from ever occurring again."[44]

The emperor thus believed that the army insurgents violated the *kokutai* as he understood it. However, four days later the Office of the Aide-de-Camp suggested that the emperor tone down his message and reword it as follows: "This action completely violated the Imperial Rescript to Soldiers and Sailors [*gunjin chokuyu*, which demanded loyalty and obedience to the emperor] and blackened our nation's history." Looking at the suggested changes, the emperor summoned Honjo and said, "I understand that you wish to avoid using the phrase 'blacken the *kokutai*.' What is the army's interpretation of *kokutai* when it zealously calls for clarification of the *kokutai*?" Honjo responded, "Our *kokutai* is one in which the emperor, who descends from an unbroken line from time immemorial, governs the state by embracing the will of the imperial founder and the ancestors. Therefore, although the recent incident was truly deplorable, it cannot be said to have blackened the *kokutai*."[45] There was a clear discrepancy between the emperor's notion of the *kokutai* and that of the army, but Hirohito agreed to modify his statement.

The emperor not only presented the modified statement of censure to the new war minister, General Terauchi Hisaichi, but also wanted to disseminate this statement to all army personnel. However, on March 19, key military officers who met at the War Ministry decided against circulating the emperor's statement within the army on the grounds that if the entire army received the emperor's censure for "violating the imperial precepts and blackening our nation's history" because of the actions of one element within the army, "it might leave an indelible blot on the entire army." The army leadership suggested that the war minister should request an imperial rescript only if the three army chiefs failed to carry out reform of the organization.[46] Thus, while the army's highest leaders, mostly from the control faction, tightened their control over the entire army, they managed to screen the army from the emperor's message of censure by refusing to convey to all army personnel how severely the emperor had reacted against the February 26 Incident. This shows that the officers in the War Ministry and the general staff, not the emperor, held the real power in Japan's army.

The formation of a new cabinet by Prime Minister Hirota Koki in the wake of the February 26 Incident also demonstrated the army's domination of the government. Although the emperor suggested to Genro Saionji that the foreign minister and the finance minister of the new cabinet should be strong individuals who would not let the military lead them by the nose, the army publicly demanded that the new cabinet pursue aggressive policies to strengthen national defense and national power and criticized any government policy of liberalism and international accommodationism.[47] Although the military coup had been suppressed, the midranking officials of the War Ministry still had to make efforts to pacify younger subordinate officers who continued to urge the army to monopolize power in the new cabinet. A nucleus of officers in the War Ministry, especially Colonel Muto Akira in the Bureau of Military Affairs, pressured the new prime minster and war minister to select cabinet members acceptable to the army.[48]

It is no coincidence that the Hirota cabinet adopted "The Fundamentals of National Policy" on August 7, 1936, a document that outlined an aggressive policy toward the East Asian continent, especially in northern China. This document, along with two other policy documents adopted at the same time, laid out a course of action that the Japanese empire would pursue in ensuing years under the slogans "New Order in East Asia" (1938) and "Greater East Asia Co-prosperity Sphere" (1942). The primary goal of the 1936 document was to solidify Japan's informal empire by strengthening its special ties with Manchukuo, building a coalition with China under the principles of coexistence and co-prosperity, and extending Japan's influence over Southeast Asia through peaceful means. At the same time, the principles outlined in "The Fundamentals of National Policy" would provide a framework for Japan's strengthening its defense against the Soviet Union in the north, while preventing the United States from obstructing Japan's designs in China, which involved Japan's naval buildup in the Pacific.[49] Complying with the army's insistence on increasing defense against the Soviet Union, the Hirota cabinet signed an Anti-Comintern pact with Germany on November 25, 1936, and joined with Italy in this pact a year later.

THE CHINA INCIDENT

The debate over the emperor organ theory in the mid-1930s and the suppression of the coup of February 26, 1936, paved the way for the formulation of an official definition of Japan's national polity (*kokutai*). In March 1937, the Ministry of Education published a booklet, entitled *Kokutai no hongi* (Fundamentals of our national polity), which condemned Western individualism as the ultimate cause of socialism, anarchism, and communism and claimed that this individualism had led to "a season of ideological and social confusion and crisis." In order to strengthen national unity and stability, the booklet reinforced the Imperial Rescript on Education of 1890 and inculcated the virtue of Japanese imperial rule. According to this booklet, "Our country is established with the emperor, who is a descendant of Amaterasu Omikami [Sun Goddess who created Japan]. . . . For this reason, to serve the emperor and to receive the emperor's great august Will as one's own is the rationale of making our historical 'life' live in the present; and on this is based the morality of the people." Exhorting Japanese traditional virtues, especially loyalty, filial piety, patriotism, and self-effacement, the booklet preached, "Our country is a great family nation, and the Imperial Household is the head family of the subjects and the nucleus of national life." The booklet added that this convergence of filial piety and loyalty had created the unique character of Japan's national morality, which was "a factor without parallel in the world."[50] However, although the Ministry of Education publicized the official interpretation of the *kokutai* among Japan's general public, ironically the court and the emperor (supposedly the most important entities in this system) remained silent. In fact, there is no indication that the emperor himself commented on the publication.

Four months later, when the events of the Marco Polo Bridge Incident broke out on July 7, 1937, Japan's decision to invade China revealed early indications of what would be a tragic consequence of Japanese imperialist activities—that is, Japan would replace a system created by Western imperialist powers with a Japan-centered system of imperialism. To accomplish this, both civilian and military leaders in Japan were promoting an Asian ideology that consisted of two incompatible ideas. On the one hand, Japanese leaders emphasized the country's special place in Asia on the grounds of a national uniqueness and superiority that emanated from imperial ideology, in which a sacred emperor served as the core of national identity, the *kokutai*, and patriotism. On the other hand, leaders propagated the idea of Japan's commitment to maintaining peace and stability in East Asia through coexistence and co-prosperity, especially in regard to China. In the trajectory of government actions and discussions that eventually led to 1942 Pacific War propaganda of a Greater East Asia Co-prosperity Sphere, both the 1937 decision of Prime Minister Konoe Fumimaro and his government to expand military operations in China, and Konoe's 1938 declaration of Japan's commitment to the New Order in East Asia, dramatically revealed fundamental contradictions and flaws in the rhetoric of Japanese imperialism. Thus, Emperor Hirohito, Japan's sovereign and commander in chief, who was supposed to be the manifestation of the virtue of the Japanese empire, became a contradictory figure under this imperial ideology. A close examination of Hirohito's personal view of Japan's role in Asia—and the role he himself played in the expansion of Japan's empire—reveals a profound contradiction between the emperor, a moderate pragmatist who favored international accommodationism, and the top government and military leaders who used the emperor as the primary icon for Japan's quest for an empire in Asia. There was thus a huge gap between rhetoric and reality—that is, between the emperor's theoretical role under the *kokutai* and the reality of what he actually thought and did.

Japan truly stood at a historic crossroad when the Marco Polo Bridge Incident occurred. Japan had to choose between two options: localizing armed conflicts in China and continuing to work patiently with Chiang Kai-shek's Nationalist government in Nanjing to reach some sort of settlement, or resorting to a military solution in order to impose Japan's wishes on China (the option favored by the militant groups within the Japanese army). Because the army leadership was divided on this issue, Prime Minister Konoe Fumimaro had a chance to pursue a diplomatic solution—if he held firmly to the option of seeking a peaceful settlement, despite serious difficulties in negotiating with Chiang Kai-shek. However, by August 17, 1937, Konoe's government had opted to seek a military solution. In retrospect, history shows that this decision to expand Japanese military activity along the entire Chinese coast dragged Japan into an unwinnable war. Moreover, on January 16, 1938, the Konoe government issued a declaration that it had closed the door to further diplomatic negotiations with Chiang Kai-shek's government.

A close examination of the role played by Emperor Hirohito at this historic juncture in the summer of 1937 sheds new light on fundamental problems in how the Japanese empire functioned under a flawed imperial ideology. One view of this period is laid out in Herbert Bix's Pulitzer Prize–winning book, which argues that "the Konoe cabinet was taking the initiative in tandem with the army expansionists, and Hirohito was supporting that decision from the outset in opposition to the nonexpansionists on the Army General Staff."[51] However, Bix's oversimplified interpretation misrepresents the role of Emperor Hirohito both at a formal and a personal level. Instead, there is another, equally valid interpretation of events: if the pragmatic, accommodationist Hirohito had in fact possessed any real authority to make decisions, he might not have authorized Japan's aggressive military expansion of 1937. This would mean that, in reality, the publicly declared wishes of the imperial throne, which were conveyed by both civilian and military authorities, had little to do with the actual desires of the emperor—a man who had no choice but to serve as the voice of the throne and to play out a role determined not by himself, but by his own military and civilian authorities. Although the emperor was supposed to be inviolable and his decisions were supposed to be sacred, what Hirohito stated did not always carry weight. Moreover, as the previous chapter shows, the court advisers, with a view to protecting the imperial throne from any ascribed responsibility and blame, advised the emperor to maintain personal neutrality and a position of imperial transcendence, which often resulted in his inaction and passivity. A disconnect existed between the imperial authority embraced by the rhetoric of *kokutai* and the actual power exercised by the emperor in the real decision-making process.

In the crucial years of 1937 and 1938, the emperor was more cautious than either the military authorities or the Konoe cabinet, and he was more eager than they to settle disputes with China through diplomatic negotiations, though his influence was considerably circumscribed. However, this does not necessarily mean that Hirohito was powerless. The emperor had enough experience to know that his interventions could make a difference in some situations, especially in cases when the prime minister and his cabinet were able to skillfully coordinate the triangular relations of the government, the court, and the military. At the outset of the Marco Polo Bridge crisis, when localizing of armed conflicts in northern China still appeared possible, the emperor hoped that Prime Minister Konoe—a charismatic court aristocrat popular with civilian and military ultranationalists—would be able to prevail over the hard-liners in the military and would pursue a moderate foreign policy toward China and the Western powers. However, the emperor watched with frustration and disappointment as the Konoe cabinet turned to an aggressive military solution in China.

By the summer of 1937, the emperor had enough experience not to fully trust "his" army stationed in northern China. A few months before the February 26 Incident, when the chief of the General Staff asked for the emperor's preauthorization to allow the Kwantung Army in Manchuria to cross the Great Wall and enter northern Chinese territory, Hirohito firmly told Prince Kanin, his uncle and the army chief of General Staff, "I will never allow the Kwantung Army to cross the Shanhaiguan pass into China proper." Such a blunt statement by the emperor is noteworthy, but what more remarkable is that the emperor came to realize that the army would not comply with his orders. Two days later the emperor said to Prince Fushimi, his uncle and the naval chief, "There were instances that the army did not listen to what I said. This is the consequence of the lack of control and failure of a subordinate to execute the will of a superior."[52] The February 26 Incident certainly increased the emperor's consciousness of his role as commander in chief of the imperial army. And when the Marco Polo Bridge Incident prompted a Sino-Japanese military clash in northern China, it is logical to surmise that this led Hirohito to feel a greater responsibility for maintaining military discipline in the army.

The emperor's primary concern about Japan's armed conflict with China was that it could lead to a spread of hostilities along the Soviet-Manchurian border. On June 30, 1937, a week before the Marco Polo Bridge Incident, the emperor received the distressing news that the trouble-ridden First Division, which had become part of the Kwantung Army, had attacked and sunk a small Russian warship off Kanchatzu Island in the Amur River. Hirohito was fearful that war might break out with the Soviet Union.[53] Therefore, when he heard of the incident at Marco Polo Bridge, he immediately summoned the army chief, Prince Kanin, and asked, "What would you do if the Soviets mobilize their forces?"[54] A vaguely optimistic response from the army chief did not ease the emperor's mind.

Three years later, looking back at the protracted war in China that his generals had not been able to bring to a satisfactory conclusion during the intervening three years, Hirohito had a noteworthy conversation with Lord Keeper of the Privy Seal Kido Koichi. Kido recorded in his diary that the emperor, who regretted his failure to insist on pursuing a negotiated settlement with China in the summer of 1937, told Kido the following on July 11, 1940:

Before the Marco Polo Bridge Incident happened, it seemed to me that war with China was unavoidable. However, since we had to be ready to defend ourselves against the Soviet threats, I thought that there was no choice but to compromise with China. Using the Kanchatzu incident as an excuse, I invited the army chief and the war minister and asked about this matter. They replied that the army had no concerns about its preparedness against the Soviets and that in the event of war with China, it could be finished within two or three months. Therefore, I left the question as it stood. In my thinking, I actually thought of contacting Konoe to hold an imperial conference to settle this issue, but if the military had been opposed to this idea, it would not have worked. That is why I talked to the military first and got this negative response.[55]

In his recollections in 1946, Hirohito was even more troubled by his 1937 failure to pursue peace with China, because by 1946 he realized that his original fears about the Western powers had been warranted—that is, his fears that the West would oppose Japanese military expansion in China. The emperor clearly understood in 1946 that Japan's decision to escalate hostilities in China in 1937 had led to the disastrous war with the United States. Looking back on May 1937 incidents in Tianjin, which had been caused by the Chinese Nationalists, the emperor said,

Sino-Japanese relations were such that war could have broken out at the slightest provocation. Therefore, I summoned War Minister Sugiyama [Gen] and Army Chief Prince Kanin, because I somehow wanted to reach a compromise with Chiang Kai-shek.

It so happened that the Kanchatzu incident broke out along the border in northern Manchuria, and the incident was used to camouflage [the purpose for] my audience with them [Sugiyama and Prince Kanin], but in fact I summoned them to hear their opinions about [our] China policy.

If the army agreed with my opinion, I thought I would ask Konoe to compromise with Chiang Kai-shek. Manchuria is countryside [i.e., very rural] and an incident there would not have developed into a serious crisis, but in case of an incident in Tianjin or Beijing I was afraid that the Anglo-American powers' interventions would definitely escalate into a clash between them and us. . . . The chief of the General Staff and the war minister were of the opinion that an incident in Tianjin would be over within a month, if we struck the first blow [against the Chinese]. I realized that their opinions were different from mine, and regrettably I did not bring up the question of potential compromise.

At this juncture the Marco Polo Bridge Incident happened. I do not believe that the Chinese provoked the fight. I think the conflict started with a minor skirmish.[56]

Thus the emperor claimed that he did not insist on compromising with Chiang Kai-shek in July 1937 because he realized that the army chief and the war minister did not agree with him. However, the emperor did not remain inactive after the Marco Polo Bridge Incident, and he continued to express his preference for an early and peaceful settlement with the Chinese Nationalists.

At the outset of the incident, on July 11, the Konoe cabinet managed to push through a resolution to localize the armed conflict in northern China, mainly because a divided army leadership did not object.[57] War Minister Sugiyama Gen and Colonel Muto Akira, head of the Operations Section in the General Staff's Operations Division, were eager to use this incident as a pretext for a military settlement of outstanding disputes with China (especially disputes over Manchukuo); but General Ishiwara Kanji, chief of the General Staff's Operations Division, was against mobilizing military divisions in Japan as well as those in Manchuria and Korea. Ishiwara's objection to the expansion of military operations temporarily carried the day, with the help of a fragile armistice that had been reached by local Japanese commanders in the Tianjin area.[58] During the first several weeks of the Marco Polo Bridge Incident, the emperor was anxious to quickly settle the armed conflicts. He asked War Minister Sugiyama to confirm that if the Chinese agreed to Japanese terms for settlement, the Japanese army would not send reinforcements. The emperor told the naval chief, Prince Fushimi, "I wish the incident in China would not expand. This has become such a trouble."[59]

In late July 1937, the emperor suggested to Prime Minister Konoe that his cabinet should settle the problems posed by the incident through diplomatic negotiations with China. Konoe's memoir illuminates his own perspective on the difficulty of working with the army at this time. Despite the prime minister's request, the General Staff refused to share its plans for military operations with members of the cabinet, and this made it impossible for Konoe's government to effectively conduct Japan's foreign and economic policies. The prime minister, therefore, complained to Hirohito that, without knowledge of what the army would do next, the governance of state affairs and the supreme command would be utterly disjointed, and this would be detrimental to the interests of the entire Japanese nation.

The prime minister begged for the emperor's good offices in solving the problem between the cabinet and the army. Realizing that there was a serious breakdown of communication between the civilian government and the military's supreme command, the emperor brought the problem to the attention of War Minister Sugiyama. But Sugiyama simply replied that he would not "be able to discuss matters concerning military strategy at a cabinet meeting where civilian ministers with political party affiliations are present." According to Konoe's recollection, the emperor offered a solution, saying, "I will inform both the prime minister and the foreign minister about the matters concerning the supreme command." If Konoe's recollection is correct, this was a noteworthy development. Hirohito's offer to serve as liaison between the Konoe cabinet and the supreme command shows that the emperor realized there was no leadership at the highest level that could unite and coordinate military and civilian state affairs at this critical moment. The emperor acted swiftly. On July 30, he asked Prince Kanin, chief of the General Staff, how far the Japanese forces intended to advance, and the prince confirmed that they were prepared to move up to Baoding, west of Tianjin. On the same day, the emperor summoned the prime minister to relay the army's intentions and suggest that the army should end military operations upon restoring peace in the northeastern district along the Yongding River.[60]

It appears that the emperor was trying to use his influence to steer the divided Japanese leadership toward a peace settlement with China in early August. Prime Minister Konoe was receptive to the court's suggestion for early termination of hostilities, but War Minister Sugiyama was either unable or unwilling to respond. Prince Takamatsu, worried about Tokyo's ability to maintain a nonexpansionist policy in northern China, went to see Hirohito on August 2 and observed that the army was badly divided on this issue, even within the General Staff itself. Takamatsu wrote in his diary, "I wondered who could bring the Army under a single authority."[61] Unfortunately, while the emperor was actively engaged in conversations with the prime minister and the chiefs of the Army and Naval General Staffs to move forward with an early settlement of the Marco Polo Bridge Incident, additional hostilities broke out in Shanghai on about August 9. Now, with the Japanese navy's involvement, Japan's military operations in southern China rapidly escalated.

The spread of hostilities to Shanghai changed the emperor's attitude. He appeared more willing to accept a military means of settling disputes with China. When Hirohito authorized sending reinforcements to the Third Fleet on August 12, he told the naval attaché, "Circumstances are such that this cannot be avoided. I suppose the Naval General Staff is thinking the same way. Since it has come to this, it is difficult to settle the conflicts through diplomacy." Behind the emperor's new willingness to seek a military solution in Shanghai was his trust in the navy leadership, including Navy Minister Yonai Mitsumasa, who was initially reluctant to support the expansion of hostilities in China but was now eager to seize the moment for a glorious naval victory. As Japanese warships began shelling Chinese ports on August 15, the emperor told the admiral, "I have full confidence in the navy's attitude and behavior to this day. Don't be carried away by the impulse of the moment, and take a wide view of things and make no mistakes."[62]

Although the emperor was now willing to use force, what separated him from his generals and admirals was his understanding that the ultimate success of Japan's China policy was political in nature and that the use of armed force was a means to achieve political objectives. Hirohito knew that should Japan go to war, the nation must not only plan for a military victory but also to secure peace. Having authorized military operations in Shanghai and along the China coast, the emperor was willing to use force with decisiveness to ensure a quick peace. In the emperor's words, "I always told [the supreme command] that we must be menacing [i.e., prepared to use force] and at the same time [be] ready to offer peace terms."[63] On August 18, the day after the Konoe cabinet officially reversed Japan's nonexpansionist policy and launched all-out hostilities along the Chinese coast, Hirohito spoke to the chief of the Naval General Staff, Prince Fushimi, expressing his worries about the spread of hostilities throughout China. He told the naval chief, "It is urgent [that we] accomplish our objective and bring an end to the hostilities. We must concentrate our main forces in one place, not in both northern China and in Shanghai. We must strike a decisive blow, and then we should offer our peace terms or let the other side propose terms."[64]

The spread of military operations in southern China, however, created a serious disagreement between the emperor, who wanted to send in large reinforcements and swiftly defeat Chinese forces in the south, and General Ishiwara, who wanted to localize the war in northern China and keep more army divisions in the north from fear of Soviet threats. Moreover, the army and navy could not even clearly identify their common enemy continued to suffer from interservice rivalry, and there was little that the emperor could do to remedy the poor coordination between the two military branches. This turned into a problem that plagued Japan throughout the Pacific War.

Behind the poorly planned military strategy lay an even more ill-conceived vision of the future relationship between China and Japan. When the Japanese leadership decided to launch an undeclared full-fledged war on China in mid-August 1937, the officials all talked about a New Order in East Asia. However, like the definition of the *kokutai*, such a "New Order" meant different things to different people. The army's basic idea of a New Order in East Asia was to achieve Japan's complete domination over Manchuria and northern China through proxy governments. To realize this, the army used the rhetoric of a trilateral "cooperation and co-prosperity" shared by Japan, Manchukuo, and a potential buffer state in northern China.[65] The army's strategic priority was to separate northern China, including the Beijing-Tianjin area, from Nationalist-controlled China and to create a puppet state under the control of the Kwantung Army.

It is difficult to know what a New Order in East Asia meant to Emperor Hirohito. He did not speak of the concept or mention this term in his private conversations with his close advisers, beyond referring to the benign concept of *hakko ichiu*, which literally means "the whole world under one roof" and suggests a world ruled under the spirit of universal brotherhood. The emperor's public speeches were prepared by his court advisers and merely repeated the Japanese government's official position. In his opening address at the seventy-second special session of the Diet on September 4, convened to approve additional expenditure for the military expedition in China, Hirohito expressed a desire "to maintain stability in East Asia" and "to realize co-prosperity" through "collaboration and cooperation" with China. But he blamed China for its failure to understand Japan's true intentions, and he asked the Chinese Nationalists to reflect on their hostile acts.[66]

Based on such limited historical records, then, what can we speculate about the kind of peace settlement with China the emperor was contemplating? According to Prince Takamatsu's diary, Hirohito supported three basic peace components: (1) creation of a demilitarized zone in northern China; (2) recognition of the Chinese Nationalist government; and (3) improvement of Sino-Japanese relations. The emperor believed that these Japanese peace terms were fair and reasonable according to international standards.[67] Apparently Hirohito did not realize that separating northern China from

Nationalist (Guomindang) rule was unacceptable from China's perspective. What seemed missing from the emperor's analysis of the situation was an interest in—or an attempt to understand—the rising sense of nationalism and aspiration for self-determination that lay behind the Chinese people's resistance to Japan's invasion. Moreover, Prince Takamatsu's account also implies that Hirohito would not have objected to Japan's territorial gain in Manchuria and northern China, even through the use of force, as long as it did not provoke an immediate armed clash with the Soviet Union or the United States.

As these military events were taking place in China, the Konoe government was appealing to the patriotism of the Japanese people and steadily guiding the entire nation to an emergency wartime footing. On August 24, 1937, one week after the cabinet decided to abandon its policy of nonexpansion in China, it outlined a general policy to bolster the people's morale throughout Japan. The cabinet resolution stated that in order to guard and maintain "the prosperity of the Imperial Throne," the government would launch a national movement to boost the people's unity, loyalty, and perseverance.[68] As hostilities rapidly escalated along the Chinese coast, in order to improve coordination between the army and navy, military authorities and the Konoe cabinet agreed to set up an Imperial Headquarters (Daihonei), which would serve as the supreme command center for Japan's entire armed forces. On November 20, the Imperial Headquarters was established inside the palace, with Emperor Hirohito as *daigensui*. (The last time the palace had been the Imperial Headquarters was thirty-two years previously, during the Russo-Japanese War, with Hirohito's grandfather, Emperor Meiji, serving as *daigensui*.) However, Hirohito was expected to rubber-stamp the General Staffs' decisions at the Daihonei imperial conference, and as expected, the emperor remained silent throughout the first of these meetings, held on November 24.[69]

However, the emperor could not ignore the Konoe government's difficulty in coordinating political strategy with military strategy, especially the resulting lack of effective peace plans, and Hirohito was looking for a way to use his influence to bring an early end to the war. On November 10, the emperor asked the lord keeper of the privy seal, Yuasa Kurahei, "In view of today's war situation, in case the other side seeks a peace settlement, I am afraid we are not prepared to respond. Don't we have to have a decision on this? I want to ask the prime minister whether we should take steps to hold an imperial conference. The way I see it, there is no mechanism to prepare for a conference at this point. I want to ask [the prime minister] whether there is need to set up such a mechanism. What do you think?" Yuasa advised the emperor that he should ask for Genro Saionji's advice first before he talked to the prime minister.[70]

In his advocacy of an effective plan for peace, the emperor had a few strange allies, who were part of the nonexpansionist group at the Army General Staff. This included Lieutenant General Tada Hayao, the vice chief of the General Staff, and the followers of General Ishiwara (who had already left the General Staff). For strategic as well as economic reasons, both Tada and the followers of Ishiwara were eager to end the war through a negotiated peace with Chiang Kai-shek's regime. These officers were more concerned about the Soviet threat to the north and did not want to exhaust manpower and resources in a broad conflict with China. While they were exploring a possibility of German mediation with Chiang's government, these officers were eager to enlist the imperial court's influence. The emperor was apparently aware of the nonexpansionists' desire to halt the war in China through an imperial decision (goshinsai).[71]

Genro Saionji's recommendation was critical in defining the emperor's role in a proposed imperial conference. The genro's recommendation illuminates the gap between the emperor's absolute power bestowed by the Meiji Constitution and the limited, ceremonial nature of the power the emperor held at an imperial conference. Genro Saionji suggested to Harada Kumao that the prime minister should take the initiative and set the stage for an imperial conference. He advised against the idea of an imperial conference convened by the emperor's own initiative. Saionji was aware of the scheme by the army's nonexpansionist faction to restrain military activity in China through an imperial order, directly issued by the emperor. But Saionji asked, "What if outpost [Japan's overseas] forces refuse to obey an imperial order? It will undermine the imperial authority." Therefore, Saionji, through Harada and Lord Privy Seal Yuasa, warned the emperor not to turn an imperial conference into an occasion to deliver an imperial order or imperial decision.[72]

Although Genro Saionji's message was unmistakable, the emperor, eager to play a more active role at an imperial conference to limit Japan's military activities in China, was still wavering. On January 10, 1938, the day before the first imperial conference, the emperor told Lord Privy Seal Yuasa, "I understand that the genro was of the opinion that I should not say anything, but the chief of the Naval General Staff's desire is such [the opposite]. What on earth should I do? Can you ask for the *genro*'s opinion one more time?" Yuasa replied, "The *genro* is not suggesting that you should remain absolutely silent. I think his point is that you ought not to say anything that may lead to a situation in which Your Majesty may have to take political responsibility."[73] Prime Minister Konoe, knowing that Hirohito was sympathetic to the Army General Staff's position to pursue negotiations with Chiang's regime, also asked the emperor to say nothing at the imperial conference.[74] In the end, when the imperial conference was convened on January 11, Hirohito followed the advice of Saionji, Yuasa, and Konoe and kept silent throughout the conference. As the emperor himself testified in 1946, his first imperial conference in 1938 created a precedent that he would follow until the end of World War II. This 1938 imperial conference did not produce the desired outcome for the emperor. The conference confirmed Japan's determination to destroy the Chinese Nationalist government unless the Chinese were willing to accept the peace terms that were advantageous to Japan. In order to realize "coexistence and co-prosperity" among Japan, China, and Manchuria, China would have to recognize Manchukuo, accept the proposed demilitarized zones in northern China and Inner Mongolia, and pay compensation for war damages, among other concessions.[75]

However, Prime Minister Konoe miscalculated the international situation and committed a series of blunders. First, when Chiang Kai-shek's Nationalist government refused to accept the high-handed Japanese peace terms, the Konoe government decided to abandon diplomatic engagement with Chiang's government. Behind this action was Konoe's attempt to replace Chiang's regime with a sympathetic faction within the Chinese Nationalist Party led by Wang Jingwei and to negotiate peace terms with the new regime. At the liaison conference on January 15, a heated debate ensued between hawkish Konoe cabinet members and General Tada of the Army General Staff, who was against continuing military operations in China. In the end, the hawkish ministers prevailed. Prince Kanin, chief of the General Staff, asked the emperor to intervene to reverse the decision, but Hirohito declined—a decision that allowed Konoe and his cabinet to pursue a military solution in China in spite of the objection of the General Staff.[76] On January 16, 1938, the prime minister publicly declared Japan's intention to treat Chiang's regime as an illegitimate government and to annihilate it.

On March 30, 1938, the Konoe cabinet put the entire nation on full-fledged war footing by issuing the National General Mobilization Law. The law allowed central authorities to control not only human and material resources but also public information for the purpose of national defense. Thus, from the summer of 1937 until 1938, under the Konoe cabinet, the entire nation of Japan was mobilized in support of war efforts in China and Manchuria.

Throughout 1938, while Prime Minister Konoe pursued inconsistent policies in China, and while Japanese troops kept moving deeper into China, the emperor continued to express his preference for an early termination of the war. Having been deeply troubled by the whole chain of military events in Manchuria since 1931, in February 1938, when the emperor had an audience with General Hata Shunroku (who had been appointed to command Japanese forces in central China), Hirohito asked for confirmation that the army would not turn the entire region into a second Manchuria.[77] With Japanese troops bogged down in inland China, by early June 1938 Prime Minister Konoe had changed his mind and become eager to put an end to the war with the Chinese Nationalists. Having heard this view from Konoe, the emperor thought of intervening with the military. However, the army leadership was determined to defeat the Chinese forces and was planning to attack Hankou. Hirohito lamented, "While one side says it wants to end the war, the other side says it will go all the way to Hankou. It is very deplorable that there is no coordination."[78] On July 4, the emperor summoned Army Chief of Staff Prince Kanin and the new war minister, General Itagaki Seishiro (who, in a historical irony, had been chosen by Konoe for the purpose of negotiating peace with China). Hirohito said to these two generals, "I think we should end this war as soon as possible: what do you think?" Both of them replied in one voice: "We will continue to fight until we defeat Chiang Kai-shek." This increased the emperor's anxiety considerably.[79]

After Japanese forces bogged down deep inside Chinese territory, Konoe tried to modify Japan's extreme position toward Chiang's regime by declaring that he wanted to build a New Order in East Asia under Japan's auspices, ostensibly with the goal of co-prosperity.[80] However, Tokyo soon realized that its attempt to negotiate a peace with Wang Jingwei's sympathetic faction in the Chinese Nationalist Party had failed. Japan would eventually try to settle hostilities in 1940 by supporting Wang in establishing a pro-Japanese regime in Nanjing, but this ill-conceived Japanese scheme would reduce Wang's government to a mere puppet of the Japanese military.

Throughout this period, the effectiveness of the Konoe cabinet was limited by its incoherent and misleading rhetoric. Prime Minister Konoe's declaration of a New Order in East Asia, based on the doctrine of cooperation and co-prosperity, was intended merely to mitigate the hostility and resistance of Chiang Kai-shek and the Nationalists. Japan had used the slogan of co-prosperity to pursue its own national interests ever since it embarked on its imperialist path; and in 1938, the Konoe cabinet used the same rhetoric to look for a way out of a war it had allowed to start but could not finish. Moreover, the Konoe cabinet and Japan's military leadership appealed to the patriotism of the Japanese people and justified their decision to mobilize the entire nation on a war footing based on national self-defense and protection of "the prosperity of the Imperial Throne." Although this allowed Japan's central authorities to appeal to the people's sense of loyalty and duty to the emperor (who was, after all, synonymous with their state), in the process, the government was enforcing the unfortunate myth of absolute imperial rule and leading the Japanese people further and further away from reality. Frustrated with his inability to settle hostilities with China, Prime Minister Konoe resigned in January 1939.

Meanwhile, in the summer of 1938, the military activity of the Kwantung Army escalated along the Manchurian border with the Soviet Union, and this intensified the emperor's fear of insubordination by that army. The Soviet occupation of a strategic hill in Zhanggufeng, where the southeastern border of Manchuria intersected with the boundaries of the Soviet Union and Korea, had led to military skirmishes between Japanese and Soviet soldiers, and this prompted the Kwantung Army and the Japanese army in Korea to propose a joint mobilization against Soviet forces. On July 19, the Army General Staff ordered the Japanese army in Korea to send the Nineteenth Division to Zhanggufeng, and on the following day, Army Chief of Staff Prince Kanin and War Minister Itagaki were planning to seek the emperor's sanction. However, Hirohito had learned that the foreign minister, the navy minister, and the lord keeper of the privy seal were all opposed to military action against Soviet forces. Therefore, through the chief aide-de-camp, the emperor communicated to both the army chief of staff and the war minister his unwillingness to meet with them because of his reluctance to authorize the proposed military mobilization. However, Prince Kanin and Itagaki asked for an audience anyway, and Itagaki sought an imperial sanction for the mobilization of the Japanese army in Korea.

Hirohito, who knew there were disagreements among the War Ministry, the Foreign Ministry, and the Navy Ministry, asked Itagaki whether he had reached full understanding with the other cabinet ministers. Itagaki's affirmative answer was interpreted by the emperor as evidence either of Itagaki's deliberate deception or of his incompetence. According to Harada's diary, the angry emperor rebuked Itagaki with unusually strong words: "The army's methods in the past have been outrageous. In the case of . . . the Manchurian Incident, and again in the early stage of the Marco Polo Bridge Incident, the army disobeyed the central authorities' order, relying only on local commanders' independent judgments. They [the local commanders] frequently employed measures that were unbecoming to my army. I feel these matters are truly outrageous. Nothing like that must happen this time." The emperor emphatically told the war minister, "You may not move even one soldier without my command."[81]

The emperor's words initially shocked Prince Kanin and Itagaki, and the General Staff ordered the Kwantung Army not to initiate any military actions against Soviet forces. However, the Nineteenth Division launched an attack across the border and occupied Zhanggufeng until the Russians rolled the incursion back and inflicted considerable casualties on the Japanese side. On August 10, the reality of Japan's military defeat—not the emperor's order—produced a cease-fire between Japanese and Soviet forces in Zhanggufeng.[82] The emperor's assessment of the situation at the outset of the incident turned out to be correct. On July 20, Hirohito pessimistically had told the lord keeper of the privy seal that Kwantung Army officers would not come to their senses until their unauthorized aggressive actions had brought about a disastrous outcome.[83]

Unfortunately, the Kwantung Army did not learn its lesson from the incident in Zhanggufeng, and in the spring of 1939 it launched several unauthorized military actions against Soviet forces in the vicinity of Nomonhan, on the border between Manchuria and Outer Mongolia. Despite the emperor's desire to localize the conflict, hostilities continued to escalate until the Kwantung Army finally decided to comply with Tokyo's order to pull back on September 7, 1939, primarily because of the difficult reality of defeat on the battlefield, not because of the authority of the emperor or the high command.[84]

At the same time, events in Europe stole the spotlight from the northeast Asian war theater. After signing the German-Soviet Nonaggression Pact of August 23 to eliminate the threat of Soviet armed intervention, Germany invaded Poland on September 1, 1939. Two days later, on September 3, Great Britain and France declared war on Germany, plunging Europe into World War II.

THE TRIPARTITE PACT

On January 6, 1939, before Germany went to war with Britain and France, Germany proposed to the Japanese government that the Anti-Comintern Pact, which Japan had signed with Germany in 1936 and Italy in 1937, be expanded. The idea was to form a military alliance against not only the Soviet Union but also other third parties. The army leadership in Tokyo, which was interested in a broader military alliance with Germany, allowed Lieutenant General Oshima Hiroshi (then Japanese military attaché, soon to be promoted to ambassador in Berlin) to explore this possibility with German authorities. But on August 23, 1939, in the midst of Oshima's investigation of a possible reshaping of the pact, Germany's sudden announcement that it was concluding the German-Soviet Nonaggression Pact came as a shock to the Japanese army. To make the situation worse, from Japan's perspective, Japanese troops were still engaged in hostilities with Soviet forces in Nomonhan. The diary of General Hata Shunroku, who was then the emperor's chief aide-de-camp, shows that by this time Hirohito was losing faith in his army's judgments and strategies on the Asian continent. According to Hata, the emperor expressed his dislike of the army's tendency to admire German military tradition and objected to the idea of forging a tripartite military alliance with Nazi Germany and Fascist Italy. Dumbfounded by the news of the German-Soviet Nonaggression Pact, Hata was sympathetic to the emperor's position. In his diary, Hata wrote of the emperor's slim hope that the way Germany had signed the nonaggression pact with the Soviet Union (without consulting Japan) might reveal the true thoughts of Germany's leaders and have a positive effect on Japan's internal debate over signing a tripartite pact with German and Italy. Hata recorded that the emperor told him, "If this misfortune wakes up the Army, it would be a blessing."[85]

However, after the announcement of the German-Soviet Nonaggression Pact and during the quiet "phony war" period of the winter of 1939–40, public discussion among Japanese leaders concerning a potential tripartite pact with Germany and Italy subsided. The emperor, who did not hesitate to reveal his anti-Axis sentiments, tried as much as possible to influence the two short-lived cabinets—that of Prime Minister Abe Nobuyuki (August 1939–January 1940) and the succeeding cabinet led by Prime Minister Yonai Mitsumasa (January–July 1940). Hirohito told Prime Minister Abe to "make use of the Anglo-American powers in diplomatic efforts" and offered his trusted chief aide-de-camp, General Hata, to serve as war minister in the Abe cabinet. However, once Germany's blitzkrieg swept through Western Europe in the spring of 1940 and after France's surrender in June 1940, the disappointed Hirohito became less eager to exert his influence. Germany's sweeping victory on the European continent was portrayed by the Japanese press as an emergence of a "new order" under Nazi Germany, similar to the New Order in East Asia that Japanese ultranationalists and militarists were advocating for the Asian continent.[86] This new development in Europe gave the Japanese army a renewed opportunity to push for a tripartite alliance with Germany and Italy. The Japanese military had been anxious to build airbases in northern French Indochina to block the supply routes used by the United States and Britain to send military aid to the Chinese Nationalists. Now that the French proxy government under the control of Nazi Germany ruled French Indochina, some Japanese leaders, both civilian and military, were eager to couple two sets of negotiations: Japan's negotiations to have access to northern French Indochina and discussions of a broader alliance with Germany.

In early 1940, after Prime Minister Abe resigned because of his cabinet's failure to deal with domestic and international problems, the emperor took an unusual step in naming Admiral Yonai as new prime minister, knowing that the admiral and his followers in the navy were reluctant to support the proposed Axis Alliance. As the emperor recalled in 1946, "I took initiative in recommending Yonai. . . . I appointed Yonai as prime minister in order to check the movement toward [forming] a German-Japanese alliance."[87] However, after the fall of France, the army brought about the collapse of the Yonai cabinet by asking General Hata to resign from his position as war minister. Following Yonai's resignation on July 16, 1940, the new cabinet, which formed under Prime Minister Konoe Fumimaro, was prepared to conclude an alliance with Germany from the very beginning. On July 19, three days before Konoe officially formed his cabinet, the new prime minister met at his residence in Ogikubo with his future foreign minister, Matsuoka Yosuke; future war minister, Tojo Hideki; and future navy minister, Yoshida Zengo. The new cabinet agreed to conclude a Japan-Germany-Italy alliance and a separate Japanese-Soviet nonaggression pact and to incorporate the European colonies in Southeast Asia into Japan's New Order.[88]

On July 26 and 27, the Konoe cabinet, along with the Army and Naval General Staffs, made a decision to pursue a twofold diplomatic and military objective: a policy of southern expansion and the conclusion of an Axis Alliance. However, the emperor clearly expressed misgivings, voicing his distrust of Germany and the Soviet Union as well as his reservations about the military's move in French Indochina. Hirohito's primary objection to the Axis Alliance and the southern advance stemmed from his fear of provoking a war with Anglo-American powers, especially the United Sates. During this period, US-Japanese diplomatic relations went from bad to worse, primarily because of Japanese military actions in China. The Roosevelt administration, which had been encouraging US business to impose a "moral embargo" on exports to Japan, had unilaterally informed Japan on July 26, 1939, that the US-Japanese Treaty of Commerce and Navigation would be terminated in six months. This meant that, beginning in January 1940, the United States would have the liberty to use economic sanctions of any kind to pressure Japan to alter its behavior. At that time the United States supplied roughly 80–90 percent of Japan's vital war materials, especially oil and petroleum products and iron and steel.[89]

Emperor Hirohito, who had a realistic grasp of Japan's national capabilities and resources, did not appear to think that, in the event of war between the two nations, Japan would be capable of defeating the United States. During his July 27 audience with army and navy chiefs, the emperor asked whether Japan would be able to win a war against the United States, and what Japan would do in the event of US embargos on oil and iron.[90] Foreign Minister Matsuoka emerged as the leading advocate of the tripartite alliance, with an idea of expanding this agreement into a quadruple alliance by including the Soviet Union. Matsuoka had also convinced himself that an Axis Alliance would strengthen Japan's bargaining power vis-à-vis the United States and would help avert a war between the two countries. However, the emperor was apprehensive about this optimistic view. On August 9, having heard Matsuoka's two-hour-long report, the emperor told Kido Koichi, lord keeper of the privy seal, "I understand that Matsuoka is trying to unify our diplomatic efforts and to avoid diplomatic isolation [for Japan] as much as possible. But it is regrettable that he [Matsuoka] is unable to see far into the future of our relations with the United States."[91] The emperor also commented, "[Matsuoka's] theory sounds plausible but its prosecution will be quite difficult."[92]

The Tripartite Pact of Japan, Germany, and Italy was formally signed on September 27, 1940, with only lukewarm approval by the emperor. On the eve of the signing of the pact, Hirohito was still apprehensive and reluctant to endorse the alliance, but he had no one to turn to for support. Opponents of the alliance in the navy, such as Prince Fushimi and Admirals Yonai Mitsumasa and Yamamoto Isoroku, could not prevail over the concerted efforts of the entire army, the Konoe cabinet, and a Foreign Ministry led by Matsuoka. Ailing Genro Saionji, who till his death on November 24, 1940, believed that the Anglo-American powers would triumph, was unable to intervene.[93] Lord Privy Seal Kido chose not to be in close communication with Saionji, because he knew very well that the *genro*, who had declined to approve the appointment of Prime Minister Konoe, were opposed to the alliance with Germany. This angered Saionji, and the attempt by Saionji's secretary, Harada Kumao, to create an opposition by contacting some naval officers (including Prince Takamatsu) did not make much difference in the overall course of events.[94] The still-anxious emperor had to rely on the counsel of Prime Minister Konoe, Foreign Minister Matsuoka, and Lord Privy Seal Kido.

Konoe and Matsuoka insisted that the 1940 Axis Alliance was intended to prevent the United States from declaring a war on the Axis Powers. This might actually have been true for Germany at the time, but Emperor Hirohito was not fully convinced of this argument. On September 15, four days before the imperial conference that would decide on a tripartite pact, Hirohito was still afraid of possible US retaliation. He told Kido, "We will be in trouble if Prime Minister Konoe abandons [his government] again when things become difficult. I will be hard pressed unless Konoe is really prepared to go through a lot with me."[95] The following day, the emperor directly asked Konoe's opinion: "If there are no other means to deal with the United States, it probably cannot be helped. However, in the event that we should have to go to war with the United States, how can the navy perform? I often heard that in the war games at the Naval Staff College, Japan is always the loser in a Japanese-US war. Can you reassure me about that?" The emperor continued: "I am really worried about this situation. What would happen if by any chance Japan should become a defeated nation? Are you prepared to share the pains and toil with me?" Konoe told the emperor the story of Ito Hirobumi, who was determined to sacrifice his life to support Emperor Meiji at the time of Russo-Japanese War (1904–5). Konoe assured the emperor that he was as determined as Ito to serve the emperor.[96]

Lord Privy Seal Kido, on the other hand, shared the emperor's concerns about the Axis Alliance's impact on Japan's relations with the Anglo-American powers. On September 21, Kido advised the emperor that Japan must immediately readjust and repair its relations with China, "[because] it is obvious that we must eventually oppose England and the United States when we conclude a military alliance with Germany and Italy."[97] The fear of a war between Japan and the United States lingered, and the emperor was of two minds about sanctioning the Axis Alliance. In the end, though, Hirohito went along with Foreign Minister Matsuoka's recommendation, and the alliance was concluded on September 27. History shows that the Konoe government's miscalculation about the US reaction to the Tripartite Pact was costly. In his recollection in 1946, the emperor regretted his action. He said, "Although I ultimately approved of the Japanese-German alliance, I never approved of it with full satisfaction. Matsuoka was convinced that the United States would not enter into war. [However] I was not certain that German Americans would support Germany as Matsuoka suggested. But I could not think Matsuoka would lie: I halfheartedly accepted his words. As for the question of [relations with] the Soviet Union, I warned Konoe that he should further ascertain the state of German-Soviet relations."[98]

CHAPTER 3

The Road to Pearl Harbor

E MPEROR HIROHITO WAS PERSONALLY AGAINST THE WAR WITH the United States and Great Britain, but this did not mean that he was an absolute pacifist who believed in avoiding war at all cost. Although he did not support reckless and aggressive military action, neither did he preclude war as a means to protect and advance his country's national interests if circumstances dictated. In 1941, the emperor did not support a war with the United States and Great Britain because he believed that it was in Japan's interest to avoid a costly and most likely unwinnable conflict. What he feared most was the collapse of his country not only through war with the Western great powers but also through civil war at home. Ironically, the military's pressure and breakdown of diplomatic negotiations with the United States eventually forced Hirohito to sanction a war he did not want, because he feared a military coup d'état and disintegration of his country from within. And this leads us to a number of interesting questions.

If the emperor was against war with the United States, did his opposition make any difference in the course of events in the fall of 1941? To what extent could he exert influence over war decisions initiated by military leaders in his unique capacity as commander in chief as well as political unifier/ratifier? Did his intervention or nonintervention make any substantial difference in Japan's decision to go to war with the United States? Documents reveal that Hirohito and his close advisers did act together as a brake to slow the final decision for one and a half months, from mid-October to the beginning of December 1941. Yet, in the end, despite his doubts and reservations, the emperor felt partly compelled and partly persuaded to sanction the Tojo government's war decision at the imperial conference of December 1. This was a result of overwhelming pressure from the Japanese high command, compounded by the failure of diplomatic negotiations with the United States. During the critical months between July and December 1941, every time an imperial conference was convened for the emperor to ratify a national decision, the resolution was presented to Hirohito *after* a consensus had been reached by the chiefs of the Army and Naval General Staffs, the ministers of war and navy, and the cabinet. This, however, did not mean that the emperor had no alternative but to accept, against his will, the military and government's recommendation for war. There was still a slight chance for him to prevail over the triangular power relations among the imperial court, the military, and the cabinet by exploiting the undefined power of the throne, despite Hirohito's own precarious and ambiguous position. From late July to early December 1941, the emperor had serious reservations about the military's eagerness to go to war with the United States, and during this period neither the army nor the navy could completely ignore the emperor's will because they needed his sanction, however ceremonial it might be, to render their decision a sacred state decision to maintain national unity.

In the trajectory of US-Japanese relations that led to Japan's attack on Pearl Harbor, the imperial conference of July 2, 1941, became an important turning point. In response to the outbreak of hostilities between Germany and the Soviet Union, the decision of July 2 gave the Japanese military the green light to take over bases in southern French Indochina in order to force the capitulation of the Chinese Nationalist government by severing its links with the United States and Britain. In carrying out this plan, the Konoe government and the Army and Naval General Staffs decided, "Our Empire will not be deterred by the possibility of being involved in a war with Great Britain and the United States." According to the plan, Japan would not go to war with the Soviet Union for the time being and would continue its military preparedness in the north. According to the record, the emperor gave ceremonial sanction to the decision that accepted the possibility of war with the United States and Britain without uttering a single word.[1]

However, Hirohito's approval of the July 2 decision did not necessarily reflect his own opinion. In late July 1941, when the supreme command in Tokyo was pressing the emperor to sanction plans to send Japanese troops

into southern French Indochina, the emperor repeatedly expressed his preference for peaceful means over use of force and warned the military to avoid
war with Britain and the United States. For example, on July 22, Hirohito
bombarded the chief of the General Staff, General Sugiyama Gen, with questions: "Is there any better way to settle the China Incident?" "Is there a better
means other than the use of force?" When Sugiyama replied in the negative,
the emperor said, "But our national strength, especially material strength, is
not sufficient. Can we achieve our objectives through use of force in such a
condition?" The emperor reminded the general that Japan's natural resources
were scarce. Apparently unconvinced by the general's estimate that military
operations should be over in a year, the emperor again asked, "You are not
going to resort to force in French Indochina, are you?" Sugiyama replied that
Japanese military commanders in Indochina were expected to peacefully
deploy their troops. The emperor concluded the audience with the following
words: "Well, it is better if you do not use force." Sugiyama, who was fully
aware of the emperor's position, recorded his observation after his audience
with the emperor: "Judging from the emperor's questions today, it seems that
the emperor is firmly determined not to use force." However, the emperor's
personal inclination for peace had no bearing on the general's thinking. Sugiyama was determined to persuade the emperor to accept the General Staff's
position. He wrote, "From now on, whenever I have an opportunity, I intend
to persuade him [the emperor] to change his mind. I think we need to guide
him step-by-step to make him understand what sort of resolve [to use force]
is necessary in the North and the South. This matter requires strict secrecy."[2]

The officers of the Operations Bureau in the Army General Staff fully
shared Sugiyama's opinions, and they were determined to persuade the
emperor that the national emergency warranted the use of force, if necessary. Lieutenant General Tanaka Shinichi, chief of the Operations Bureau,
recorded his opinion on the same day, July 22:

> The emperor's idea of no use of armed forces is fine, but in view of the cur-
> rent overall situation, the stage has reached a critical point that demands
> his resolve to resort to the use of armed forces if necessary. We must
> explain this point to the emperor and earn his approval. In order to do
> so, we need to prepare persuasive data. We must not only persuade the
> emperor that we are at the critical point that demands his resolve but also
> present a rationale that will convince the emperor of positive outcomes of
> the military solution.[3]

Three days later, on July 25, Japanese troops moved into southern French Indochina. The following day, in retaliation, the Roosevelt administration issued an executive order to freeze all Japanese assets in the United States, which eventually allowed the US State and Treasury Departments to implement a virtual oil embargo that President Roosevelt had not originally intended to impose on Japan.[4] The British and Dutch governments followed suit, which in turn pushed the Japanese military further toward war preparations.

The emperor did not conceal his frustration with the military leaders who were apparently misadvising him. He complained to Sugiyama that, contrary to the general's earlier estimate, "[Japan's] move into southern French Indochina induced further United States sanctions."[5] The emperor was reportedly "extremely unhappy" when Admiral Nagano Osami, chief of the Naval General Staff, during an audience on July 29, spoke of Japan's need to resolve to go to war with the United States in the wake of its economic sanctions. Hirohito made it clear that as far as he was concerned, a war with Britain and the United States was "out of the question." Navy Minister Oikawa Koshiro, in an attempt to ease the emperor's concern, explained that Admiral Nagano's belief in the need to go to war with Britain and the United States was his own opinion. The navy minister assured the emperor that Nagano's opinion by no means represented the navy's position. The following day, the emperor, who was still concerned about Nagano's attitude, reminded the admiral, "[Former] Chief of the Naval General Staff Fushimi told me that he would avoid war with Britain and the United States. Have you changed that?" Nagano replied, "I have not changed that principle, but because our supplies are gradually diminishing, if we are going to fight, I think the sooner we do [so], the better."[6]

The lord keeper of the privy seal, Kido Koichi, also recorded in his diary what the emperor told him about his verbal exchanges with Nagano. Although the admiral repeated the navy's desire to avoid war, he told the emperor that without new oil supplies, Japan's oil reserves would last for only two years, and that in case of war with the United States, Japan would run out of oil in one and a half years. The admiral expressed his conviction that there was thus no other alternative but to strike first. The emperor asked Nagano, "What do you think will be the outcome of war with the United States?" Hirohito continued, saying that he wanted to believe the navy's explanation for the prospect of victory, but he wondered whether Japan could achieve a sweeping victory like the Battle of the Japan Sea in the Russo-Japanese War of 1904–5.

Admiral Nagano answered, "A victory like the one in the Battle of the Japan Sea is out of the question, and I cannot tell you whether Japan will win or not." The emperor confided to Kido his uneasiness about the admiral's statements: "This means that Japan is going to fight a war out of desperation [*sutebachi no tatakai*], and it is truly dangerous."[7]

Hirohito's anxiety continued to increase in August. He repeatedly expressed his concern over, and even his distrust of, the army's intentions. On August 5, the emperor complained to Prince Higashikuni, who was serving in the army, that he (Hirohito) was troubled by the army's abuse of the prerogative of the supreme command. Pointing out the disastrous consequences of Japan's advance into southern Indochina, contrary to the General Staff's initial optimistic estimate, the emperor told the prince, "The army justifies everything on the ground of operational necessity, and since they do not tell me their true intentions, I am quite at a loss."[8] The next day, on August 6, General Sugiyama requested imperial sanction for the liaison conference's decision to reinforce Japanese defenses in Manchuria but recommended avoiding provoking war with the Soviet Union, except for a war of defense. The emperor reluctantly approved the decision but made it clear that he was compelled to do so against his wishes. He also added a rather strongly worded warning: "In any case the army has a tendency to start a fight. You must keep a vigilant eye on them [in Manchuria] so that they will not engage in a conspiracy."[9]

※

There is no doubt that the imperial conference held on September 6, 1941, was the turning point that set Japan on a direct course for Pearl Harbor. The final conference decision consisted of three parts. First, Japan would "complete preparations for war" with the United States, Great Britain, and the Netherlands by the last ten days of October. Second, Japan would "concurrently take all possible diplomatic measures vis-à-vis the United States and Great Britain" to attain its objectives. Third, if there was no prospect of Japan's demands being met "by the first ten days of October through the diplomatic negotiations . . . [Japan would] immediately decide to commence hostilities against the United States, Great Britain, and the Netherlands."[10] In other words, Japan would start war preparations against the United States and Britain while continuing its diplomatic efforts, commencing hostilities if diplomacy failed to produce the desired outcome by mid-October.

Historians disagree as to whether Hirohito had any options at this crucial juncture. Robert Butow offers the widely accepted interpretation that the decision to expand hostilities was made by army and navy staff officers before September 5, 1941, and that "war was inevitable" unless the United States made concessions or "the monopoly of decision making held by the supreme command was broken."[11] Butow suggests that even the emperor could not have changed course without changes in the decision-making process. Herbert Bix, on the other hand, borrows from the work of a Japanese leftist historian, Koketsu Atsushi, and argues that the emperor "clearly had options at this moment" and could have changed national policies had he wanted to.

As evidence to support this argument, Koketsu and Bix cite Takagi Sokichi's account of Hirohito's audience with Prime Minister Konoe Fumimaro and the chiefs of staff on the evening of September 5, arguing that the emperor had accepted the General Staffs' position the night before the imperial conference. According to Takagi, the emperor initially expressed serious doubts about General Sugiyama's estimate of a probability of victory against the United States and Britain. Hirohito even asked, "Sugiyama, are you lying to me?" However, Admiral Nagano came forward and made a persuasive analogy comparing Japan to a dying patient in need of surgery: Nagano urged the emperor to accept the liaison conference's resolution that would be presented at the imperial conference the following day. According to Bix, the emperor seemed impressed by the admiral's eloquent argument, and, now in a better mood, said to Nagano, "All right, I understand." At that point, Prime Minister Konoe raised a question that Bix thinks was crucial. Konoe asked the emperor, "Shall I make changes in tomorrow's agenda? How would you like me to go about it?" Hirohito replied, "There is no need to change." Bix argues that at that moment, the emperor was presented with "a chance to stop, or slow, or lengthen the countdown to all-out, unbound war," but, according to Bix, the emperor chose not to do so because he "accepted" Nagano's "rapid decline" arguments and "ruled to set time conditions—ruled, that is, in favor of opening hostilities once certain conditions were met."[12]

The problem with this argument (that Hirohito could have changed the outcome of the imperial conference on September 6) is that it relies on selected evidence. According to the emperor's own 1946 recollection, on September 5, when Prime Minister Konoe reported to Hirohito on the agenda for the imperial conference (to be held the next day), the emperor asked Konoe to give diplomatic negotiations priority over a military solution by changing the order of the resolutions that had been reached by the liaison conference. Konoe told the emperor that he could not do this; instead, the prime minister proposed summoning the chiefs of staff so that Hirohito himself could "ask questions."[13] Konoe's memoir supports the accuracy of the emperor's recollection.[14]

General Sugiyama's more detailed record of what happened on September 5 shows that in the beginning, the emperor clearly expressed his desire for peaceful diplomatic efforts. Hirohito stated in the imperative form, "Continue peaceful diplomatic means as much as possible. Do not pursue war preparations in parallel with diplomacy, and put diplomacy first."[15]

According to the general, the emperor then asked questions about specific military operations, apparently to point out that General Sugiyama's past estimates had been unreliable.[16] Hirohito asked, "In the event of a war with the United States, is the army confident that it can dispose of the matter within a scheduled time frame?"[17] When Sugiyama replied that the initial phase of operations in the south would take about three months, the emperor reminded the general, "You were War Minister when the China Incident broke out [in 1937]. I remember you, as War Minister, told me that the incident would be over in about a month. But, after four long years, the fighting has not yet been settled." When Sugiyama tried to explain that China's continent had a vast hinterland, the emperor said, "If you call the Chinese hinterland vast, would you not describe the Pacific as even more immense? With what confidence do you say three months?"[18] In the end, the emperor became impatient, raised his voice, and asked, "Can you guarantee our victory?" Sugiyama's evasive answer did not satisfy the emperor, and Admiral Nagano came to the rescue as described earlier.[19] At this point in the narrative, Prime Minister Konoe's own account includes another important point that Takagi's record does not: consequently, Koketsu and Bix fail to mention it. According to Konoe, after hearing Admiral Nagano's persuasive analogy of Japan as a dying patient, the emperor continued to press the point: "Thus far, I take it that the supreme command will place an emphasis on diplomacy. Is that correct?" Both Sugiyama and Nagano answered in the affirmative.[20] Therefore, one can argue that when the emperor told Prime Minister Konoe that there was no need to change the agenda for the imperial conference, he did so because he believed that the supreme command had already agreed to give priority to diplomacy, not to war preparations.

The record compiled by Lieutenant General Tanaka Shinichi, who worked in the Operations Bureau of the Army General Staff, supports the above interpretation. According to Tanaka, at the end of the September 5 meeting,

Admiral Nagano assured the emperor that the three-part draft resolution did not favor war and that the resolution was designed merely to cope with the situation in case war was deemed unavoidable. The admiral's statement was followed by Prime Minister Konoe's words: "As both General Staff chiefs stated, our top priority is diplomatic negotiations." Finally, the emperor said, "I understood. I will approve."[21]

If Bix believed that Takagi Sokichi's account was reliable, he should also have mentioned the record of Takagi's lengthy interview with former prime minister Konoe on October 27, 1943, which is contained in the same source that Bix cites. Konoe's detailed recollection of the September 5 meeting, as told to Takagi, confirms the accuracy of Konoe's later memoir as well as General Sugiyama's memo. Takagi's record also reveals that Konoe believed it was extremely important to set the record straight—namely, that the chiefs of the Army and Naval General Staffs had agreed with his cabinet's position to emphasize diplomacy over war preparations. Therefore, Konoe asked the president of the Privy Council to repeat, at the imperial conference on September 6, the questions the emperor had asked the chiefs of staff on the prior day.[22]

There is another possible explanation for why the emperor did not force the reluctant chiefs of staff to change the agenda of the imperial conference. Aware of the futility of his personal attempts to change the liaison conference's unanimous decision, Hirohito might have wanted to *encourage* further discussion of the entire agenda when the imperial conference convened, rather than automatically sanction the decision presented to him the day before. Here is a dilemma and perhaps an ironic contradiction for leftist historians: the emperor who wanted to act like a constitutional monarch had to exercise his authority like an absolute monarch if he was to avoid war with the United States. Actually, in mid-August the emperor had attempted to change the imperial conference from a ceremonial venue for ratification of premade decisions to a real deliberative institution that decided national policy. In August, Hirohito was deeply concerned about the mounting tension with the United States and asked the lord keeper of the privy seal, Kido, to consult with the prime minister to determine whether the emperor could engage in discussion with participants in the imperial conference.[23] However, there is no indication that Kido pursued the matter at that time.

The emperor engaged Kido in a similar discussion on the morning of September 6: while talking with Kido right before the imperial conference convened, Hirohito expressed his desire to ask "various questions" at the conference. Kido, however, advised against doing so and told the emperor that the president of the Privy Council was supposed to ask questions. Kido suggested that the emperor should make a brief statement at the end of the conference, emphasizing the need for the supreme command's cooperation to achieve successful diplomatic negotiations with the United States.[24] The emperor, following Kido's advice, remained silent and listened to the ceremonial presentations throughout the conference. At the end of the conference, Hirohito read the now famous poem composed by his grandfather, Emperor Meiji: "All the seas, in every quarter, are as brothers to one another. Why, then, do the winds and waves of strife rage so turbulently throughout the world?"[25] There was no doubt in anyone's mind at the conference that the emperor wanted the supreme command to pursue diplomatic means, not war preparations. Yet, in the end, the imperial conference made no change in the decision reached by the prior liaison conference.

The above attempt by the emperor shows both the extent and limitation of his ability to influence decision making. Certainly, Hirohito's unprecedented expression of his desire for peace served as a brake on Japan as it moved toward Pearl Harbor. However, the nebulous power relationships among the emperor, the supreme command, and the prime minister allowed the military to keep intact the ambiguous decision of September 6, which in turn allowed each party to pursue war preparations and diplomatic negotiations simultaneously. In other words, there was no real consensus. Since the prewar Japanese system depended on the leadership's ability to build a consensus, there was a danger that the failure to do so could lead to a breakdown of the entire system, unless someone was willing to compromise.

Between the imperial conference of September 6 and the next turning point—namely, the appointment of General Tojo Hideki as the new prime minister in mid-October—the supreme command, particularly the Army General Staff, was determined to persuade the emperor of the inevitability of war with the United States. During this period, the General Staff presented the emperor with a series of seemingly realistic strategic plans that would win a war against the United States and Britain. So successful was this effort that by the mid-October deadline (which had been set by the September 6 decision), the emperor, despite continued personal reservations, was no longer able to dismiss the need for war preparations. Although there is no specific evidence to suggest that Hirohito had accepted the inevitability of war before the US government rejected Japan's proposal of November 20, he most likely realized by mid-October that the possibility of going to war was very real.

The unprecedented expression of his own clear preference for peace, expressed by Hirohito on September 6, could be considered a real test of pro-war officers' loyalty to the emperor. After all, the Imperial Rescript to Soldiers and Sailors, issued by Emperor Meiji in 1882, had commanded absolute loyalty to the emperor, and military education in early Showa Japan required every soldier and sailor to internalize this virtue.[26] For a while after the September 6 imperial conference, even the hard-line pro-war army officers had mixed feelings over the proper pace of war preparations. The officers exhibited a curious mixture of emotions: uneasiness about the emperor's opposition to war, along with an audacious hope of prevailing over the emperor's personal opinion. In the end, however, these officers were united in the conviction that sooner or later they would have to persuade Hirohito to accept military solutions to settle a probable confrontation with the United States.

Two men who best represented the army officers' ambivalent loyalty toward the emperor were Major General Muto Akira, chief of the Military Affairs Bureau of the War Ministry, and Lieutenant Colonel Ishii Akiho, Muto's right-hand man in the ministry. Major General Muto was a leading war advocate in the army, but he gathered his subordinates immediately after the imperial conference and told them that they must respect the emperor's wish: "The emperor's wish is to pursue diplomatic solutions at all cost. Although I am convinced that a war [with the United States] is unavoidable in the long run, we must not press it on the emperor. We must wholeheartedly concentrate on diplomatic efforts, and work diligently until the emperor realizes the futility of diplomacy and comes to a decision in favor of war, on his own. I am going to tell this to the Minister [War Minister Tojo Hideki]."[27] In his memoir, Lieutenant Colonel Ishii pointed out the contradiction in Muto's argument, writing that it was illogical as well as disloyal (*fuchu*) to the throne, because while Muto realized that the imperial wish (*seii*) was to avoid war at all cost, he was still telling his subordinates that he believed war to be inevitable. Nevertheless, Ishii defended Muto, calling his view farsighted despite the imperial wish for peace; Muto considered war unavoidable because there were limitations to Japan's concessions to US demands. Ishii was even sympathetic to his superior, who was caught between imperial pressure from above and his responsibility to the army under his command. Perhaps Ishii, too, exhibited a typical military officer's ambivalence between his personal loyalty to his military superior and his impersonal loyalty to the emperor. In their comments, both Muto and Ishii clearly demonstrated their belief that their expert knowledge made their judgment superior to that of the emperor.[28]

This conviction (that their own judgment was superior to that of Emperor Hirohito) was even more apparent among the hawkish officers in the Operations Bureau of the Army General Staff. This group was determined to appeal to the emperor about the necessity for war preparations until he changed his mind. According to Lieutenant Colonel Ishii, when he visited Colonel Hattori Takushiro of the Operations Bureau, Hattori passionately told him, "We won't be able to make any move later unless we go to war now. I can give you many specific reasons if you want. What he [Tojo] should do right now as war minister is to go to the palace day and night and appeal to the emperor for the urgent need to go to war."[29]

From late September to early October, the records of both the Operations Bureau (in the First Department) and the War Guidance Section in the Army General Staff show that the pro-war officers engaged in intense discussions of how to win over a peace faction that included the emperor, Prime Minister Konoe, and Navy Minister Oikawa Koshiro. On September 30, the War Guidance Section recorded its resolve to prepare a "written report to the emperor" (*josobun*) concerning the need to open hostilities against the United States, Britain, and the Netherlands. Under Lieutenant Colonel Hattori's supervision, Takayama Shinobu, a thirty-four-year-old major in the Operations Bureau, began to prepare a report to persuade the emperor that a war with the United States and Britain was winnable. The document was eventually completed on October 20, 1941, as a *hoto shiryo*, under the title "Materials to Be Submitted in Reply to the Throne: The Operational Outlook, Both at the Beginning and Several Years Later, in Regard to a War with America, England, and Holland."[30] The document offered detailed, logical explanations for military strategies in Southeast Asia and the Pacific in order to overcome the emperor's deep concern about there being little prospect of victory if a war dragged on for several years. More specifically, the document argued that Japan would gain material advantages over the United States and Britain by the third year of a war, and it provided specific estimates of necessary military supplies and probable consumption rates of war materials. In addition it outlined plans to secure needed supplies in Southeast Asia, the Pacific, and North Asia.[31]

However, as noted above, this was a *hoto shiryo*: a collection of prepared answers in reply to anticipated questions from the emperor that were used by the chief of the General Staff during his audience with the emperor. Such documents were usually not submitted to the emperor. Therefore, contrary to the suggestion by some historians that the emperor's thinking was influenced by the October 20 *hoto shiryo* on the prospect of a war with the United States, there is no clear evidence to prove that Hirohito had actually received this particular document and read it.[32] Whether the emperor read it or not, there is no doubt that, throughout late October and the entire month of November, the document gave the Army General Staff ammunition to use in its continued attempts to influence Hirohito's thinking.

While the Army General Staff and pro-war officers in the navy continued to build their arguments in favor of war, the emperor himself started to show some indications that his support for a peaceful settlement had begun to waver, for at this point Hirohito started to talk about what Japan should do in the event of a war with the United States. On October 9, Hirohito summoned Prince Fushimi, the emperor's uncle and former chief of the Naval General Staff, and asked for his opinion about ongoing problems with the United States. According to the recollections of Prince Fushimi, when the prince expressed his conviction that a war with the United States was inevitable and argued that Japan should go to war sooner rather than later, the emperor replied, "Even if it may be so, I would rather wait a little longer. I know that eventually we might reach the point where we have to fight. I am prepared to accept that eventuality [*kakugo ha itashiteiru*]."[33] Perhaps Prince Fushimi's recollection exaggerated the emperor's willingness to accept the inevitability of war. After his meeting with the prince, Hirohito complained to the lord privy seal that he was "painfully" (*itaku*) disappointed with Prince Fushimi's "radical" advice.[34] However, whatever the emperor's true feelings, this episode shows that he was deeply troubled by the option placed in front of him and was struggling in vain to search for an alternative.

The emperor even suggested to Prime Minister Konoe that Chief of the General Staff Sugiyama should be replaced by Prince Higashikuni. Hirohito knew that although the prince was well respected within the army, Higashikuni was in favor of a peaceful diplomatic solution with the United States.[35] Even more importantly, the emperor trusted him. In contrast, the emperor repeatedly questioned General Sugiyama's reliability and at one point even asked if he was lying. However, Prime Minister Konoe did not support the emperor's proposed military reshuffle. Konoe reminded the emperor that the court must be careful not to interfere in the supreme command's personnel decisions. Konoe was afraid that the appointment of an imperial house member to such an important and responsible military position might disrupt the working relations between the supreme command and the government, as in the cases of Prince Kanin and Prince Fushimi in the previous decade.[36]

Thus, it can be seen that the people surrounding the emperor offered little help, and Hirohito was losing hope for a peaceful solution. On October 13, the emperor told the lord privy seal that the possibility of a diplomatic settlement with the United States seemed to be fading. Hirohito talked about specific matters that must be addressed in the event of war. For example, he suggested to the lord privy seal that the declaration of war must reflect the emperor's sincere regard for world peace, and he emphasized the importance of carefully studying the question of how to end a war.[37] Apparently, the tense situation made the emperor feel that war might happen at any moment regardless of his opposition.

Prime Minister Konoe's resignation on October 16 was a devastating blow to the emperor's hope for peace. Hirohito was counting on the prime minister's ability to resist the military's pressure and continue diplomatic negotiations with the United States. After the war, the emperor retrospectively expressed his disappointment in Konoe's "lack of firm conviction and courage." In the emperor's view, Konoe created his own predicament at the time of the imperial conference of September 6. Despite the emperor's personal plea to place priority on diplomatic negotiations over war preparations, Konoe had refused to amend the liaison conference decision and had allowed the September 6 decision to include the mid-October deadline for going to war. According to the emperor, Konoe resigned because he could not extricate himself from this decision and the army and the navy pressed him to take action when the deadline arrived.[38]

Leftist historians who like to emphasize the emperor's inclination toward a military solution often quote Konoe's statement regarding the circumstances surrounding his resignation, which was recorded by his chief cabinet secretary, Tomita Kenji:

> Of course his majesty is a pacifist, and there is no doubt that he wished to avoid war. When I told him, as prime minister, that to initiate war is a mistake, he agreed. But the next day he would tell me, 'You were worried about it yesterday; but you don't have to worry so much.' Thus, gradually, he began to lean toward war. And the next time I met him, he leaned even more toward war. In short, I felt that the emperor had absorbed the views of the army and navy high commands and gave me the impression that he

thought that the prime minister did not understand military matters and that he [the emperor] knew much more. Consequently, as a prime minister who lacked authority over the high command, I had no way of making any further effort because the emperor, who was the last resort, was this way.[39]

Certainly, Konoe might have liked to blame others, including the emperor, when he chose to resign because of his inability to overcome pressure from his hawkish war minister, General Tojo, as well as from the Army and Naval General Staffs.[40] However, in the light of the Army General Staff officers' determination to persuade the emperor of the inevitability of war, the circumstances then surrounding Hirohito are reminiscent of Max Weber's words quoted by Maruyama Masao: "Even an absolute monarch—or, in a sense, *especially* an absolute monarch—is impotent in face of the superior specialized knowledge of the bureaucracy."[41]

Weber's words were prophetic, given what happened at the imperial court from mid-October to November 1941. There is ample evidence to suggest that Hirohito was still personally against war with the United States at the time of Prime Minister Konoe's resignation, and that he and Lord Privy Seal Kido wanted Konoe's successor to be someone capable of reversing the September 6 decision and giving diplomacy a chance. Yet the emperor and Kido chose as Konoe's successor the war minister, General Tojo, who, as spokesman for the supreme command, was the leading advocate of war in the cabinet and was instrumental in forcing Konoe's resignation. Why? Hirohito and the lord privy seal were fully aware that the emperor had the respect and loyalty of his ministers and generals but did not possess real power to reverse the September 6 decision, and both opted to gamble on Tojo's loyalty to the throne and his ability to control the war factions in the military. Tojo's loyalty to the emperor was well known to the palace as well as to the army. The lord privy seal, acting as "cabinet midwife,"[42] recommended Tojo as the new prime minister at the senior statesmen's meeting (*jushin kaigi*) on the grounds that only Tojo could control the militant elements in the army, forge cooperation between the army and the navy, and reexamine the September 6 decision. Kido later admitted in an interview in 1967 that although he did not mention it explicitly to the senior statesmen at the time, he believed that Tojo was an exemplary soldier who would obey any order if it came from the throne. Kido even confessed that he "used the emperor" to reverse the decision Hirohito himself had sanctioned on September 6 and that, with his back against the wall, Kido had no other recourse but to resort to this unusual measure of recommending Tojo as prime minister.[43]

The emperor was obviously a willing participant in Kido's scheme. He never doubted General Tojo's loyalty to the throne. After the war, Hirohito told one of his most trusted chamberlains, Kinoshita Michio, "There was nobody who followed my opinions and carried them out as closely as he [Tojo]."[44] The emperor also commented, in his "Monologue," that in October 1941 he had thought that Tojo, "who grasped the sentiments within the army," would be able to restrain the army and carry out his wishes, if he (the emperor) imposed certain conditions when he appointed Tojo as prime minister.[45]

On October 17, in order to carry out this unusual maneuver to avoid a decision for war, the emperor and Kido played their respective roles without creating the appearance of impropriety. First, Hirohito summoned Tojo and directed him to form a cabinet. Reminding the new prime minister of the "exceedingly grave situation" Japan was confronting, the emperor emphasized the utmost importance of cooperation between the army and the navy. Then, the emperor summoned Navy Minister Oikawa and repeated the urgent need for interservice cooperation. Shortly after this, the lord privy seal met Tojo and Oikawa, who were still in the waiting room of the palace, and conveyed the emperor's wish that, in determining the fundamental policies of the nation, the new cabinet ought "to deliberate very carefully and to undertake a thoroughgoing study of the situation at home and abroad *without being bound by the imperial conference decision of September 6.*"[46] This was the emperor's so-called clean slate (*hakushi kangen*) message.

General Tojo's loyalty to the emperor was evident in an episode that took place at the War Ministry, on the afternoon of October 17, right before Tojo went to the palace to have an audience with the emperor. According to Lieutenant Colonel Ishii's memoirs, Ishii anticipated an imperial order to withdraw Japan's troops from China in the near future under the new cabinet, and he drafted a memorandum arguing in favor of keeping Japanese forces in China. He then submitted the memo to War Minister Tojo. Although Tojo did not expect the premiership to fall on his shoulders at that time, he returned the memorandum to Ishii and said, "I have read your finely crafted memorandum. But, if the emperor declares that it should be so, I will say 'yes' and retreat."[47] Tojo was caught by surprise when he was ordered to serve as both prime minister and war minister. However, once he received the imperial command, Tojo faithfully and diligently carried out his task: he conducted a thorough reexamination of national policy without being bound by the September 6 decision. Tojo's secretary, Akamatsu Sadao, recalled that the prime minister always told his subordinates that "the emperor is a sacred being [*shinkaku*]":

> We subjects, regardless of how important we become, cannot overcome our existence as human beings [*jinkaku*]. Even the prime minister is unimportant in front of the emperor. He [the emperor] is beyond everything, and standing in his noble light, we first come to be respected by the people. . . . Since our people are like the children of the emperor, it is important to disseminate the imperial will to all corners and at the same time to unite the people's will under the emperor. Here lies the important duty of the emperor's ministers.[48]

Because of Tojo's unquestionable loyalty to the emperor, Tanaka Shinichi, in the Operations Bureau of the Army General Staff, called the Tojo government a "court cabinet" (*kyutei naikaku*).[49]

Appointing Tojo was a double-edged sword, however. The failure of the final attempt at diplomatic negotiations with the United States by the Tojo cabinet certainly meant war. The chief of the Combined Fleet, Vice Admiral Ugaki Matome, aptly observed in his diary, "If the decision is not to go to war, [the prime minister chosen from the army war faction] will serve as a means of restraining the army. If the decision is in favor of war, [Tojo] has enough vigor to push the nation toward war."[50] The emperor's brother, Prince Takamatsu, who was also serving the navy at that time, had a similar impression of Tojo's appointment as prime minister. The prince wrote in his diary on October 17, 1941, that the decision was unexpected, but he continued, "Upon careful consideration, I thought it might be an inevitable conclusion for those who knew what they were doing. . . . They made a clever move, but I also feel that this could be an end of diplomatic negotiations and an ultimate decision for war."[51]

The emperor and the lord privy seal were fully aware that they might gamble away peace if this final attempt at negotiations failed. In a sense, therefore, it can be argued that when Hirohito sanctioned Tojo's appointment as the new prime minister, the emperor had to be prepared to accept the worst possible scenario—war with the United States. The emperor's words to the lord privy seal on October 20 reflected this fact: "There is a saying, isn't there? You cannot get a tiger's cub unless you brave the tiger's den."[52]

If the emperor's intent was to let the Tojo cabinet continue diplomatic negotiations with the United States, and if the prime minister was willing to comply with the emperor's wish, what went wrong? When and how did Hirohito come to accept the inevitability of war and give up his hope for diplomacy? From October 23 to November 1, Prime Minister Tojo convened, almost daily, a liaison conference (the highest-level meeting between the Tojo cabinet and the supreme command) to reexamine Japan's fundamental policies.[53] Although the prime minister's intentions were sincere and he acted as a moderating force to build a consensus between the government and supreme command, his approach had some intrinsic problems. One was Tojo's blindness to his own predisposition in favor of military solutions. Perhaps he was deceiving himself, but he had little ability or imagination to push forward an alternative to military solutions or to consider pragmatic concessions.

The liaison conference agenda set up by officers of the War Ministry was biased toward war from the beginning, but there is no indication that Tojo had difficulty accepting it. According to the record of the liaison conference, out of ten matters discussed, nine concerned strategic and operational considerations of war, and only one item had a two-part question regarding diplomatic negotiations: "What are the prospects of the Japanese-American negotiations?" and "What are the limits to the concessions that can be made?" The answer to the first question was, "There is no hope of success over the short term." The second question provoked a lengthy discussion and focus shifted to the issue of "How much can we concede?" This question led to another question: "What would happen to Japan if the American proposals were accepted in their entirety?" The conference record says, "All except the Foreign Minister [Togo Shigenori] judged that the Empire would become a third-rate country." At the end of the meeting on October 30, Tojo proposed, perhaps too hastily, that on November 1 the liaison conference must decide which course Japan should choose. Tojo offered the following three alternatives: (1) "Avoid war and undergo great hardships" (*gashin shotan suru*), by which the military usually implied that Japan would become a third-rate nation and might plunge down the path of national suicide; (2) "Decide on war immediately and settle matters by war"; and (3) "Decide on war but carry on war preparations and diplomacy side by side." The following words in parentheses were attached to the third option: "(We would like to do it in such a way that diplomacy will succeed.)" Tojo was determined to reach a decision one way or the other, saying, "A decision must be reached on November 1, even if we have to meet all night." Obviously, the structure of the liaison conferences agenda reinforced the General Staff's eagerness to resolve any doubts about Japan's ability to wage war against the United States and strengthened its case for war.[54]

Moreover, the only reason Tojo made an effort to reexamine the decision of September 6 was the emperor's personal opposition to war. Tojo personally did not have any strong reason or conviction to continue diplomatic negotiations with the United States. The conversation between Tojo and General Sugiyama on the morning of November 1, right before the critical liaison conference, shows the weakness of Tojo's position. Because of the emperor's doubts about war, Tojo expressed his preference for the third alternative ("Decide on war but carry on war preparations and diplomacy side by side"). Sugiyama laid out the supreme command's demands: (1) abandonment of diplomatic negotiations, (2) resolution to go to war, (3) commencement of hostilities in early December, and (4) diplomatic maneuvers to support war strategies. Tojo responded, "I will not stop the supreme command from maintaining its arguments, but I do not think it is easy to persuade the emperor." Sugiyama concurred, saying, "I know how hard it is to ask the emperor to accept our position. We will choose the third alternative, if there is no other option left for us." Tojo again replied, "I am afraid that the emperor will not listen." However, he did not offer any other argument to buttress the emperor's case in favor of diplomacy.[55]

Without a consensus between Tojo and Sugiyama, the liaison conference began deliberation of the three alternatives that the Tojo cabinet had proposed. After seventeen hours of heated discussion, the conference adopted the third proposal. According to the minutes, "(a) A decision for war was made; (b) the time for the commencement of war was set at the beginning of December; (c) diplomacy was allowed to continue until midnight, November 30, and if diplomacy was successful by then, war would be called off."[56] The Foreign Office was to submit "Proposal A" to the United States, in which Japan promised to withdraw from French Indochina and part of China (except for designated areas in north China, Inner Mongolia, and Hainan Island) after settlement of the China Incident and expressed willingness to "act independently" of the Tripartite Pact. If this proved unsuccessful, Japan would try "Proposal B" as its final offering, in which Japan would agree to retreat from southern Indochina in return for the United States' restoring trade relations to the conditions prior to freezing Japanese assets.[57] Although the supreme command's proposition to go to war immediately was rejected, the liaison conference's decision for war first, and then setting a clear deadline for diplomatic negotiations in Washington (midnight, November 30), meant that practically the Tojo government favored a military solution over its ability to maintain the diplomatic option. Japan could now avoid war only if the United States accepted one of the two Japanese proposals before December 1.

According to Tojo's testimony after the war, when the prime minister, accompanied by the two chiefs of staff, reported the liaison conference's decision to the emperor on November 2, Hirohito's face was filled with despair. After a moment of silence, the emperor asked in a somber voice, "When our efforts to break the deadlock through diplomatic negotiations fail, does Japan have no other choice but to decide to go to war with the United States and Britain?" He added, "Under the circumstances, it may be unavoidable to go ahead with war preparations, but I want you to try your very best to find a way out through diplomatic negotiations." Tojo testified that the emperor's grave look made such a strong impression on him that he took the trouble to convene an unprecedented meeting of the army and navy councilors (*gunji-sangiin kaigi*) on November 4 in the emperor's presence. However, the participants simply reaffirmed the liaison conference's decision, and the emperor listened in silence.[58]

The record of the imperial conference on November 5 indicates that the cabinet members and supreme command shared the urgent sense that war was inevitable unless the United States accepted Japan's proposals. Even so, Prime Minister Tojo's statement at the end of the meeting suggests that he did not dismiss the prospect for diplomatic success, however small it might be. He defended the liaison conference's decision with something of a brinkmanship argument, saying that only the actual show of Japan's determination to fight would bring a chance for diplomatic success vis-à-vis the United States, which simply expected Japan to succumb to its economic pressure.[59]

Some critics of Emperor Hirohito, such as Herbert Bix, argue that at this imperial conference the emperor made the actual decision for war by sanctioning both the completion of preparations for operations and a deadline for terminating diplomatic negotiations with Washington.[60] Certainly, it is most likely that at this point Hirohito had accepted the inevitability of war with the United States, in the event that Japan's Proposal B failed. However, in the emperor's mind, was the result of final diplomatic efforts a foregone conclusion, as Herbert Bix suggests? Even Hirohito's foremost Japanese critic, Yamada Akira, argues that on November 5 the emperor approved the impe-rial conference's decisions, most likely because he thought that Japan's Proposal B, which included the possibility of Japan's withdrawal from southern Indochina, might break the diplomatic deadlock in Washington.[61]

The emperor's hesitation in accepting the inevitability of war can also be explained by his knowledge of how the Japanese military planned to open hostilities against the United States, if the Roosevelt administration refused to accept Japan's final proposal. On November 3, in order to influence the emperor's decision in the imperial conference to be held two days later, the chiefs of the Army and Naval General Staffs, General Sugiyama and Admiral Nagano, jointly had an audience with the emperor and informed him of the operational plans for Southeast Asia and the Pacific in the event of war. Admiral Nagano reported that the navy would launch air attacks simultaneously on the Philippines, Malaya, and Hawaii. About four hundred planes would approach the island of Oahu and initiate a "surprise attack" (*kishu kogeki*) on the aircraft carriers and battleships as well as on the aircraft on the ground. This surprise attack could be as bold and daring as the Battle of Okehazama,[62] according to the admiral, and its success would depend on the fortunes of war.[63] The emperor asked when the navy planned to make the attack and learned that the date would be December 8 (Japan time), which would be December 7 in Hawaii.[64] Although the emperor made no further comments, it is possible to argue that the navy's bold plan for a surprise attack on Pearl Harbor made the emperor not only more cautious but also more anxious to exhaust last-minute diplomatic negotiations, even though he realized that the chance of success was slim.

Even after the United States rejected Japan's Proposal A, the emperor appeared to pin his hope on last-minute diplomatic success in Washington. On November 15, when General Sugiyama had an audience with the emperor to report on the army's strategies in the southern regions, in the event of an outbreak of war, the emperor asked the general, "You are going to halt the advancement of the forces if we reach a diplomatic understanding with the United States, aren't you?" The general assured the emperor that he would issue orders to withdraw troops in the event that diplomacy succeeded. The emperor made a rare positive reply to the chief of the General Staff: "That is good."[65]

On this same day, November 15, the liaison conference adopted a "Draft Proposal for Hastening the End of the War against the United States, Great Britain, the Netherlands, and Chiang [Kai-shek in China]."[66] The document was designed to alleviate the emperor's apprehensions about Japan's ability to prosecute the war successfully. On November 5, right after the imperial conference, Tojo ordered the officers in the Military Affairs Bureau to create (1) a rationale for going to war with the countries identified in the draft document and (2) a plan for ending the war.[67] Apparently, these orders were prompted by questions raised by Hirohito on November 2 during an audience with Tojo. The emperor asked whether the prime minister had thought about the rationale for the war and how to terminate the conflict.[68] This draft proposal drawn by the army is one more case of the military bureaucracy's effort to remove the emperor's doubts about going to war.

It is difficult to tell exactly when the emperor realized that war with the United States was unavoidable. Perhaps the realization came to him gradually. The lord keeper of the privy seal, Kido, wrote in his diary on November 19 that he advised Hirohito to consider several measures in case the United States rejected Japan's final proposal, including the idea of convening a meeting of *jushin* (senior statesmen) before reaching a decision for war. Kido did not think it wise for Japan to declare war purely on the technical ground of passing the deadline.[69] The US formal rejection of Japan's Proposal B came on November 26. Those in favor of war believed that the harshness of the counterproposal offered by the so-called Hull Note allowed them to label it an ultimatum. The officers in the War Guidance Section of the army General Staff called it a "godsend" (*tenyu*).[70] Kido wrote in his diary, "The tables were turned against us."[71] The emperor himself admitted, in his postwar "Monologue," that US secretary of state Cordell Hull's "so-called ultimatum" brought an end to diplomatic negotiations with a sense of finality.[72] By that time, the emperor may have felt that his country had already passed the point of no return.

The final decision to commence war with the United States, Britain, and the Netherlands was made at the imperial conference on December 1. The nearly two-hour-long meeting simply formalized the decision for war that had already been made a month earlier, and "His Majesty, ever the silent spectator of the scene," as Robert Butow puts it, "left the chamber."[73] It is not too difficult to document the emperor's personal agony and hesitation to sanction the final decision for war. Deputy Grand Chamberlain Kanroji Osanaga recalled in his memoir,

> The anguish he [the emperor] suffered on the eve of war with America was extreme. . . .
>
> At such times the emperor would be in his room alone. . . . But we could hear him pacing the floor, sometimes muttering to himself, and we knew

that something had happened again, and was worrying him, but it was not our place to ask what. The pacing would continue for a long time, each step resounding painfully in our minds, so that we wished to stop up our ears.[74]

On November 26, the emperor suggested to Tojo that the *jushin* attend the imperial conference to deliberate the war question, but the prime minister did not accept that idea.[75] Instead, the emperor invited eight *jushin* to a luncheon on November 29 and listened to their opinions for about an hour afterward. Although recognizing the grave situation Japan was facing in the wake of the failed negotiations with the United States, most of the *jushin* expressed doubts or hesitation about making a hasty decision for war, but without directly saying that it was not the right time to go to war.[76] If the emperor was looking for a strong voice against war from the *jushin*, he must have been disappointed. Later he recalled, "The opinions of those who were against war were abstract, but the cabinet argued for war by providing numbers to back up its case, and therefore, to my regret, I did not have power to curb the argument in favor of war."[77]

On November 30, the day before an imperial conference was to be convened to endorse a final war decision, the emperor briefly withheld his order to convene the meeting, after being told by his brother, Prince Takamatsu, that the navy still had lingering doubts about going to war with the United States. Neither the emperor nor his brother was able to get rid of worries that Japan might not be able to win the war. The emperor consulted with Kido, who in turn advised him to summon Navy Minister Shimada and Chief of the Naval General Staff Nagano and ask for their candid opinions.[78]

According to Navy Minister Shimada's November 30 diary entry, the two admirals had an audience with the emperor for twenty-five minutes in the evening. The emperor asked them, "The time is getting pressed: an arrow is about to leave a bow. Once an arrow is fired, it will become a long-drawn-out war, but are you ready to carry it out as planned?" Admiral Nagano expressed the navy's firm resolve to carry out an attack, upon receiving an imperial mandate (*taimei*), and told the emperor, "The task force will arrive 1,800 *ri* [4,392 miles] west of Oahu by tomorrow." The emperor turned to Admiral Shimada and asked, "As navy minister, are you prepared in every aspect?" Shimada replied, "Both men and supplies are fully prepared and we are waiting for an imperial mandate." The emperor continued, "What would happen if Germany stopped fighting in Europe?" The navy minister replied, "I do not think Germany is a truly reliable country. Even if Germany withdrew, we would not be affected." At the end of the audience, "in order to make the emperor feel at ease," in Shimada's words, the navy chief and the navy minister guaranteed a successful attack on Pearl Harbor and the navy's resolve to win the war at all cost. The navy minister observed that "the emperor appeared to be satisfied."[79] After the audience, the emperor told Kido that Shimada and Nagano were "reasonably confident" about the war, and consequently he approved of holding an imperial conference the next day, as originally scheduled.[80] This was the point of no return.

Thus, the role that Emperor Showa played in Japan's decision to go to war with the United States could be compared to Max Weber's discussion of the absolute monarch who is "impotent in face of the superior specialized knowledge of the bureaucracy." The emperor was personally against war with the United States and exerted his influence to delay the war decision for one and a half months; but his influence was circumscribed within the nebulous triangular power relationship among court, government, and military. Emperor Hirohito eventually succumbed to the persistent pressure of the military bureaucracy and accepted the argument that war was inevitable and possibly winnable. But though Hirohito eventually sanctioned the government's war decision, he was never free from the fear that his country might lose the war.

CHAPTER 4

An Uneasy Commander in Chief

W HAT DO WE KNOW ABOUT EMPEROR HIROHITO'S PERSONAL
views and actions concerning the prosecution of the Pacific War?
Was he an active and willing leader? Or did he seek to end the war as soon
as possible? After the war, Deputy Grand Chamberlain Kanroji Osanaga
claimed that Hirohito had begun to think of the termination of hostilities
as early as December 8, 1941.[1] However, historians must be cautious about
concluding that the emperor's primary concern was to end the war as soon
as possible. Certainly, he had been against the gamble of war with the United
States and Great Britain; and in late 1941 he had been reluctant to support the
decision to go to war. But once Japan commenced the war with the United
States and the Allied Powers, the official task of Emperor Hirohito as *daigensui* (commander in chief) was to command both the army and the navy and
to lead Japan to victory. Under the Meiji Constitution, in the realm of state
affairs, ministers who assisted (*hohitsu*) the emperor took full responsibility
for the decisions they made during peacetime; but when the country was
at war, the chiefs of the Army and Navy General Staffs aided (*hoyoku*) the
emperor who commanded (*tosui*) the entire Japanese armed forces. Both
the army and the navy were required to obtain the emperor's sanction to
change their overall strategic plans. Therefore, because both branches of the
military went through this formality, we can conclude that throughout the
Pacific War the emperor was indeed expected to participate in the military
decision-making process.[2]

During the first year of the Pacific War with the Anglo-American powers,
Emperor Hirohito—as well as Japan's military and civilian leadership—pros-

ecuted the war in order to win advantageous peace terms for the country. In other words, the emperor believed that an early termination of the war would be in the best interest of Japan, because his country would be able to negotiate an advantageous peace while it still maintained a position of relative strength. The emperor had been reluctant to approve a risky war with the United States and Great Britain partly because his military advisers were unable to give firm assurance that Japan could win the war. Because of the emperor's reluctance, the supreme command had to produce an operational plan created specifically to persuade him that Japan would be able to conclude the war successfully.

From the outset the emperor was haunted by the possible negative consequences of a prolonged war. His initial optimism about winning an advantageous peace through swift military action and diplomatic strategies disappeared quickly in 1942, as news of Japanese military defeats began to arrive at the palace. From the early stages of the Pacific War, the emperor was nervous about any sign of US counteroffensive in the southern theater and possible Soviet attack in the northern theater. He was also anxious to end the stalemate in China. Emperor Hirohito's understanding of Japan's military situation was more pessimistic than that of the highest-ranking military leaders in the Imperial Headquarters, and his strategic thinking was more cautious. His cautiousness came from not only his own careful and prudent personality and his sense of responsibility as head of state but also his unique role as *daigensui*. In this role, Hirohito was the only person to receive reports from both the army and naval chiefs of staff about the war situation on all fronts. As Japanese forces found it increasingly difficult to hold their ground against Allied counteroffensives, the rivalries and disagreements between the army and the navy became more and more serious and undermined effective cooperation between the two branches. While the two service branches were competing for state resources and preoccupied with their own survival, the emperor was able to look more objectively at the weaknesses and problems of each strategy, based on the war intelligence he received from both branches. Frequent complaints from both the army and navy about the other's inability and unwillingness to cooperate frustrated the emperor and caused him to worry about successful prosecution of the war. The emperor had to play a lonely role as the sole link between the army and navy, while at the same time encouraging both sides to cooperate in order to roll back the enemy in the South Pacific.

Anxious to conclude the war successfully, the emperor was eventually persuaded to support a strategy of quick engagement and victory in decisive battles that, it was hoped, would allow Japan to avoid a prolonged war and conclude favorable peace terms with the enemy. However, when his original fear of a prolonged and unwinnable war became a distinct possibility, the emperor began to waver between his hope for winning a final decisive battle before beginning peace negotiations, and his search for a way out of the nightmarish war through third-party mediation or, in the worst scenario, surrender. But when did the emperor realize that Japan's initial plan to win the war with an early victory was ill-conceived and unrealistic? When did he lose hope that Japan would win a decisive battle and be able to negotiate favorable peace terms? When and how did he begin to lean toward terminating the war at all costs in order to avoid the further destruction of his country? How did the emperor communicate his views to his government officials and military leaders? And what role did he play in changing the course of a war that was not going well for Japan?

%

Despite Japan's spectacular initial success in the surprise attack on Pearl Harbor, the Pacific War did not begin auspiciously. Contrary to Emperor Hirohito's desire to justify Japan's action by delivering a declaration of war *before* hostilities commenced, there was an unexpected delay in handing over the Japanese government's final note to terminate diplomatic negotiations with the United States. Moreover, this note failed to serve as a declaration of war. Thus, Japan's attacks on December 7, 1941, took the United States by surprise, and an enraged President Roosevelt called December 7 "a date which will live in infamy."

At the outset of the war, the Imperial Headquarters followed the strategy for concluding the war outlined in the "Draft Proposal for Hastening the End of the War against the United States, Great Britain, the Netherlands, and Chiang [Kai-shek in China]." This had been adopted on November 15, 1941, by the Tojo cabinet, as part of its effort to win the emperor's approval for going to war. The document proposed that Japan should create an international environment that would precipitate US surrender through (1) occupation of the footholds of the United States, Great Britain, and the Netherlands in the southern theater of war and elimination of US naval presence; (2) development of the occupied territories to build Japan's self-sufficient economic sphere; (3) defeat of the Chiang Kai-shek regime in China; and (4) defeat of

Great Britain through cooperation with Germany and Italy (which included Japan's efforts to mediate between Germany and the Soviet Union).[3]

It is important to note that at the initial stage of the war, the Japanese leadership believed that, in order to break the US will to fight, Japan had to first work closely with Germany and Italy to hasten the surrender of Great Britain. To that end, the Japanese military leadership considered brokering a peace between Germany and the Soviet Union.[4] The emperor fully supported this idea as part of Japan's strategy to conclude the war swiftly. According to Colonel Matsutani Sei at the Army General Staff, when the chief of the General Staff, General Sugiyama, reported the army's intention to draw up a plan for German-Soviet mediation on January 6, 1942, the emperor, who was "always afraid of the Soviet Union's entry into the war [against Japan]," told the general, "That is good. Act upon it immediately."[5] This suggests that the Japanese leadership was looking at many options, excluding neither diplomacy nor military action as means to a swift and victorious conclusion of the war.

However, the success of Japan's initial military operations in the southern theater exceeded Tokyo's expectations and allowed the military leaders in the Imperial Headquarters to move away from their original strategy of wrapping up the war early through both military and diplomatic means. The leaders' thinking shifted toward a strategy of finishing the war through military expansion and defeating the enemy. On February 5, 1942, less than two months after the commencement of war in the Pacific, Lord Privy Seal Kido was alarmed by his country's euphoric attitude toward the initial victories: so he gathered his courage and cautioned the emperor not to be too optimistic about the prospects for overall victory. Kido's warning may have been effective, for a week later the emperor asked Prime Minister Tojo Hideki to pay close attention to the issue of how to end the hostilities. The emperor told General Tojo, "I suppose you are paying enough attention not to miss any opportunity to conclude the war; for the sake of mankind's peace it is undesirable to prolong the war recklessly and expand the devastating damage."[6] However, the news of the fall of Singapore, which reached the emperor on February 15, appeared to alleviate the emperor's anxiety over Japan's military prospects, for after this, Kido and the emperor did not discuss the question of how to bring an end to the war for an entire year.

Other factors also subverted moves toward relying on diplomacy to end the war. For example, liaison conferences between the Imperial Headquarters and the Tojo cabinet in 1942 did not reach any resolution to use diplomacy and mediation to win the war; consequently, the emperor's concern about possible Soviet participation in the war against Japan was never really addressed by the government. Despite Foreign Minister Togo's proposal for German-Soviet mediation as well as peace negotiations with Chiang Kai-shek's government in Chongqing, the liaison conference on March 7 decided to maintain a wait-and-see policy. As Japanese forces continued to expand their occupation of Southeast Asia and the South Pacific, it became increasingly clear that neither the army nor the navy was interested in mediation: both forces wanted to secure Japan's northern border with the Soviet Union by letting the Soviet Red Army continue fighting with Germany. Moreover, the German government repeatedly told the Japanese ambassador in Berlin that Germany would not appreciate Japan's mediation efforts with the Soviet Union. Instead, in July 1942, the German foreign minister requested Japan's participation in the war against the Soviet Union—a request that, on July 25, 1942, the Japanese government and Imperial Headquarters decided to decline. Tanemura Sako, in the Army General Staff, recorded in his diary on September 7, 1942, that the idea of Soviet-German mediation had "reached a deadlock."[7] Faced with such discouragements, the Foreign Office stopped exploring the possibility of German-Soviet mediation after January 6, 1943; in the meantime, at the imperial conference of December 21, 1942, the Tojo cabinet decided not to negotiate a peace with the Chinese Nationalist government under Chiang Kai-shek.[8]

Throughout 1942, although Emperor Hirohito continued to sanction the supreme command's military plans, the gap continued to increase between the emperor's personal concerns about Japan's war situation and the military leadership's view of the war. The emperor's elation with Japan's military success may have reached its peak on March 9 when he heard of the Dutch surrender in Bandung, Dutch East Indies, and the fall of Rangoon in Burma. The emperor told Kido with a smile, "We are achieving war results too quickly."[9] However, as military historian Edward J. Drea observes, "At heart he [the emperor] remained cautious and conservative."[10] While the General Staffs of both the army and navy continued to pursue the strategy of rapid military expansion in the south, the emperor exhibited increasingly cautious tendencies in the following months. From the very beginning of southern operations, in January and February 1942, what set the emperor apart from his military leaders were his nervous questions about Japan's initial military success and his skepticism about the military's confidence in its own capabilities. For example, the emperor repeatedly questioned General

Sugiyama, chief of the General Staff, about the army's optimistic strategy to capture Bataan in the Philippines. As the emperor feared, the capture of Bataan turned out to be a costly and difficult operation.[11]

Because of his uneasiness about war with the United States and Great Britain, the emperor tended to prefer a cautious containment of hostilities. He frequently asked General Sugiyama about Japan's possible occupation of the Portuguese territory in East Timor. He was concerned lest Portugal, which had stayed neutral to that point, enter the war against Japan and its allies in Europe, in the event that Japan expanded its military occupation into East Timor.[12] In another example, concerning the stalemated war in China, after Hirohito received the report that the initial phase of Japan's military operations in the southern theater had been completed, on May 29, 1942, the emperor asked General Sugiyama, "Can't you somehow figure out a way to settle the China Incident?"[13]

The emperor's reaction to the capture of eight Americans who had participated in the "Doolittle Raid" on Tokyo on April 18, 1942, demonstrated his concerns about Japan's international image and about the safety of his overseas subjects, both military and civilian. On May 6, Tanemura Sako, of the Imperial Headquarters, recorded that within the military there were voices supporting the execution of these American prisoners of war (POWs). "Perhaps, this reached the emperor's ears," Tanemura wrote, adding that the chief aide-de-camp at the palace conveyed the emperor's following words to the vice chief of the General Staff: "Treat the prisoners of war with civility." The emperor was worried about the negative impact that Japan's cruel treatment of prisoners of war might have on Japan's international relations. The emperor was especially worried about the safety of Japanese POWs in enemy hands and about his civilian subjects who lived overseas. His personal intervention through an imperial sanction spared the life of five of the American POWs, but the Army General Staff ordered the execution of the other three.[14]

In addition to his involvement in such policy decisions, Emperor Hirohito believed that, as *daigensui*, one of his important responsibilities was to raise military morale—especially when his country was faring badly in the war. On June 8, 1942, when the emperor received the detailed report of the disastrous naval defeat at Midway, including the loss of four aircraft carriers, he remained composed. Hirohito told the chief of the Naval General Staff, Admiral Nagano, "Be careful not to allow it to affect the morale of the forces, and do not retreat to passive and conservative tactics." Apparently, the emperor wished to believe the defeat to be a temporary setback, rather than the beginning of a long retreat for the Japanese navy.[15]

When the news of fierce fighting in Guadalcanal and eastern New Guinea reached the palace in August 1942, the emperor's countenance changed. Fearing any sign of Anglo-American rollback, the emperor began to exhibit discomfort with the existing military strategy and to frequently ask questions about operational details. In contrast to the optimistic calculations of the supreme command, the emperor, who had enough education in military history to grasp the strategy in Guadalcanal, foresaw grave dangers from the early stage of the operation. As early as August 24, the emperor called the strategies in Guadalcanal and New Guinea "disastrous," and by September 15, Tanaka Shinichi, the army chief of operations, observed, "The emperor appears to be of the opinion that there is little hope of securing Guadalcanal."[16] Throughout the fall of 1942, the emperor continued to receive disappointing reports from the fronts in Guadalcanal and New Guinea, and he asked his aides daily about military operations in the region. On December 11, the night before his visit to Ise Shrine to pray for his country's success in war, the emperor confided to his military aide-de-camp, Colonel Ogata Kenichi, about his frank opinions of the war. According to Colonel Ogata's diary entry of that day, "Tonight, contrary to his habit, [His Majesty] expressed his frank reflections on past history, political affairs after the Manchurian Incident, the war, and so on. He said that it was easy to start a war but hard to end it. What [His Majesty] told me contained his significant and confidential opinions on the issues concerning the army's war guidance and war preparations. I cannot record the details here."[17]

From the end of 1942 to the beginning of 1943, the emperor became increasingly frustrated by what he considered an inconsistent and indecisive military strategy in Guadalcanal. In his eyes, the biggest obstacle to victory was the lack of coordination between the army and the navy, for this relationship was plagued by serious interservice rivalry. Fully aware that he stood above the two military branches as *daigensui*, the emperor apparently felt compelled to intervene actively in this case. He asked the military aide-de-camp to convey the following to both General Sugiyama and Admiral Nagano: "I want to know just what strategy you are going to employ to defeat the enemy. The situation is quite serious. I think the staff of the Imperial Headquarters should hold a meeting and deliberate this matter. There is no time to waste even during the New Year's celebration. I will be ready to attend the meeting at any time." These strong words from the emperor prompted the

Imperial Headquarters to convene a meeting on December 31, 1942. General Sugiyama emphasized the emperor's uneasiness about inconsistencies in the army's and navy's strategies in the Solomon Islands and New Guinea, and he ordered his staff to reconsider the entire strategy in these areas and to draw a new plan that clearly outlined how to destroy the enemy and bring an end to the war. Before the meeting, the vice chief of the General Staff, Tanabe Moritake, commented, "What the emperor fears the most is the possibility that Japan might lose the war. The Imperial Headquarters' meeting must address this issue." This led to the supreme command's decision to retreat from Guadalcanal and concentrate on securing eastern New Guinea.[18]

After Japan's withdrawal from Guadalcanal, completed by February 1943, the army's strategy was to secure Lae and Salamaua in eastern New Guinea. However, Allied air attacks blocked the Japanese attempt to transport troops from the Island of New Britain to Lae. Out of 6,912 Japanese troops, only about 1,200 reached Lae. When this tragic news reached the palace, Emperor Hirohito told General Sugiyama that this failure had to serve as a hard lesson, and the emperor asked him to think carefully about the next move so that Lae and Salamaua would not fall the way Guadalcanal did. Historian Yamada Akira suggests that the emperor was more acutely aware of how inadequate airpower contributed to Japan's loss of Guadalcanal than his military advisers were and was deeply concerned about Japan's ability to command the air in eastern New Guinea.[19]

This series of serious defeats disturbed the emperor so much that he brought up the matter with Lord Privy Seal Kido. During a routine meeting with Kido in the spring of 1943, the emperor initiated a conversation about possible ways to end the war. According to Kido, on February 5, 1943, he reported to the emperor on certain discussions with former prime minister Konoe Fumimaro and Matsudaira Yasumasa (Kido's chief secretary), both of whom were by that time affiliated with a peace-oriented faction. The emperor's response made Kido realize that Emperor Hirohito shared his own concerns about the continuation of the war and felt an urgent need to take steps toward early termination of the war. Until that moment, Kido said, he had been afraid to bring up this subject with the emperor because he had no idea how the emperor might respond to pessimistic views concerning the war's progress. Once the emperor and Kido realized they both favored early termination of the war, the two men started to spend about an hour, almost daily, exchanging intelligence and expressing frank opinions about how to deal with a war that was not progressing well for Japan.[20] Kido consistently stated, in his diary, his postwar recollections, and his 1967 interview, that their forthright discussions continued for the next two and a half years.[21]

For example, on March 30, 1943, during his meeting with Kido, the emperor himself initiated a discussion about the war situation and expressed his candid opinion in favor of an early conclusion of the war. According to Kido, this conversation lasted for one and a half hours. Because it was unusual for the emperor to initiate such a conversation, Kido made a special note of it in his diary but did not give further details of their conversation. In addition, in Kido's postwar commentary on his diary, in which he explains several important diary entries in detail, Kido recalled that this March 30 conversation with the emperor was the first step toward paving the way for ending the war.

By March 30, because of defeats at Midway and Guadalcanal, the emperor was becoming pessimistic about Japan's ability to maintain command of the air in the Pacific, and he asked for Kido's opinion on Japan's prospects for winning the war. According to Kido's recollection, the emperor said,

> In view of the series of situations that has developed, I do not think the prospect for the current war is good. Although the supreme command is telling me that both the army and the navy are determined to fight and win at all costs, I wonder if we can recover the airpower that we have lost at Midway: I am afraid that it will be extremely difficult. If we lose command of the air to the enemy, I am afraid that it will become difficult to sustain ongoing operations throughout the vast region and [I am afraid] that they [the military operations] might begin to fail at every turn. Kido, what do you think?[22]

In response, Kido expressed his own doubts about the probability of a Japanese naval victory and suggested that the best Japan could do would be to strike a devastating blow to the enemy fleet and thus bring an end to the war. Kido clearly remembered the emperor's pessimistic response: "If only we could do so."[23]

The emperor's frustration turned to indignation when he learned that Japanese forces at Attu in the Aleutian Islands, having had no hopes for reinforcement, had fought to the last man. Tragically, on May 29, 1943, these forces had committed *gyokusai* (they all perished in suicidal attacks against the enemy). A week later, on June 6, the emperor expressed his displeasure to General Sugiyama saying, "It is regrettable that we had to adopt this kind of strategy [*gyokusai*]." Realizing how badly coordinated the naval operations on Attu Island had been, the emperor asked Sugiyama, "Are the army and the navy seriously trying to work together?"[24] The emperor was clearly frustrated by the navy's inability to lay out a clear long-range plan and by the obvious lack of cooperation between the army and navy. Two days later, on June 8, the emperor complained to the chief aide-de-camp, who in turn quoted the emperor's words to General Sugiyama:

> They [the army and the navy] should have been able to anticipate this kind of military outcome [at Attu] ahead of time. . . . There has to be a long-range prospect [of victory] from the beginning.
>
> Can there ever be a serious discussion of true intentions between the army and the navy? Isn't it the case that one side advances a demand vigorously, and the other side accepts it irresponsibly? . . . Even if the army and the navy make a brilliant agreement, if they cannot fulfill their promise, simply because it is impossible to carry it out, it is worse than failing to make a promise at all.
>
> When there is friction between the army and the navy, we cannot prosecute this war.[25]

The emperor was afraid that his country's complete defeat in the Aleutian Islands might encourage American and Chinese efforts, as had happened at Guadalcanal. He feared that this might give neutral observers and third parties a negative impression of Japan's military ability. Thus, on June 8 the emperor asked General Sugiyama one more question: "Is there any way we can defeat American forces in a frontal attack somewhere?"[26]

Quoting these last words, historian Yamada Akira argues that because of the disaster at Attu Island, in June 1943, this date became the turning point in the emperor's thinking. Yamada argues that from then on, the emperor began to urge a policy of frontal attack and decisive battle in order to defeat the United States.[27] However, it is not clear whether this idea was initiated by the emperor himself or by Prime Minister Tojo. According to Kido's diary, when Tojo came to Kido's office after his audience with the emperor (on the morning of June 7), Tojo told Kido that the war had come to the point that required a decisive battle. Tojo added that, in view of the changing situation on the European front (which was becoming unfavorable for Japan's European allies), Japan had to review its future strategy and closely monitor Germany's moves.[28] In any event, from June 8 onward the emperor began insisting on a decisive, frontal attack against US forces in the Pacific so that Japan could claim a victory.

The next day, June 9, 1943, when the emperor received reports from General Sugiyama regarding the situation in New Guinea, the emperor first inquired about the condition of the military and food supplies. Then Hirohito stated, "Somehow we have to defeat the United States." During the same audience, the emperor also touched on the incident of a Soviet airplane that had fired on Japanese installations within the boundaries of Manchuria and had been shot down by the Kwantung Army on June 7. The emperor wondered if the Allies had requested this action by a Soviet aircraft. General Sugiyama dismissed that possibility, but the emperor continued: "In any event, you must make sure not to expand the hostilities and not to make any mistake. What do you think the Soviet Union would do if the Allies asked it to act?" After the audience, General Sugiyama noted that the emperor was "extremely apprehensive" about the Soviet motives for its plane's aggressive act in Manchuria.[29] This exchange suggests that the emperor's concerns about the possible spread of hostilities in the northern theater made him even more anxious to stop the American counteroffensive in the south. However, despite Hirohito's repeatedly urging decisive frontal attacks on US forces throughout June, neither the army's operations in northeastern New Guinea nor the navy's efforts to defend its bases in the Solomon Islands were successful.

The emperor's biggest preoccupation in the summer of 1943 seemed to be the urgent need to build consensus among his own generals and admirals. Hirohito still hoped that his country would be able to defeat the United States in a decisive battle—that is, if the Japanese army and the navy could truly cooperate and show the resolve to engage in such a battle. On June 30 and July 1, upon learning from both General Sugiyama and Admiral Nagano that US forces might attempt to land on Lae and Salamaua in northeastern New Guinea, as well as on New Georgia and Rendova in the Solomon Islands, the emperor urged the army and navy leaders to coordinate joint operations on both fronts. Many people around Hirohito recorded his unusually strong words: he demanded that the army and navy unite their entire forces to forestall any attempted landing and destroy enemy forces. This unity should prevail wherever the enemy tried to land, regardless of which Japanese military force was assigned to each locality.[30] During July, as the emperor continued to receive news of Japanese retreats, one after another, from eastern New Guinea and the Solomon Islands, he became increasingly critical of ineffective military strategies, especially of navy failures. The emperor repeatedly questioned the chiefs of the Army and Naval General Staffs, as well as his military aides: "Somehow is there a way to defeat the enemy?"[31] Lord Privy Seal Kido also recorded the emperor's preoccupation with the situation in New Guinea in late July.[32]

Disturbing developments in Europe further increased the emperor's anxiety. On July 26, 1943, Prime Minister Tojo brought news of the collapse of Benito Mussolini's government in Italy. Tojo warned the emperor that the new regime under General Pietro Badoglio might favor Italy's surrender. In a separate meeting with Foreign Minister Shigemitsu Mamoru, on the same day, the emperor expressed his opinion that Japan should pay more attention to its relations with the Soviet Union and not be so bound by Germany's attitude. Both the emperor and the foreign minister agreed that Japan must start thinking about what to do if Germany dropped out of the war. Earlier, Kido had told Prime Minister Tojo that if Germany chose to end the war, and asked Japan to seek peace (in accordance with the Tripartite Pact's stricture for no separate peace agreement), then Japan should improve its relations with the Soviet Union and ask the Soviets to mediate remaining problems in the Pacific with the United States and Britain. From Kido's diary, it appears that he discussed this idea with the emperor on same day.[33]

Although the emperor did not give up hope of winning a decisive battle against the United States in the summer of 1943, he was deeply troubled by both his military's inability to defeat the enemy and the grim outlook for Italy and Germany on the European front. As his military aide, Colonel Ogata Kenichi, wrote in his diary on August 2, "[The emperor] seems to be worried about recent developments in international and other affairs, and I have reason to believe that he is occasionally deeply preoccupied." The colonel added that he had heard the emperor was so absorbed in thought that on the way to performing religious rites he had not even realized he had passed the entrance (to the shrine).[34]

The mounting tensions prompted the emperor to discuss possible alternative courses of action with his military leaders. For instance, when Emperor Hirohito met with General Sugiyama on August 5, although he continued to encourage the general to "study [ways] not to allow the Americans to claim 'We won, we won,'" he also asked if the general thought Germany would send reinforcements to defend Sicily. When Sugiyama replied in the negative, the emperor responded with agitated questions: "Are you suggesting that the Germans would be pushed back to northern Italy? That means that the oil fields in Romania may be in danger. In that case, don't you think Japan must reconsider? Don't you think the time has come for Japan to reconsider?" At the time of this conversation, Sugiyama thought that the emperor was referring to the question of Soviet-German mediation, but it later became apparent that the emperor was referring not only to Soviet-German peace but also to the broader issue of Japan's seeking peace with its enemies through possible Soviet mediation. Sugiyama concluded his audience with the emperor by saying, "The question of the utmost importance is how the supreme command will guide the course of war in case the unfavorable [European] war forces Germany to make peace with England." Major General Sanada Joichiro, who was in charge of operations at the Army General Staff, recorded that this meeting between the emperor and Sugiyama set in motion a new course of action: by the end of September, army headquarters had drafted a new strategic plan that emphasized defensive operations, defining what came to be known as the "absolute defense perimeter" (*zettai kokubo-ken*).[35]

According to the emperor's postwar "Monologue," he began to lose hope for Japan's victory in September 1943, when Japanese forces were defeated in the Owen Stanley mountain range in eastern New Guinea. He also admitted, "I thought we would be able to seize an opportunity to negotiate peace immediately after thrashing the enemy somewhere. But because of the no separate peace agreement [clause of the Tripartite Pact], we did not want to violate the international agreement and make peace before Germany. I even thought that it would be a good thing if Germany was quickly defeated."[36] Although the emperor continued to support the military's argument that Japan needed a decisive victory before entering into peace negotiations, all the sources quoted above, including the emperor's own "Monologue," suggest that September 1943 was an important turning point in Hirohito's thinking and that he was rapidly giving up hope for Japanese victory through a decisive battle.

The "absolute defense perimeter" strategy, adopted by the imperial conference with the emperor's consent on September 30, 1943, reflected a shift in the expectations of both the emperor and Japan's military leadership. Instead of seeking a victory in a decisive battle that would allow Japan to continue its expansion, Japan's leaders were now looking for a way to win a decisive battle in order to stop the enemy's advance. The strategy of absolute defense perimeter called for Japanese forces to sustain the 1943 front lines until Japanese forces could rebuild their strength for a final decisive battle in mid-1944. According to the plan, Japanese forces were supposed to hold their positions in Rabaul and the Marshall Islands as an advance-guard line (*zenei-sen*), while rebuilding forces along the absolute defense perimeter (from the Kuril Islands in the north, to the Ogasawara Islands and eastern New Guinea in the south, and the Dutch East Indies and Burma to the west).[37] But Japanese frontline forces continued to lose ground, and by the end of 1943 they were no longer able to sustain the absolute defense perimeter.

In the last few months in 1943, as the hope of a victory through a decisive battle was gradually replaced by a fear that Japan and its allies might lose the war, the emperor asked less frequently for a decisive battle during his meetings with the chiefs of the two General Staffs. Hirohito's pessimism grew as he lost confidence in the navy's ability to defend the perimeter. As early as October 1, the day after the imperial conference that adopted the absolute defense perimeter strategy, the emperor expressed to Kido his fear that the navy might not be able to sustain its will to fight if it was forced out of Rabaul.[38]

The emperor was also frustrated by the slow pace of progress in army-navy cooperation. He considered rear fortification of the absolute defense perimeter through united army and navy efforts to be essential for success of the new strategy. According to Major General Sanada Joichiro, on October 10, when the chief of the Naval General Staff, Admiral Nagano, conveyed to the emperor the navy's difficulty in securing the rear of the absolute defense perimeter in the southern Pacific, Hirohito realized that the differences between the navy and the army over execution of the absolute defense perimeter strategy had never been resolved. The emperor made an "extraordinary statement" to the admiral: "If there are still disagreements between the two General Staffs, I want to ask the chief of Naval General Staff what has been the meaning of the meetings we have held up to this point? Why have we taken the trouble to do all that?" The emperor was also worried about reports of Germany's weakness. General Sanada recorded Hirohito's questions of October 26: "Germany is weak, isn't it? Does Germany have any chance to win if it continues to fight this way?"[39] These comments clearly show that multiple problems were causing the emperor's anxiety from the end of 1943 to the beginning of 1944—that is, the repeated defeats and retreats by Japan and its allies and poor coordination between Japan's army and navy. So great was his anxiety that some historians even suggest that the emperor began to display symptoms of neurosis.[40]

Japan's inability to stop US counteroffensives in the South Pacific and the interservice rivalry between the Japanese army and navy were linked in the thinking of the emperor. As *daigensui*, Hirohito was deeply disturbed by the lack of unity between the two military organizations. In early 1944, as continued reports arrived of Japanese defeats in the South Pacific, Hirohito felt he had to intervene to ensure a unity of supreme military command. When Admiral Nagano informed the emperor that the Americans had landed on Kwajalein in the Marshall Islands on January 31, the alarmed emperor chided the admiral, saying, "The Marshalls are part of Japan's territory. Why can't you do anything when it has being taken by the enemy?"[41]

During this same period, Prince Takamatsu, the emperor's brother who was serving in the office of the Naval General Staff, pressed Hirohito to deal with a dispute between the army and the navy over the allocation of airplanes.[42] On February 9, the emperor urged the chiefs of the two General Staffs to settle this dispute in a spirit of mutual concession, and he warned that the ongoing interservice rivalry might lead to political instability and collapse of the ruling cabinet.[43] This episode reveals the depth of the emperor's concern about the internal political instability and disorder that might result from intra- and interservice rivalries. There is no doubt that the earlier military coup attempts in the 1930s continued to haunt the emperor. But in 1944, Hirohito's anxiety about a possible political coup against the Tojo cabinet was not unfounded, for there was indeed an urgent need to unite the army and the navy. Japan's retreat from the Marshalls and the crumbling of the absolute defense perimeter led to increasing criticisms of Prime Minister Tojo and his cabinet.

General Tojo's opponents, many of whom were naval officers, resented his concentration of power. They criticized him for concurrently serving as war minister and prime minister and for suppressing opposition through tight censorship and rigorous use of the military police. The most influential anti-Tojo group was led by Admiral Okada Keisuke, who had been prime minister during the February 26 Incident of 1936 and had barely escaped an assassination attempt by rebel army officers. Admiral Okada, working with his confidant, Rear Admiral Takagi Sokichi, secured the support of a group of naval leaders who realized the wisdom of a quick end to the war (this group included Admiral Yonai Mitsumasa and Prince Takamatsu). During this period, Okada and Takagi also communicated with civilian leaders, including former prime minister Konoe Fumimaro and his secretary (and son-in-law), Hosokawa Morisada, as well as Matsudaira Yasumasa, who at the time was secretary to Lord Privy Seal Kido.

On February 17 and 18, 1944, US forces seized Japanese naval bases on the Truk Islands in the Carolines, which were located within the absolute defense perimeter. This defeat was a devastating blow to the Tojo cabinet. It prompted the prime minister to propose a drastic measure: to unite civilian and military authorities by consolidating them under his sole command. Tojo proposed that he serve concurrently as prime minster, war minister, and chief of the Army General Staff and that Navy Minister Shimada serve as chief of the Naval General Staff. This plan was supposed to establish a unity of the civilian government and supreme command under General Tojo and ensure that Tojo, who would control both military and civilian affairs, could prosecute the war effectively. This plan was also supposed to unite the army and the navy under the joint command of General Tojo and Admiral Shimada, which, in the eyes of Tojo's opponents in the navy, meant only that Shimada would be Tojo's yes-man. When Kido conveyed Tojo's proposal to the emperor on February 19, the emperor asked whether it would affect the integrity (*kakuritsu*) of the supreme command. Kido replied that he would ask the prime minister to study this issue further.[44]

General Sugiyama, who had been asked to resign as army chief of the General Staff, disagreed with Tojo's proposal and argued that the civilian government and supreme command should *not* be merged. Sugiyama submitted his opinion to the emperor on February 21, warning that should the prime minister (who was already serving as war minister) assume the highest military office as chief of the Army General Staff, Japan would revert to a shogunate: this, said Sugiyama, should never be allowed. However, in the end the emperor supported Tojo's proposal, although with some hesitation. Hirohito told Sugiyama, "I thought about the same point that you were concerned about. I clarified that point with Tojo. Tojo assured me that he would carry it out with great caution, so I was relieved. . . . As you said just now, the arrangement is an exceptional measure at this time of emergency and requires caution. But do offer your cooperation to make it work."[45]

The extraordinary times that allowed General Tojo to concentrate both administrative and military power in his hands reveal that Japan's decision-making process, which relied on consensus within a triangular power relationship between the government, military, and imperial court, was paralyzed when faced with the possibility of national defeat in 1944. Moreover, implementation of this measure demonstrates that the power of the emperor as commander in chief was too abstract and unreal to unite and coordinate the army and navy. General Tojo's efforts to unite the government and military were, in a sense, a desperate attempt to tip the balance of power in favor of the army, to ensure more efficient management of the war effort.

Tojo was able to push through these changes because he enjoyed the full confidence and trust of the emperor. Hirohito indeed trusted Prime Minister Tojo and respected the decisions of the Tojo cabinet. Up to this point, the emperor had tried to follow official channels of communication between the government and supreme command, and he had refused to listen to criticisms of the Tojo cabinet's war policy that came from unofficial channels through the palace chamberlains, senior statesmen, or most importantly, imperial family members. Even the emperor's younger brother, Prince Takamatsu, could not easily talk to Hirohito about national policy. In late March, the prince admitted to Hosokawa (the prime minister's secretary) that the emperor did not like people trying to reach his ear through imperial family connections.[46] Hirohito therefore supported Tojo's reorganization efforts as the best way to unite the mutually antagonistic army and navy and reverse the tide of a war that was not going well for Japan. Probably, without the emperor's support, Tojo would not have been able to make such an unprecedented move.

Tojo's action, however, backfired and provoked further anti-Tojo sentiments among naval officers and political moderates. Tojo was able to stay in power for several months after the February 1944 reorganization, using the emperor's confidence in him to shield against mounting opposition. But Japan's repeated military retreats in the Pacific and Southeast Asia—especially the shattering blow at Imphal on the Indo-Burmese border and Japan's utter defeat on Saipan in June-July 1944—enabled the anti-Tojo faction to persuade Emperor Hirohito and the lord keeper of the privy seal, Kido, that their confidence in Tojo was misguided. As Robert Butow has pointed out, Prime Minister Tojo's ouster from office was "tremendously significant since it brought the possibility of a termination of hostilities closer to realization than even the most ardent end-the-war advocate had dared hope prior to this time."[47]

Two main questions need to be examined regarding the removal of Tojo from power in July 1944. How did this come about? And what role did the emperor play? Advocates for termination of the war were able to use the emperor's voice to tip the delicate balance of power in their favor, and in this way they forecast how they would set the stage for Japan's decision to surrender through the emperor's *seidan* (sacred imperial decision) a year later. Although many historians might wonder why it took so long for the end-the-war faction to succeed, the circumstances of Tojo's resignation show how difficult it was for this group to prevail over the diehards who were determined to stay the course with the existing war strategy and fight to the bitter end.

By June 1944, Japanese military leaders who had access to top military intelligence, especially officers in the navy, knew that Japan must at all costs defend the Mariana Islands against the Americans. These leaders understood that Saipan and Tinian, in the Marianas, were vital for the protection of Japan's home islands against US air assaults. The battle in Saipan, therefore, was a decisive battle that Japan could not afford to lose, and Emperor Hirohito fully understood the island's significance. Having heard that American troops had started to land on Saipan, the emperor told General Tojo on June 18, "Our soldiers on the front line are putting up a good fight, but aren't our forces inadequate compared with the enemy forces? If we lose Saipan, there will be more and more air raids in Tokyo. We must hold [Saipan] at all costs."[48] After Japan's defeat in a major naval battle near the Marianas on June 19–20, loss of Saipan appeared inevitable. The Tojo cabinet and army decided not to send reinforcements to retake Saipan and reported that decision to the emperor on June 24. Hirohito did not want to give up Saipan and asked Tojo to call a meeting of the Supreme Military Council (Gensui Kaigi), but the council endorsed the Tojo cabinet's decision to abandon the island. The loss of Saipan shocked the emperor deeply. In a diary entry of June 26, Chamberlain Irie Sukemasa wrote, "Today the emperor was again gazing at fireflies in the garden of the Fukiage [Palace]. Under the circumstances, there is nothing better for him than to divert himself and to recuperate."[49] Although Hirohito recalled in his 1946 "Monologue" that his trust in Prime Minister Tojo and Navy Minister Shimada remained unchanged during this period,[50] the defeat in Saipan apparently began to shake the emperor's confidence in Japan's ability to hold its absolute defense perimeter.

The anti-Tojo momentum in the navy increased as Japan's chance to regain Saipan slipped away. As early as June 3, Rear Admiral Takagi and his friends arranged a secret meeting of three influential admirals—Okada and Yonai, who had served as prime ministers in the 1930s, and Suetsugu Nobumasa, who had been home minister in the Konoe cabinet. The three admirals agreed that the Tojo cabinet must go and that, as a first step, they would force the resignation of Navy Minister Shimada, who remained loyal to Tojo and was also chief of the Naval General Staff. At the same time, Prince Takamatsu, another end-the-war advocate, pleaded with Prince Fushimi to persuade his protégé, Shimada, to step down. Prince Fushimi did talk with Shimada, but Shimada resisted the prince's advice. After the Tojo cabinet formally decided not to send reinforcements to Saipan, Okada and Tojo had a tense meeting on June 27 that ended in a rupture over the issue of Shimada's resignation. Admiral Yonai was disgusted by Japan's loss of Saipan and despairingly told Takagi on June 30, "Although I do not know [the] exact details, Japan has lost the war. We have been defeated beyond doubt. Whoever leads the war, there is nothing to be done. Old ones like me have nothing else to do but take a nap." Takagi's own observation on the same occasion illuminated what was wrong with the Tojo cabinet's policy. He pointed out to Yonai that Japan had lost the Marshalls, the Carolines, and New Guinea and was about to lose Saipan, an island well within the absolute defense perimeter adopted in September 1943. However, according to Takagi, the Tojo cabinet could not accept the reality, insisting that the war was a draw and refusing to modify Japan's strategy.[51]

As we have seen, Tojo had many opponents in the navy, but not everyone in the army agreed with General Tojo's policies either. The army officers of the War Guidance Section of the Imperial Headquarters, who were studying long-term war plans, independently reached a conclusion similar to Yonai and Takagi's by late June 1944. As early as January 4, 1944, the section's chief, Colonel Matsutani Sei, had warned the chief of the General Staff that if Japan made a strategic mistake against the Allies, the nation might face a crisis that would endanger the preservation of the *kokutai* (national polity). Again on March 15, Matsutani wrote a report to the chief of the General Staff to the effect that both Japan and Germany were cornered and defending their respective absolute defense perimeters. Matsutani predicted that after July or August, Japan's national strength and military power would gradually decline. He recommended that Japan concentrate all its forces on a final decisive battle in June or July, which he predicted would determine Japan's fate. Matsutani also recommended that the leaders of the government and supreme command draw up draft peace terms by June or July and report to the emperor.[52] However, Colonel Matsutani's superiors, including General Tojo, did not pay attention to these reports. In the colonel's mind, the Allied cross-channel invasion at Normandy on June 6 and the US landing on Saipan on June 15 were decisive turning points. Like the navy officers who advocated early termination of the war, Matsutani was shocked when Japan could not defend the Marianas for even a week after the US assaults began. He realized that Japan's absolute defense perimeter was broken.

When the Imperial Headquarters decided to abandon Saipan on June 23, Matsutani and his team (Lieutenant Colonel Tanemura Sako and Major Hashimoto Masakatsu) drafted a new report and finalized it on July 2. This report shows that some of the best minds in the army were able to make an objective assessment of Japan's position in the war: "Strategically speaking, the empire has no future prospect of reversing the general situation of the war, and moreover, Germany's situation is roughly the same as the empire's. Since Japan will face a *jiri-hin* [gradual decline] from now on, we all came to the conclusion that Japan should make plans to end the war. . . . Therefore, although it is very difficult, the empire must seek to conclude the war through political maneuvers and offensives. In such a case, the only condition for peace should be the preservation of the *kokutai* [national polity]."[53]

Matsutani and his team were fully aware that the Army General Staff would not appreciate this assessment of the war situation, but Matsutani nevertheless risked his job by meeting with both the chief and vice chief of the Army General Staff on June 29, 1944, and orally conveying his recommendation. Tojo was displeased with Matsutani's report and reassigned the colonel to the command post in China on July 3. In this action, Tojo followed his usual policy of sending those who disagreed with him to remote and very dangerous war fronts.

Prime Minister Tojo was determined to stay in power, on the grounds that he had the emperor's trust, and members of the anti-Tojo faction could not easily force his resignation until they could persuade the emperor to come around to their way of thinking. However, the main challenge faced by the opposition was how to gain access to the emperor. Tojo, who was both prime minister and chief of the Army General Staff, practically monopolized the emperor's access to official civilian and military communication channels, and the lord keeper of the privy seal reinforced this system of control. According to Hosokawa's diary entry of June 13, Prince Takamatsu warned Hirohito that he (the emperor) was not receiving any information that did not pass through official channels, but the emperor insisted that this was not true, and the two brothers got into an argument. The prince later admitted that the emperor did not like his family members' interfering in the official decision-making process.[54]

On July 8, when Prince Takamatsu learned of Japan's utter defeat in Saipan, the prince expressed his frustration at his brother's inflexibility and reluctance to exercise his discretionary power, as emperor, in what the prince considered a righteous cause:

His majesty's personality—his dislike of wrongdoing and his fastidiousness in following the rules—is a strength when the system functions normally, but it becomes a fatal shortcoming once the system stops functioning as it is truly intended. Because I am afraid that his shortcoming might bring great harm in the face of a grave situation expected in the near future, it is necessary [for him] to adjust his thinking and prepare himself as to how to approach and deal with such a case. Therefore, I told [his advisers] that we needed an adviser who could guide the emperor to nurture an appropriate frame of mind. Since the emperor utterly dislikes deviating from a methodical way of doing things, he expects the lord keeper of the privy seal to attend to political affairs, the chief aide-de-camp to military affairs, the minister of the imperial household to the affairs of the court, the grand chamberlain to the matters of chamberlains; and if they [these officials] bring up matters outside their responsibilities, he is displeased, and he will never comment on such matters. The grand chamberlain had initially intended to speak to [the emperor] about everything, but it became impossible. Of course, events like the February 26 Incident, in which [the emperor] lost the grand chamberlain and the lord keeper of the privy seal, shocked him so deeply that he hardened his determination to prevent such tragedies, making a clear distinction [between official and unofficial channels]. The lord privy seal is grateful for the emperor's consideration, but he also feels it [the emperor's position] is too rigid.[55]

This quotation illuminates the contrast between the reserved emperor, who was overly cautious about the impacts of his personal decisions, and his younger brother, who had more freedom to speak his own mind and was inclined to use his influence more freely to achieve his goals. These differences may be attributed partly to the difference in the two men's personalities but also to differences in upbringing and training. The personal differences between the emperor and his younger brother, as well as their difference of position within Japan's leadership, continued to resurface periodically during the rest of the war.

For the opposition to undermine the emperor's confidence in Tojo, it was necessary to gain the support of one key person—Lord Privy Seal Kido. Because he had been instrumental in selecting General Tojo as prime minister on the verge of Japan's decision to go to war with the United States in the fall of 1941, Kido avoided criticizing the Tojo cabinet's war policy as long as he could. However, Kido was a realist who understood that the authority of the emperor, which in the end justified Kido's own position and influence, depended on the preservation of an equilibrium between Tojo's followers and the anti-Tojo coalition. Kido maintained close contact with both sides, but he sensed increasing anger and frustration among naval officers and senior civilian statesmen about the inflexible and ineffective policy of the Tojo cabinet. Tojo's insistence on staying the course and continuing the fighting turned the division between Tojo's followers and the anti-Tojo group into a division largely between a war faction and a peace faction. The Tojo government's official acknowledgment of the fall of Saipan on July 7, 1944, eventually forced Kido to side with the peace faction. Kido's decision was also influenced by the passionate pleas from the navy's end-the-war advocates and their civilian sympathizers.[56]

About the time of the fall of Saipan, certain groups were plotting to assassinate Tojo, and Kido and some other court advisers felt compelled to respond to this threat. Among those groups, the most noteworthy scheme was led by Rear Admiral Takagi, with the secret support of Prince Takamatsu.[57] According to Takagi, on July 8 Kido told Professor Yabe Teiji of the Imperial University of Tokyo that the lord keeper of the privy seal had no authority to replace the prime minister. However, Kido suggested that he would "steer the situation" when got out of control, for instance if there were an act of "terrorism" or a further deterioration of the war situation. Although Kido was against a coup to place a particular individual in power, he stated that an act of terrorism to eliminate undesirable elements could not be prevented.[58] In this statement, Kido showed an apparent general knowledge of the assassination plot of Takagi and his group.

There is no evidence to prove that the emperor himself heard about attempts to assassinate Tojo, but Kido's diary indicates that Kido daily informed the emperor of the tense political situation that was developing between the Tojo government and opposition groups. For instance, on July 7 Kido wrote in his diary, "From 10:25 to 11:45, during my audience [with the emperor] I explained in detail the continuously deteriorating domestic political conditions."[59] There is no doubt that the emperor realized that the unpopularity of Prime Minister Tojo was creating a dangerous situation at home. By the time Kido had a crucial meeting with the prime minister on July 13, Kido and the emperor seemed to have an understanding that Tojo should seriously consider stepping down.

In the Kido-Tojo meeting of July 13, Tojo expressed his determination to stay in power and reinforce existing efforts to win the war at all costs. To Tojo's surprise, Kido offered a counterproposal, suggesting three changes, all of which could be construed as an expression of no confidence in the Tojo cabinet. First, the government must be separate from the supreme command, which meant that Tojo (who was prime minister as well as war minister) should not concurrently serve as the chief of the Army General Staff. Second, Navy Minister Shimada, who was unpopular within the navy, must resign. Third, some senior statesmen (*jushin*) should be appointed as cabinet members to maintain national unity. Tojo was willing to consider inclusion of senior statesmen in his cabinet and he did not reject the idea of separating the government and supreme command. But Tojo would not accept the resignation of Navy Minister Shimada. Kido and Tojo ended the meeting without further discussion. Tojo eventually accepted Kido's proposals later that day, but only after Tojo had learned directly from the emperor that he supported Kido's proposals.[60]

Although Prime Minister Tojo was badly shaken by the realization that he had lost the emperor's confidence, he tried to preserve the composition of his cabinet by accepting Kido's proposals. However, at this point, the forces of opposition against the Tojo cabinet were too strong to reverse. Seven former prime ministers, known as the *jushin*, met on July 17 to discuss whether they should support the continuation of the Tojo cabinet, and six of them refused. The *jushin*'s collective recommendation was conveyed to Kido, who in turn reported it to the emperor on the following day. Realizing that the *jushin*'s action sealed the fate of his cabinet, Prime Minister Tojo submitted his resignation on the same day (July 17) and the emperor accepted his resignation on July 18.[61] In retrospect, after the war, the emperor commented that Tojo did not seem to understand the key objective of the cabinet reform, which was to put an end to the concentration of authority in one person. The emperor also added, "Tojo was good at bureaucratic management, but he was unable to understand the wishes of the people . . . and especially, he could not comprehend the inclinations of 'intellectuals.'"[62]

Why did the emperor not encourage Prime Minister Tojo to step down earlier? According to his own recollection in 1946, the emperor did not believe he could initiate a dissolution of the Tojo cabinet, despite its unpopularity, because of "the bitter experience of the Tanaka cabinet" in 1928. Hirohito did not want Tojo's supporters to be able to blame the destruction of the general's cabinet on court intrigue, and at that time the emperor did not believe he could find a man with more influence over the army than Tojo. Moreover, because Tojo had cultivated personal connections with leaders in many of the countries that the Japanese empire considered part of the Greater East Asian sphere of influence, Hirohito was afraid of losing these international connections if Tojo left the government.[63]

The end of General Tojo's term of office did mark a change in direction, however difficult and slow, in Japan's path toward conclusion of the war. Tojo's resignation came as a great relief to those who were plotting to assassinate him. If he had refused to resign and had stayed in power for a few more days, it is likely that one of several planned assassination attempts would have been carried out. This would have created an interesting historical coincidence, because on July 20 there was an assassination attempt against Adolf Hitler— an attempt that revealed to the outside world the existence of internal dissent in Nazi Germany. One may argue that, ironically, this failure to carry out an assassination attempt against Tojo effectively kept Japan's enemies from understanding the internal divisions and power struggles within the Japanese leadership. Some may even ask this hypothetical question: if American war leaders had understood the instability of Emperor Hirohito's government and realized the vulnerability of Japan's internal unity, would that have made any difference in their strategy to achieve Japan's unconditional surrender?

CHAPTER 5

Imbroglio

Moves to End the War

O N THE QUESTION OF JAPAN'S DECISION TO END THE WAR, historians, especially in the United States, tend to focus on the final months of the war in the summer of 1945. These historians generally limit their discussion to two possible causes for Japan's surrender: the dropping of atomic bombs on Hiroshima and Nagasaki or the Soviet Union's declaration of war on Japan. This approach presupposes that only the external physical power of the enemies' military could force the militaristic Japanese government to lay down arms. If the Allied Powers had utterly destroyed Japan's home islands and occupied Japan with ground forces, certainly there would have been fewer controversies over the proximate cause of Japan's surrender. However, the fact that Japan was itself forced to make the difficult decision to surrender—and had to carry out this decision by accepting the Potsdam Proclamation—makes it challenging for historians to pin down exactly how and why Japan reached the decision to surrender and thereby end the war.

There is no doubt that the double shock of the atomic bombing of Hiroshima and Nagasaki and the Soviet invasion of Manchuria were both very important in prompting Japan to surrender. However, historian Robert Butow offered another explanation over sixty years ago in his seminal book on this subject, *Japan's Decision to Surrender*: "The atomic bombing of Hiroshima and Nagasaki and the Soviet Union's declaration of war did not produce Japan's decision to surrender, for that decision—in embryo—had long been taking shape. What these events did do was to create that unusual atmosphere in which the theretofore static factor of the Emperor could be made active in such an extraordinary way as to work what was virtually a political miracle."[1]

This "political miracle" contributed to the creation of the myth of Emperor Hirohito's *seidan* (sacred decision) to end the war. In the collective memory of the Japanese people, the emperor's unprecedented radio announcement of August 15, 1945, in which he accepted the Potsdam Proclamation, became the convergent point of the twofold myth that both the emperor and atomic bomb served in the role of peacemaker: that is, the atomic bombs forced the emperor to issue his *seidan* to surrender, and he was thus able to save Japan from national suicide.[2] However, what appears to be a "political miracle" was in reality a series of actions carried out by a group surrounding the emperor that could be considered a "peace faction." This group included government officials, military officers, and the emperor's formal and informal advisers—all of whom shared a sense of urgency about the need to conclude the war.

Some thirty years ago, Akira Iriye produced a study of the dynamics of power and culture in Japan, in the United States, and in the relations between the two countries. In this work he also argued that "there was sufficient interest and intelligence in both Japan and the United States in the middle of July [1945] to end the war then and there." Iriye concluded that "the Japanese-American war could have been terminated" on the eve of the Potsdam Conference.[3]

Documents pertaining to internal developments in Japan with regard to Emperor Hirohito and the imperial court allow a reexamination of internal forces that shaped Japan's decision to end the war "in embryo." How did political efforts of the end-the-war faction pave the way for a final decision to terminate the war—even before the externally caused double shocks of the atomic bombs and the Soviet declaration of war? What role did the emperor actually play in this political maneuvering? What do we know about his personal views and actions concerning the termination of the war? How important were the emperor's interventions in the triangular power relations of the court advisers, government leaders, and military leaders? What role did the emperor play as commander in chief in dealing with an intensifying rivalry between the army and navy—the former dominated by diehards willing to fight to the bitter end, the latter now led by end-the-war advocates like Navy Minister Yonai Mitsumasa, Admiral Okada Keisuke, and Prince Takamatsu?

Even though the emperor came to realize sometime between March and September 1943 that Japan must end the war as soon as possible, Japan was still not boxed in at this point and there were a number of ways to seek to end the war. However, documents show that the emperor continued to share the opinion of his military and court advisers that Japan must win a decisive battle before it could open peace negotiations with the United States. The problem with this strategy was that Japan was never able to win such a battle. When did the emperor realize that it was unrealistic for Japan to pursue a decisive battle before negotiating favorable peace terms? When did he face up to the distinct possibility that Japan's defeat was unavoidable? And did he begin looking for an alternative way to end the war? What were the minimum acceptable peace terms for the emperor? Was he prepared to accept the unconditional surrender that the Allies publicly demanded?

For the emperor, the eight-month period in which Japan was governed by Prime Minister Koiso Kuniaki became a time for a painful rethinking of Japan's position and search for an exit from a disastrous war. Hirohito approved the appointment of General Koiso as new prime minister on July 20, 1944, but in later years he did not have positive recollections of Koiso. He stated in 1946 that he "reluctantly approved" of Koiso's appointment as prime minister because a more desirable candidate, General Terauchi Hisaichi, was needed on the southern front to defend the Philippines. The emperor was also apprehensive about Koiso's alleged involvement in the failed military coup plot of March 1931 (known as Sangatsu Incident) as well as his tendency toward an ultranationalist type of "mystic fanaticism." The emperor commented, "The Koiso cabinet turned out to be ineffective, as I predicted," adding that Koiso had "no convictions or confidence [in himself]" and was easily swayed by the people around him.[4] Apparently, from the outset the emperor did not consider General Koiso a competent and reliable leader. Although questioning Tojo's judgments on wartime policy, Hirohito still counted on General Tojo's ability to control the military. Unable to find an alternative to Koiso, the emperor even asked Kido if Tojo might be able to remain as war minister in the Koiso cabinet, but Kido advised against such an idea for political reasons.[5] The idea of forming a coalition cabinet of national unity with General Koiso as prime minister and Admiral Yonai as navy minister apparently alleviated the emperor's reservations about General Koiso's leadership qualities.[6]

Members of the peace faction, who hoped that Tojo's resignation would bring the beginning of the end of the disastrous war, were also frustrated by the new prime minister. Koiso at least accommodated the wishes of the navy's anti-Tojo faction by forming a coalition cabinet with Admiral Yonai, an action that the peace faction interpreted as the first step toward ending the war. The new prime minister also stopped his predecessor's practice of monopolizing both military and political power by appointing General Sugi-yama Gen as war minister, restoring the authority of the supreme command (i.e., by removing the supreme command from the office of the prime minis-ter), and appointing General Umezu Yoshijiro as chief of the Army General Staff. Koiso originally wanted his war minister to be either General Yamashita Tomoyuki or General Anami Korechika (whose leadership was later cov-eted by the peace faction as well), but Generals Tojo, Sugiyama, and Umezu blocked Koiso's wish.[7] Moreover, having been unable to secure the prime minister's participation in the Imperial Headquarters' meeting, on August 5, 1944, Koiso proceeded to reorganize the liaison conference that served as a coordinating body between the cabinet and the military headquarters. This group was renamed the Supreme War Leadership Council (also known as the Council of Big Six) and officially became the highest decision-making body in Japan.

All these concessions to political rivals and Koiso's inexperience and unfamiliarity with central government politics made it difficult for him to effectively explore an alternative to the existing policy of fighting to the bitter end. The Koiso cabinet turned out to be a transitional government that was not ready to abandon the policy set previously by the Tojo cabinet, and that disappointed the end-the-war advocates. The emperor shared their disap-pointment in Prime Minister Koiso. However, the last few months under the Koiso cabinet witnessed a quiet but substantial shift in the power relationship between the army faction in favor of continuing the war and the peace faction that included both civilian and military officers, especially officers within the navy. This shift in power turned out to be an important factor that eventually paved the way for Japan's decision to surrender.

※

Under the Koiso cabinet, from the summer of 1944 to the spring of 1945, Japanese forces continued to retreat from Southeast Asia and the Pacific. During this period, it is not clear if the emperor fully grasped the precarious situation of Japanese forces in the Pacific. For example, Japan suffered seri-ous naval losses near Taiwan on October 24–25, 1944. As historian Yamada Akira argues, "The emperor must have been familiar with the details of the losses the Japanese forces suffered [off the coast of Taiwan]." But at the same time, Yamada also notes that the Imperial Headquarters' reports to the emperor concerning the battle gave a picture of an "illusionary victory." Having investigated this discrepancy between the reports of victory submitted to the emperor versus actual battle losses, Yamada points out a crucial factor: although the emperor received fairly accurate information about Japan's losses (in terms of warships and airplanes), he also received grossly exaggerated reports on damages allegedly inflicted on the enemy. Therefore, Yamada concludes, the overall effect of these reports likely led the emperor to the mistaken belief that Japan had not, in fact, been badly defeated. Although Yamada is a harsh critic of the Japanese military, his analysis suggests that exaggerated reports to the emperor of Japanese military accomplishments were not intentionally fabricated by the Imperial Headquarters but rather were due to headquarters' wishful thinking and blind reliance on reports coming from the front lines, where field commanders wrote optimistic reports in haste, without verifying the facts.[8]

In a similar manner, the emperor did not seem to understand how badly the Japanese navy had been defeated in the waters surrounding the Philippines. Hirohito received detailed and fairly accurate reports on Japan's losses there, but he also received exaggerated reports on Japanese military accomplishments. Japan's strategy to defend the Philippines was plagued by numerous disagreements—not only between the army and the navy but also within each military branch—over the best location for engaging in a decisive battle, Leyte or Luzon. There were also breakdowns of communication between the Koiso cabinet and the Imperial Headquarters in Tokyo, as well as between Tokyo officers and field commanders in the south. In November 1944, Prime Minister Koiso resorted to waging a nationwide propaganda campaign, calling for a marshaling of forces for a battle on Leyte, which would be Japan's ultimate decisive battle—despite the fact that General Yamashita Tomoyuki (who commanded the Japanese forces in the Philippines) argued for engaging in a decisive battle on the main Philippine island of Luzon, not on Leyte.

In 1946, Emperor Hirohito admitted that, in retrospect, General Yamashita's Luzon strategy would have made more sense; but in late 1944, the emperor admitted, he was confused and misguided by the resolute insistence of the Koiso cabinet and the Army General Staff that the best strategy was to pursue a decisive battle in Leyte. As a result, Hirohito gave his own sanction to that fatal strategy. By December 19, the disastrous outcome of Japan's badly coordinated and halfhearted naval engagements at Leyte forced Imperial Headquarters to change its strategy. The Army General Staff quietly abandoned the goal of a Leyte victory and decided to concentrate available forces to defend Luzon. Afterward, when the emperor asked Prime Minister Koiso how the government could explain to the Japanese people the decision to abandon Leyte, Koiso was baffled and had to admit that the shift of the army's strategic goal from Leyte to Luzon had taken place without the prime minister's knowledge and that Koiso had been forced to deal with the new and unexpected situation. With incidents like this one, the emperor's confidence in Prime Minister Koiso rapidly eroded as Japan lost more and more ground in the Philippines.[9]

On January 6, 1945, the emperor received a report that US forces had entered Lingayen Gulf on the main Philippine island of Luzon and had begun a landing attempt. He summoned Lord Privy Seal Kido and, according to Kido, "[The emperor said that] the war situation in the Philippines was becoming increasingly grave, and depending up its outcome, he wondered if there was need to solicit advice from *jushin* [senior statesmen]." Kido advised Hirohito against conferring with *jushin* at that time and suggested instead that the emperor should have a frank discussion with the chiefs of the Army and Naval General Staffs.[10] On January 13, the emperor again brought up the war situation in the Philippines and potential enemy attacks on the coast of French Indochina and asked Kido about the possibility of meetings with *jushin*. And on January 19, obviously unsatisfied with reports of the chiefs of the General Staffs, the anxious emperor questioned the chiefs, not without sarcasm, "Your plan sounds good, as usual; but so far you have failed to execute your previous plans. Are you sure about [your plans] this time?"[11]

Thus, based on historical circumstances and later reports, the emperor himself likely initiated the plan to meet discreetly in the palace with seven *jushin*, one by one. Between February 7 and February 26, 1945, Hirohito met with six former prime ministers and former lord keeper of the privy seal Makino Nobuaki. The emperor did not meet with Admiral Yonai, who was then serving as navy minister, or with General Abe, then serving as governor-general of Korea. According to the published memoir of Grand Chamberlain Fujita Hisanori, who attended most of these meetings, the emperor was particularly interested in hearing from the *jushin* about how Japan should bring an end to the war. Fujita's memoir notes that, at the time, it was taboo for any Japanese subject to speak about a cessation of hostilities; the military police could immediately arrest anyone suspected of antiwar sentiments. Perhaps Fujita was sincere when he wrote that in these conversations with the *jushin* the emperor was struggling to find an opportunity to talk about making peace. However, when Fujita commented, "It is not too much to say that [the emperor] was thinking about a policy to end the war more earnestly than anyone else in charge of government," Fujita was probably speculating and very likely exaggerating the emperor's desire for early peace.[12] There is no doubt that the emperor was anguished by his country's deteriorating position in the war with the United States and that he was searching seriously for a way to save his country. However, from the sources available to us, it is difficult to tell how far the emperor was ready to commit himself to making peace in February 1945. It is easier to conclude that the emperor was genuinely troubled by the situation and was seeking advice from the senior statesmen.

Most of the meetings with the *jushin* did not appear to have been helpful to the emperor, but their exchanges do give us a glimpse of the emperor's changing perceptions. For example, Hirohito recalled that even though he had asked for the *jushin*'s views on the future outcome of the war, "nobody was able to offer convincing opinions." The emperor also recalled that although Admiral Okada and Baron Makino held moderate views, neither had been able to recommend a convincing policy course. The emperor thought that Prince Konoe Fumimaro's plea for an immediate termination of the war was based on "an overly pessimistic view."[13]

However, the meeting between Hirohito and Konoe on February 14 sheds some light on the emperor's thinking about the war at that time. That is, Hirohito may have had a negative recollection of Konoe's advice because he did not fully share Konoe's sense of urgency about the need to immediately terminate the war, or perhaps because Konoe could not offer specific suggestions on how to end the hostilities. Perhaps the emperor's negative recollection was also a product of Konoe's touching what the emperor most feared: internal disorder and the destruction of the *kokutai* (national polity). In the February 14 conversation, Konoe argued for ending the war at the earliest possible opportunity on the grounds that prolonging a hopeless war would certainly make a defeated Japan vulnerable to the influence of communism. Konoe emphasized his concerns about the rise of radicalized, lower-class elements in the Japanese military who believed in "the compatibility of the *kokutai* and communism."[14]

Both Konoe and the emperor knew that propaganda from the die-hard faction that advocated fighting to the bitter end was based on the argument that the Allies' ultimate goal was to destroy Japan's *kokutai*. Konoe suggested that removing the die-hard faction from power might soften the Allied position and allow Japan to negotiate more favorable peace terms. The emperor asked Konoe a pointed question: "With regard to the *kokutai*, unlike your idea, the army is of the opinion that the United States is even thinking of changing our *kokutai*. What do you think?" Konoe replied that the army was taking a hard line in order to "boost the people's fighting spirit." Pointing out that some Americans, such as former ambassador Joseph C. Grew, had a good understanding of the Japanese court, Konoe emphasized the importance of concluding the war as soon as possible, before American public opinion turned against the imperial court. The emperor asked Konoe, "You mentioned the need for a purge of certain elements from the army, but what should be the goal of a purge in the army?" When Konoe replied that ideological orientation should be the determining factor in deciding who should go, the emperor asked again, "It comes down to the question of personnel. Konoe, what is your opinion on this point?" Konoe, however, was not able to offer a convincing option; he merely suggested placing General Anami Korechika or General Yamashita Tomoyuki in the highest military office. Konoe said he hoped that the emperor would take a personal initiative in the matter. The emperor responded, "I think it is difficult to do so unless we achieve a military victory one more time." The meeting ended with Konoe's pessimistic questioning of whether such a victory would ever be possible. Unless it happened very soon, Konoe added, it would be of no use.[15]

The same day, the emperor told his military aide, "I believe that this war is certainly winnable if we make our best efforts, but I am anxious about whether or not the people will be able to endure until then."[16] This statement, in conjunction with the exchange with Konoe, indicates several things about the emperor's thinking in February 1945. The emperor obviously shared Konoe's concern that a protracted war might result in internal disorder in Japan, which might include uprisings instigated by discontented leftists. However, even though the emperor was sympathetic to Konoe's proposal to purge the army of overly militant leaders, Hirohito was not sure how to replace these military men with others, and he did not find Konoe's vague advice very convincing. Therefore, the emperor was not persuaded to abandon the hope of seeking a negotiated peace after Japan's symbolic victory in a decisive battle. The emperor's nonaction to this point suggests that he was probably looking for a way out of this policy drift, waiting for a decisive moment or set of circumstances that would force him to decide what to do concerning the strategy of a decisive battle, one way or the other.

Another *jushin*, Admiral Okada, met with the emperor on February 23 and also recommended that Japan should seize an opportune moment to make peace and end hostilities. However, according to Grand Chamberlain Fujita, Okada's recommendation was limited to merely an "abstract" argument without a specific policy recommendation on how to lead the nation toward peace.[17] However, it is not clear from Fujita's report if the emperor was aware of what lay behind the cautious words of Admiral Okada. In any case, the admiral, who had narrowly escaped assassination in the February 26 Incident of 1936, was unable to articulate his honest views about the course of the war; Okada knew that any expression of doubt about or opposition to the war might cost him his life. He at least had the courage to use the term *shūsen* (to end the war) during his audience with the emperor. Prior to the admiral's interview, the term *shūsen* had been taboo at court and the euphemism "change of direction" had to be used in the emperor's presence.

※

In the meantime, some end-the-war advocates in the navy were quietly trying to prod the nation toward a termination of the war. When Admiral Yonai assumed the position of minister of the navy in the Koiso cabinet, he persuaded Rear Admiral Inoue Shigeyoshi to serve as his vice minister. Together, they unobtrusively began gathering political forces to move toward an early termination of the war. On August 29, 1944, with the tacit approval of Navy Minister Yonai and Chief of the Naval General Staff Oikawa Koshiro, Navy Vice Minister Inoue secretly ordered Rear Admiral Takagi Sokichi to conduct a clandestine survey of Japan's decision makers and recommend "what need[ed] to be done to wind up the war."[18] Following these orders, Takagi communicated with numerous political and military leaders and meticulously recorded their frank views about if, when, and how to end the war. The extensive records Takagi accumulated during this period survived the war and now provide valuable information about the thinking (across Japan's governmental organizations) of the various peace factions; these records show clearly how, in 1944, these peace advocates were quietly searching for the best possible scenario for the war's end.

One of the most outspoken proponents of an early termination of the war was the emperor's own younger brother, Prince Takamatsu, who did not hesitate to express his frustration with the emperor's reluctance to listen to the end-the-war advocates. According to Rear Admiral Takagi's record of his interview with the prince on September 17, 1944, Prince Takamatsu was so assertive—and spoke with such conviction—that Takagi felt the prince was speaking on behalf of the emperor. During this meeting, the prince told Takagi that the ultimate objective of the policy to conclude the war was to protect Japan's *kokutai* and that the only terms for peace, on Japan's part, should be the preservation of the *kokutai*. Prince Takamatsu argued that the whole country must unite and resolve to survive at all costs in order to defend the *kokutai*. He believed that army propaganda advocating *gyokusai-shugi* (death and no surrender) was impracticable and that the navy must take the initiative in proposing a course to terminate the war.[19] Takagi might have been too eager in wanting to believe that Prince Takamatsu was expressing the will of the imperial court, but there is no doubt that the assuring words from the prince strengthened Takagi's conviction that the survival of the nation required early peace negotiations based on realism, not fanaticism.

From these records of Takagi's interviews and Prince Takamatsu's diary, it is clear that the voices of the end-the-war faction were increasingly being heard in early April 1945—that is, on the eve of Prime Minister Koiso's April 5 resignation—and well before the beginning of the Battle of Okinawa, the first battle fought in Japan's home territory.[20] These records show a strengthening of the end-the-war proponents and a relative increase of their political influence over the hard-liners who were still insisting on continuing the war to the bitter end. During this period, the tide appeared to be slowly shifting, at the highest level of the Japanese government, in favor of the peace faction. The strengthened position of the end-the-war advocates was due to a number of factors, but one was clearly Japan's utter defeat in the Battle of Iwo Jima (February 16–17), which coincided with the emperor's confidential interviews with seven *jushin*. During the spring of 1945, Takagi's clandestine survey continued to expand, and he began exchanging information and ideas with the peace faction within the navy as well as with civilian leaders, including the office of the lord keeper of the privy seal and Foreign Minister Shigemitsu Mamoru.

Continual interservice rivalry made the situation very complex: army hard-liners who still believed in Japan's superior spiritual strength, like the followers of General Tojo, were determined to keep fighting. They began circulating a proposal to merge the two military branches and create an overarching ministry of defense. In practice, this would mean that the army would virtually absorb the navy, for the latter's capabilities had been dramatically reduced by devastating defeats in the Marianas and the Philippines. However, the Navy Ministry, then under the leadership of Yonai and Inoue, resisted this move because the two men knew that the army was trying to silence the end-the-war advocates in the navy. The proposal to integrate the army with the navy eventually reached the emperor. He summoned Navy Minister Yonai and War Minister Sugiyama separately on March 3 and asked for their opinions. Admiral Yonai expressed his firm opposition to the idea of integration, while General Sugiyama, apparently unfamiliar with this army initiative, promised to study the matter carefully. The emperor simply listened to the both chiefs without expressing his own preference.[21] However, according to Takagi's record, Admiral Okada told Admiral Nomura Kichisaburo in early March that the emperor was seriously displeased with the idea of placing the two military branches under one command.[22] Given the emperor's own leanings toward moderation, Hirohito was probably afraid of the army's attempt to control moderate groups in the navy (which was then under Admiral Yonai's command). In the end, the proposal to integrate the services was effectively abandoned after the new Suzuki cabinet was formed on April 7, with Admiral Yonai continuing as navy minister.

In March, there was another important development at the highest level of the Japanese leadership. Several civilian and military leaders close to the emperor started to discuss a *seidan* scenario, that is, a way to conclude the war by means of a formal decision by the emperor. As noted earlier in this chapter, during Konoe Fumimaro's audience with the emperor on February 14, Konoe had already hinted that, in order to facilitate an early negotiated peace with the Allies, a purge of military hard-liners might have to be carried out through the emperor's *seidan*. At that time, however, the emperor was not yet ready to follow Konoe's suggestion.[23]

The possibility of utilizing the emperor's *seidan* to end the war was explored further by Kido and Foreign Minister Shigemitsu. On March 8, Kido wrote in his diary that he met with the foreign minister and "discussed the prospects of the war, the disposition of the emperor's close advisers, and so on." However, Kido did not record the details of their discussion.[24] After the war, Kido provided brief commentaries on his wartime diary, in which he explained what he had discussed with Shigemitsu during their meeting of March 8, 1945. According to Kido's recollection, he agreed with the foreign minister's opinion that there was no prospect for a "negotiated peace" and that Japan would have no choice but to "surrender." Kido told Shigemitsu that he had himself been agonizing over when and how to bring up the question of ending the war with government leaders, admitting the difficulty of making a 180-degree turn from war to peace under the circumstances. Kido suggested to the foreign minister, "I think that there is no other way but to set the stage in extreme secrecy for the occasion in which we eventually realize [peace through virtual surrender] by the emperor's order." Kido added that the *jushin* were in reality powerless and unreliable, adding, "When the time is ripe, you in the government and I in the palace shall [have to] give it our best efforts to carry it out." Shigemitsu fully agreed with Kido and promised to do his best to secretly work toward that end.[25]

Consequently, according to Kido, when he had an audience with the emperor on the following day (March 9), Kido warned Hirohito that the military situation was becoming increasingly serious, and Kido explained the gist of his conversations with Shigemitsu. Kido asked the emperor to be prepared to perform his task in case of such an eventuality.[26] This is an important indication that the emperor was aware of the understanding between Kido and Foreign Minister Shigemitsu (however vague it might have been), that, when an opportune moment arose, the emperor should use the prestige of the throne and an imperial *seidan* to end the war.

Though Kido's postwar recollection alone may not be sufficient to prove that the emperor was aware of this *seidan* proposal, notes written by Shigemitsu on March 4, 1945, support Kido's claims. In the wake of Japan's defeat at Iwo Jima, anticipating an American invasion of Okinawa, Shigemitsu wrote in a private memorandum to himself,

Today Japan is on the verge of collapse, and today's question is how to preserve *kōtō* [imperial reign] and cultivate the future of the Japanese race.

Whenever I have the chance, I have been reporting to His Majesty and communicating clearly with the *jushin* and with the lord keeper of the privy seal about the current situation. Therefore, I trust that the highest leadership has been prepared [for the worst]. From His Majesty I have already heard about his personal wishes that Japan must take necessary measures to conclude the war at the appropriate time—even at the expense of [having to make] territorial concessions; and now is the time that we should examine this matter thoroughly.[27]

The increasingly desperate foreign minister also wrote in a private note to himself on March 7, "Prime Minister Koiso has already been abandoned by the Diet, the people, and the *jushin*, and even by his cabinet members."[28]

In another private notation, dated March 9, Shigemitsu offers a valuable account of a meeting with Kido the previous day. Shigemitsu visited Kido to discuss the urgent need for action by Japan's top leadership. Kido explained to Shigemitsu that his efforts to unite the army and navy by order of the emperor had not been successful, saying,

> In order to save the Japanese race and the imperial court, in the event that the appropriate time for diplomatic negotiations comes, I have made up my mind to offer counsel to the emperor, and you and I can jointly send the imperial order to the cabinet to carry it out. The question is how we should negotiate [with our enemies]. If the Soviet Union stays neutral, we should determine in advance how to do it through the Soviet Union.
>
> We cannot count on the *jushin*. Nor can we count on members of the imperial family. When it comes to the prime minister, I cannot even have a frank discussion with him. His Majesty asked me if he should talk to the prime minister concerning measures to conclude the war, but I advised against it. I responded that the foreign minister fully understood the situation and he should be the one to know this matter.
>
> Konoe is absolutely against the idea of Soviet mediation, [and] the *jushin* are divided on the issue. However, as a last resort, we can arrange for a hearing with the emperor. Until then, I will take full responsibility for what is happening within the court. I will leave it to historians of later generations to judge. I must ask you to take care of foreign and government affairs.[29]

At the close of the conversation, Shigemitsu, who had been impressed by Kido's firm determination, wholeheartedly agreed with Kido.

Shigemitsu concluded his personal memorandum of March 9 with an important observation about the emperor's position with regard to Japan's possible peace terms, if not surrender. He wrote, "His Majesty's wishes are increasingly crystallized. Now that my conjectures [regarding the emperor's point of view] are confirmed, the direction in which our nation must go has been all decided." The most important point, however, appears in the margin of Shigemitsu's memo: "His Majesty had already conveyed, through the lord keeper of the privy seal, his desire that the foreign minister should contemplate ways to conclude the war. The conditions [for surrender] should be primarily the preservation of imperial reign [*kōtō*] and then the avoidance of punishment for those who were responsible for the war as well as [the avoidance of] disarmament."[30] The picture that emerges from these sources is the possible existence of a tacit understanding, however vague, among the emperor, Kido, and Shigemitsu that when the time was ripe, the emperor would endorse the Japanese government's decision to end the war through a *seidan* if a few conditions were met: preservation of the imperial court, no trials to determine Japan's war responsibility, and no disarmament of Japanese forces by the Allies.

In another indication of the changes taking place in Japan, on March 16, Takagi—who was then studying specific steps that could be taken to end the war—recorded a noteworthy conversation he had with Matsudaira Yasumasa, aide and private secretary to Lord Privy Seal Kido. After discussing possible diplomatic channels that could be used for mediation (which included the Soviet Union, Sweden, and England), the two men exchanged ideas about a *seidan* scenario. Both agreed on a general outline that the next cabinet under a new prime minister would set the stage for the emperor to appear in public and formalize a policy to conclude the war. This public appearance would be at an imperial conference, to be attended by the heads of government agencies and the supreme command. In the meeting with Takagi, Matsudaira stated, "The emperor's public intervention should be a stately, dignified offer of peace." Matsudaira added that Kido alone would take responsibility. Apparently, Matsudaira was using this conversation with Takagi to convey Kido's *seidan* scenario to the peace faction in the navy.[31] Since this scenario presupposed the appointment of a new prime minister, the replacement of Prime Minister Koiso was simply a matter of time.

In the meantime, the emperor had a growing sense of urgency about the need to do something about the war that Japan was rapidly losing. On the night of March 10, following Matsudaira's conversation with Takagi, Tokyo witnessed the most devastating destruction that Japan experienced during the war. Three hundred and thirty-four US bombers carried out an incendiary bombing operation (developed under the command of Major General Curtis E. LeMay) and burned down almost sixteen square miles of Tokyo, destroying some 267,000 buildings. According to military historian Ronald H. Spector, "It was the most destructive single bombing raid in history," killing "more than 83,000 people" and injuring 41,000 in a single night.[32] Shocked by hourly reports of increasing civilian casualties, the emperor expressed a desire to see the damage with his own eyes. On March 18, Hirohito was able to inspect the ruins of Tokyo. He had not been outside the imperial palace since October 26, 1944. Looking at the ruins, the emperor commented to Grand Chamberlain Fujita, who had accompanied him, that the damage was more horrifying than the Great Tokyo Earthquake of 1923, because the the remains of the concrete buildings (i.e., not wooden buildings as in 1923) made the scene painful to view. The emperor remarked to Fujita, "Grand chamberlain, Tokyo has been reduced to ashes."[33]

Although Japan's prospects for victory were now close to nil, at the beginning of April 1945 the emperor had not yet been asked to intervene to change the course of the war. Nor had he received any information to change his mind about considering the anticipated Battle of Okinawa as Japan's last chance for a decisive battle that could facilitate negotiating an advantageous peace. However, the situation soon deteriorated, and on April 5, 1945, in the wake of the initial Japanese defeat on Okinawa, Prime Minister Koiso (who had lost the trust of his cabinet as well as the chiefs of staff) tendered his resignation. Koiso's ill-advised attempt to use a former Nationalist (Guomindang) official, known as Miao Ping, as an informal diplomatic channel to negotiate a truce with Chiang Kai-shek's regime in Chongqing had sealed his political fate.

Seventy-seven-year-old Admiral Suzuki Kantaro, who had served Emperor Hirohito as grand chamberlain from 1929 and 1936 and had survived gunshot wounds inflicted by military fanatics during the February 26 Incident, was called to the imperial palace to form a new cabinet. There was a consensus among five former prime ministers (Okada Keisuke, Yonai Mitsumasa, Hiranuma Kiichiro, Wakatsuki Reijiro, and Konoe Fumimaro) and Lord Privy Seal Kido to nominate Suzuki as the new prime minister. Historians disagree about the extent of Prime Minister Suzuki's determination to bring an end to the war, but various statements by court advisers indicate that there was a tacit understanding among the emperor, Kido, and Suzuki that Japan must terminate the war under the leadership of a Suzuki cabinet. It is safe to say that the *jushin* and the court envisioned the Suzuki cabinet as having the mission to end the war. According to Grand Chamberlain Fujita, who attended Suzuki's audience with the emperor, Hirohito urged the reluctant admiral to accept appointment as prime minister, using some extraordinary expressions: "You are my one and only hope" and "I beg you to accept it." The implication of accepting this appointment was quite obvious to the grand chamberlain. Although Prime Minister Suzuki never stated clearly the objectives of his cabinet, his selection of Togo Shigenori (the leading figure among end-the-war advocates) as the new foreign minister clearly indicated what was expected of the Suzuki cabinet. In fact, Togo wrote in his memoir that he had agreed to join the cabinet only after he and the prime minister had reached an understanding that the foreign minister's task was to negotiate a termination of the war. Togo also testified after the war that soon after he was appointed as foreign minister, during his audience with the emperor, the emperor informally conveyed to Togo his desire for an early termination of the war.[34]

In his 1946 recollections, the emperor attributed Japan's devastating defeat in Okinawa to poor coordination between the army and navy. He also noted that reports of kamikaze attacks had deeply distressed him and that this "unreasonable" tactic had increased his sense of urgency. It is important to note that Emperor Hirohito thought at that time that the Battle of Okinawa would be Japan's final decisive battle and that, should Japan lose the battle, acceptance of an "unconditional surrender" might be unavoidable.[35]

CHAPTER 6

The "Sacred Decision" to Surrender

GIVEN JAPAN'S DIRE MILITARY SITUATION IN 1945, CAN WE identify any single factor or combination of factors—such as the dropping of atomic bombs on Hiroshima and Nagasaki, the Soviet entry into the war against Japan, or the internal situation in Japan—that finally caused Japan to surrender? Can we also determine what role Emperor Hirohito played in the decision to surrender? Certainly, the double shock of the atomic bombs and the Soviet declaration of war significantly accelerated Japan's surrender.[1] However, these two external military pressures would not, by themselves, have accomplished the immediate orderly surrender of Japan. As Tsuyoshi Hasegawa suggests, "Japan's decision to surrender was above all a political decision, not a military one."[2] It is important to reexamine Japan's internal decision to surrender, especially with regard to the role Emperor Hirohito played in that decision.

Since the time of Tokyo Trial, many American analysts and historians have debated one question: if the emperor possessed the power to stop the war in August 1945, why did he permit the war to start in the first place?[3] A shift from the America-centered point of view to Emperor Hirohito's viewpoint requires reversing the question: if the emperor could not stop Japan from going to war in the first place, how and why was he able to play a critical role in ending the war through his *seidan* (sacred imperial decision)?

Over the years, scholars have offered various accounts of the ending of the war. Herbert Bix portrays Emperor Hirohito as an active commander in chief who refused to accept surrender for his own self-serving reasons until it was too late, but Bix's selective use of evidence makes his work unpersuasive.[4] Sadao Asada, Edward Drea, and Tsuyoshi Hasegawa offer other interpretations.[5] These scholars utilize newly available Japanese sources and partially modify the conclusion of Robert Butow, who argued in 1954 that the atomic bombing of Hiroshima and Nagasaki and the Soviet declaration of war created "that unusual atmosphere in which the theretofore static factor of the Emperor could be made active in such an extraordinary way as to work what was virtually a political miracle."[6] Butow illustrated that, in August 1945, the peace faction among the emperor's court advisers and members of the Suzuki cabinet accomplished this "political miracle" by setting the stage for the emperor's act of *seidan*. Although Asada, Hasegawa, and Drea partially incorporate this point of view, they all suggest that external factors for surrender were more important than Japan's internal reasons. Asada emphasizes the shock of the atomic bombs on the military's confidence; Hasegawa stresses the shock of the Soviet Union's war declaration on the Japanese military's thinking; and Drea recognizes the significance of both. However, none of these scholars have given enough credit to efforts by the peace faction within the imperial court or the Suzuki cabinet for their contributions to creating this political miracle. Neither have these scholarly examinations sufficiently explained how the peace faction and the emperor cooperated in setting the political stage for the miracle—nor why this stage setting eventually led to the emperor's act of *seidan*.

Hasegawa argues that in 1945 the peace faction lost three opportunities for peace prior to August—Germany's surrender in May; Japan's defeat in Okinawa in June; and finally, the Potsdam Proclamation of July 26—and he admits that the emperor's *seidan* was indeed a decisive factor in Japan's surrender.[7] However, ultimately Hasegawa concludes that it was the Soviet declaration of war that made *seidan* possible. In *The End of the Pacific War* Hasegawa summarizes the effect of the Soviet invasion: "In the tortuous discussions from August 9 through August 14, the peace party, motivated by a profound sense of betrayal, fear of Soviet influence on occupation policy, and above all by a desperate desire to preserve the imperial house, finally staged a conspiracy to impose the 'emperor's sacred decision' and accept the Potsdam terms, believing that under the circumstances surrendering to the United States would best assure the preservation of the imperial house and save the emperor."[8]

Although Hasegawa conveys the mounting pressure from the Soviet invasion that led to the emperor's *seidan*, in his assessment the efforts by the imperial court and the Suzuki cabinet to terminate the war are reduced to a last-minute desperate action—what Hasegawa calls "a conspiracy to impose the 'emperor's sacred decision.'" Hasegawa does describe the peace party's efforts to seek the Soviet mediation prior to the Potsdam Conference in his book *Racing the Enemy*, but he does not attach much emphasis to the period before the atomic bombs and Soviet invasion, which Butow describes as a time in which a decision to surrender was forming "in embryo" in Japan.

How significant were the peace faction's embryonic political efforts to end the war in the period before the double shock of the atomic bombs and Soviet declaration of war? How did the Suzuki cabinet and Emperor Hirohito's court advisers lay the groundwork for peace? And how did their internal political maneuvers set the stage for the emperor's *seidan*? Would their efforts have gathered enough momentum to stop the war without the atomic bombs or Soviet invasion? Evidence suggests that the efforts of the peace faction made the emperor's intervention possible and that the peace faction prevailed over the military faction by taking advantage of the throne's undefined power and, according to Lord Privy Seal Kido, by resorting to the unprecedented use of the emperor's *seidan* with some "recklessness [*mucha*]."[9]

By June 1945 the peace faction realized the bankruptcy of the military's strategy to win a decisive battle in the homeland in order to negotiate favorable peace terms. At this point the peace faction began to seek a political solution to end the war. With the emperor's tacit approval, Lord Privy Seal Kido and the peace faction within the Suzuki cabinet began to explore what kind of peacemaking process and what peace terms would be acceptable to their own military leaders. For the peace proponents, the internal matter of finding a workable political process to manage the military's resistance to surrender was as important as the external issue of obtaining acceptable peace terms from the United States and the other Allied Powers.

More specifically, what role did the emperor himself play in bringing about the *seidan*? According to Butow, the emperor was not the prime mover in this process: "Although the trend of the decision should be ascribed to the personal preference of the man himself, the real significance of the role of the Emperor lies in *the influence of the Throne* and not in the authority or personality of its occupant. Despite the wording of the Constitution, the Emperor had never possessed the actual power to decide on war or peace. Even under the pressing circumstances of August 1945, the Emperor was only the instrument, and not the prime mover, of Japan's momentous decision."[10] This interpretation, however, raises further questions, for even if the emperor was not the prime mover, he was not merely a robot-like instrument of other decision makers. Although the military leadership often ignored the emperor's personal opinions, his words could make a difference in extraordinary circumstances—for example, when the triangular power relations between the imperial court, the government, and the military allowed the emperor to impose the court's will over the other two, especially when the military needed the emperor's approval as commander in chief to execute its objectives. Thus, in order to understand the political miracle of the emperor's *seidan*, we need to reexamine how the dynamics of the power triangle shifted throughout the summer of 1945.

Although it may be possible to argue that the physically powerless peace faction used the *seidan* process as a tool to end the war, the emperor's personal opinion did make a difference in the implementation of the *seidan*. The key question here is when and how the peace faction transformed the emperor's personal opinion in favor of ending the war into a *seidan* and a state decision that in effect forced Japanese decision makers to end the war. When did the emperor realize that Japan's surrender was unavoidable and when did he start working for the termination of the war? What did the emperor think were realistic peace terms? How did he communicate his views to his government officials and military leaders? And how did the emperor's opinion influence these leaders?

It is important to repeat here that available reports to the throne from the Army and Naval General Staffs (*joso, naiso*), as well as the testimonies of both Emperor Hirohito and Lord Privy Seal Kido, show that the information the emperor received regarding the status of the military situation on every front and at home was extensive and detailed, if not completely accurate. The emperor as the head of the state and *daigensui* had to be well enough informed to function as a unifier and ratifier of Japan's national decisions on military and political affairs, however ceremonial his role may have been.[11] The summer of 1945 in Japan was an extraordinary time, when the emperor's voice carried an unusually heavy weight because the government and military were unable to reach a decision over a question that would determine the fate of the nation.

///

From late April to early May 1945, a series of discouraging reports reached the emperor in Tokyo: the Soviet Union's notice on April 5 not to renew the

Soviet-Japanese Neutrality Pact when it would expire one year later in April 1946, Germany's surrender on May 7 (May 8 in Japan's time zone), Adolf Hitler's death, and the Soviet occupation of Berlin. The diary of Rear Admiral Takagi Sokichi, who was secretly ordered by Navy Minister Yonai Mitsumasa to study how to end the war, offers valuable information about this period. When former prime minister Konoe met Kido on May 5 and asked a pointed question about the emperor's attitude toward terminating the war, Kido told Konoe that the emperor had recently become more outspoken about taking steps to end the war, explaining,

> Until very recently, [the emperor] refused to concede the complete disarmament of Japanese forces and [rejected] the punishment of the leaders responsible for war [as part of peace terms] under any circumstance; and he insisted on fighting to the bitter end rather than accepting these terms. He [the emperor] was of the opinion that Japan's disarmament would allow a Soviet invasion. Therefore, it took me a long time to soften His Majesty's opinions, but recently (a few days before May 5), he changed his mind.
>
> [The emperor] now feels that the acceptance of these two terms [disarmament and the punishment of war leaders by the Allies] may be unavoidable. Not only that, on the contrary, he is now even thinking that [once we decide to end the war] the sooner we act, the better.
>
> We have to wait for an opportune moment, but I think that the time for us to ask for the emperor's decision [to end the war] will come in the near future.[12]

This passage confirms, as Emperor Hirohito stated in his 1946 "Monologue," that after Japan's defeat in Okinawa, sometime between late April and early May, the emperor sensed that one way or the other, it was unavoidable that Japan had to accept unconditional surrender. By early May the emperor was prepared, however reluctantly and vaguely, to consider accepting terms of surrender that he had previously opposed, including disarmament and punishment of Japan's war leaders by the Allies, as long as Japan could preserve its sovereignty.

Shigemitsu Mamoru's private note of March 9, 1945, also supports the conclusion that the emperor was changing his mind during this period. Specifically, Shigemitsu addresses the question of the *kokutai* (national polity) and states that Emperor Hirohito was prepared to narrow the preservation of the *kokutai* to the protection of imperial reign (*koto*) alone, while the army leadership insisted on protecting the *kokutai* in the broadest possible sense for the purpose of self-preservation.[13]

The emperor's 1946 "Monologue" and his advisers' testimonies clearly mark June 1945 as when the emperor explicitly expressed to the highest levels of Japanese leadership his personal desire for peace. Although the imperial conference of June 8 formally reaffirmed the decision to fight to the bitter end, both the emperor and Kido were well aware of the confusing atmosphere surrounding this bellicose resolution: that is, since mid-May, the Supreme War Leadership Council (the Big Six) had been secretly discussing the idea of approaching the Soviet Union to act as a mediator with the Allied Powers.[14] At this juncture, two alarming reports about the lack of Japanese military preparedness reached the emperor, prompting him to speak up in favor of seeking peace. First, on June 9, the day after the imperial conference's resolution to continue the war, the emperor received discouraging reports from General Umezu Yoshijiro, chief of Army General Staff, regarding Japanese forces in China. The general confessed that he had no confidence in defending China from a possible American invasion. The emperor noted that for the first time General Umezu looked defeated and appeared to have lost his nerve. Three days later, on June 12, the emperor received another shocking report from Admiral Hasegawa Kiyoshi about the terrible condition of Japan's material strength—a shortage of raw materials, the poor condition of its military industry, and an inadequate defense capability at home.[15] Foreign Minister Togo wrote in his memoir that when he had an audience with the emperor on June 20, the emperor talked about the inadequate military preparations in Japan as well as China. The emperor expressed his personal desire that the foreign minister take steps to bring an end to the war as quickly as possible.[16]

KIDO'S GROUNDWORK FOR
THE EMPEROR'S *SEIDAN*

Around this time, the emperor quietly allowed Lord Privy Seal Kido to initiate the groundwork for bringing an end to the war. Kido noted that it was unusual and even unconstitutional for a lord keeper of the privy seal to initiate a policy. Kido knew that his job was to serve as catalyst or liaison between the emperor and the cabinet, and he realized that he was about to step outside the traditional boundaries of power granted to the lord privy seal. However, even though Kido's postwar accounts may have exaggerated his role in ending the war, his actions during the summer of 1945 show that he believed that the emperor had personally sanctioned his exploration of possible peace negotiations. It is important to note here that the legitimacy of Kido's work to end the war was based on an imperial mandate, however personal and informal this mandate may have been, and Kido shrewdly used this unofficial imperial mandate to influence cabinet members and military leaders. Here we see manifest the peace strategy of Kido (and of the court's peace faction) to exploit the emperor's personal wish to end the war by putting this personal wish forward as if it were a formal expression of imperial will, namely *seii* or *seidan*, the will of the state sanctioned by the emperor upon approval of the cabinet and supreme command.

Kido's approach evolved from the suggestions of seven Tokyo University professors, including Takagi Yasaka and Nanbara Shigeru. Sometime between February and March 1945, Kido and members of the peace faction (such as Konoe Fumimaro and Takagi Sokichi) started to circulate the advice of these professors, and some of the scholars' writings reached the emperor. When Konoe had an audience with the emperor on February 14, Konoe recommended that Hirohito control the army diehards through a *seidan*.[17] The peace faction's written pleas to the emperor that Japan conclude the war through his *seidan* continued to reach Hirohito throughout the summer.[18] The military considered the authority to declare a cease-fire as belonging to the supreme command, not the cabinet; and since the army was still dominated by diehards determined to fight to the bitter end, the peace faction's only hope was to seek the emperor's intervention through a *seidan*.

During the Kido-Konoe meeting of May 5, Kido explained his strategy for termination of the war. Kido believed that the most effective way, in the end, would be for Navy Minister Yonai to approach the army leadership and ask for its consent. However, Kido thought that at that point neither the army command nor War Minister Anami Korechika were ready to take this step. Kido was afraid that hasty action might cause open disagreements within the Suzuki cabinet and lead to its collapse. Both Kido and Konoe realized that close cooperation between Navy Minister Yonai and Kido would be crucial to carry out Kido's plan. Kido also promised to work with the *jushin* (senior statesmen). Konoe was favorably impressed by Kido's unusually firm determination to carry out what might be called a conspiracy for peace.[19]

Kido's first task was to reverse the June 8 imperial conference resolution reconfirming that the war would be fought to the bitter end; next, he had to quietly build a consensus among government and military leaders to move them toward accepting the imperial decision to terminate the war. On June

8, almost immediately after the imperial conference concluded, Kido drafted "A Working Plan to Terminate the War." His speed demonstrates Kido's eagerness to assume the role of unofficial imperial agent in carrying out a "peace plot." Kido had firm grounds for believing that he was carrying out Hirohito's will, for immediately after the imperial conference, the emperor took the unprecedented action of showing Kido the complete transcript of the imperial conference. Kido believed that the emperor did this because Hirohito was deeply troubled by the conference's resolution to continue the war. Therefore, Kido quickly drafted the "Working Plan" that same day and submitted it to the emperor the following day. The emperor read the plan, readily approved of it without asking any questions, and simply told Kido to try it out. Kido did so.

Kido's plan contained two key strategies that he pursued over the next few months: (1) the government would seek the emperor's decision and move toward termination of the war; and (2) the emperor's letter requesting peace mediation would be sent, most likely to the Soviet Union.[20] By June 18, Kido secured the willingness of Prime Minister Suzuki, Navy Minister Yonai, and Foreign Minister Togo to pursue actions to terminate the war, along the lines laid out in the "Working Plan." Although Kido hesitated to approach War Minister Anami for a while, on June 18 he did tell the war minister that the emperor desired termination of the war and approved Kido's plan. At that time Kido believed that he had obtained the war minister's reluctant concurrence.[21] Kido's ability to communicate with General Anami was crucial to this process, because the war minister was the key to keeping the army's hard-liners in check.

What Kido did not realize was the strong impression War Minister Anami received from Kido's revelation that the emperor favored termination of the war. On June 18, marking "secret history" in the margin of his diary, General Anami wrote, "From Lord Privy Seal Kido, [I] heard [His Majesty's] personal wishes."[22] Four days later, at the imperial conference of the Big Six, Anami would hear directly from the emperor himself that he favored immediate action in seeking peace mediation.

Understanding that Kido, Prime Minister Suzuki, and Foreign Minister Togo wanted to seek peace, the emperor took an unusual step: he convened another imperial conference of the Big Six on June 22.[23] At this conference, Emperor Hirohito personally opened the discussion and asked the council members to search for ways to terminate the war without being bound by the previous resolution of June 8, which had reaffirmed the continuation of the war. Then, the emperor asked for opinions of the cabinet and supreme command. After he made it clear to attendees that he favored immediate action in seeking peace mediation, the rest of the meeting lasted only thirty-five minutes. And these thirty-five minutes produced a major new decision: "the overtures toward Moscow would be carried forward with a view to obtaining a negotiated peace."[24] In his 1946 "Monologue," the emperor commented, "I was relieved that [the government] was now resolved to start peace negotiations, although everyone had a different opinion regarding [acceptable] peace terms."[25] This suggests that in the emperor's mind, an embryonic decision to surrender was taking shape. On July 7 Hirohito pressed Prime Minister Suzuki to more aggressively pursue the possibility of a Soviet mediation, proposing to send a special envoy to Moscow. On July 12, acting on the prime minister's suggestion, the emperor personally asked Konoe Fumimaro to go to Moscow.[26] However, the plan to send Konoe as a special envoy did not materialize because the Soviets were unwilling to engage in negotiations before the Potsdam Conference. As history shows, Joseph Stalin had no intention of serving as mediator on behalf of Japan, for he had already promised at the Yalta Conference in February 1945 to enter the war against Japan "two or three months" after Germany's surrender.[27] By refusing to engage in negotiations with Japan, Stalin was trying to prolong the war so that Soviet forces could enter the war and take over Mongolia and Manchuria.[28]

Moreover, the steps the Japanese government took to seek mediation via the Soviet Union were ineffective. Japan's official request did not outline specific peace terms. It merely stated that the emperor wished to restore peace and send Prince Konoe to Moscow as a special envoy. The Japanese leadership was deeply divided, and at that point the peace faction and the war faction were not even ready among themselves to engage in any discussion of specific peace terms. Konoe was expected to go to Moscow without any concrete peace proposals to find out what would be acceptable to all parties—including the Russians as well as the Japanese hard-liners. Once he obtained Stalin's consent to the terms of mediation, Konoe had intended to first seek Emperor Hirohito's sanction and then make it Japan's formal decision in order to overcome the military's oppositions.[29]

As mentioned earlier, by early May the emperor had started to consider the possibility of accepting unconditional surrender, so long as Japan could preserve its *kokutai*. He did not publicly clarify what constituted the *kokutai*. That is, did it only include the preservation of the imperial house? Or did it also include protection of the entire imperial system of Japan? However, as seen in his conversation of March 9, 1945, with Foreign Minister Shigemitsu, when the emperor discussed the preservation of the *kokutai*, the emperor was thinking about the preservation of *koto* (imperial reign), some form of constitutional monarchy. As we will see later, on the verge of Japan's surrender Hirohito was clearly willing to let the Japanese people decide what form of political system they wished to have. However, the emperor would not agree to accept the abolition of the imperial house.

That same summer, leaders of the Allied Powers met in Potsdam and sent Japan an ultimatum on July 26, 1945. The Potsdam Proclamation was issued jointly by three Allied leaders: US president Harry S. Truman, British prime minister Clement Attlee, and president of the national government of the Republic of China, Chiang Kai-shek; the head of the Soviet Union, Joseph Stalin, was not included by name in the ultimatum. Declaring that the Allies were ready to strike a final blow and eliminate Japan's "irresponsible militarism," the Potsdam Proclamation demanded "the unconditional surrender of all Japanese armed forces" and warned, "The alternative for Japan is prompt and utter destruction." The ultimatum did not mention what would happen to Emperor Hirohito and the Japanese imperial system.[30]

Although the Truman administration later explained that the United States dropped the atomic bomb because the Japanese government had rejected the Potsdam Proclamation, it is important to point out that, from Tokyo's perspective, Japan had never *officially* rejected the Allied ultimatum. The Suzuki cabinet had simply ignored it and failed to send its official reply to the United States: the Japanese word *mokusatsu*, used by the Japanese press, literally meant "to kill it with silence." According to Kido's recollection, neither the emperor nor Kido had any serious problems with accepting the Potsdam Proclamation when they saw the text. Kido believed that the emperor shared Kido's impression that the proclamation was more generous than they had originally expected. The Suzuki cabinet's chief secretary, Sakomizu Hisatsune, explained later in his memoir that the Suzuki cabinet believed the proclamation provided Japan with an opportunity for a "negotiated peace," not a "surrendered peace," because cabinet members thought that, although the proclamation demanded "the unconditional surrender of all Japanese forces," it did not demand the unconditional surrender of the sovereign state or the *kokutai*. In the end, the reasons for Japan's failure to respond the Potsdam Proclamation were twofold: first, because Stalin had not signed the Allied ultimatum, Foreign Minister Togo wanted to ascertain the Soviet response to Tokyo's request for mediation before Japan replied; and second, the overwhelming majority of Japanese military officers, especially in the army, were still in favor of fighting to the bitter end, and the Suzuki cabinet was unable to prevail over their resistance.[31]

Therefore, in the opinion of Emperor Hirohito, Kido, and the peace faction, there was no doubt that the combination of two catastrophic events—the atomic bombs dropped over Hiroshima on August 6 and Nagasaki on August 9; and the Soviet declaration of war against Japan on August 9—provided the final impetus for Japan's decision to end the war. The Potsdam Proclamation had already given the Japanese government an outline of surrender terms almost acceptable to Japan. Kido and the Suzuki cabinet needed to find some way to use the momentum of these extraordinary events to set the stage for an imperial *seidan* to end the war. In a sense, this was an abuse of the system defined under the Meiji Constitution. Theoretically, the Japanese emperor was an all-powerful sovereign. But in reality, when the government and the supreme command were united in favor of a national policy (as in the decision to attack Pearl Harbor), the emperor more closely resembled Max Weber's absolute monarch who was "impotent in face of the superior specialized knowledge of the bureaucracy."[32] For a few critical days at the end of the Pacific War, however, Japan's government and military leadership lacked consensus. This gave a unique opportunity to those within the bureaucracy and court who sought peace to request that the emperor dictate his opinion as a state decision in order to overcome resistance of the war faction. In other words, Hirohito's most trusted men found a way to transform the emperor's personal opinion into a state decision through the discreet but unprecedented manipulation of an existing system that usually made decisions collectively. The most important point was that the *seidan* had to be issued by the emperor in his role as *daigensui* (commander in chief) so that the military would have no choice but to obey the order. The question was when and how to ask the emperor to act.

FIRST *SEIDAN*

The shock caused by the atomic bombs over Hiroshima and Nagasaki was a major factor that allowed the peace faction to overcome the military's resistance to terminating the war. There are certain elements of truth in Masumi Junnosuke's argument that the Pacific War started with the so-called Hull Note as a godsend for Japanese leaders who advocated war and ended with the atomic bombs as another godsend for those who wanted to restore peace.[33] With regard to the question of which had more effect on Japan's surrender decision, the atomic bombs or Soviet entry into the war, Kido's postwar statements were fairly consistent. When the investigative team from the US Strategic Bombing Survey asked Kido this very question on November 10, 1945, Kido answered that it was hard to tell exactly which had more impact.[34] During his interview with Japanese historian Oi Atsushi at Sugamo Prison in April 1950, Kido stated,

> On the eve of the atomic attacks, the peace faction's influence was becoming strong enough to constitute a counterweight against the war faction; and the atomic bombs drastically reduced the sway of the war faction, and the peace faction gained momentum. In addition, the Soviet declaration of war further reduced the dominance of the war faction and gave the peace faction the upper hand. Therefore, I think that the atomic bombs alone could have allowed us to terminate the war. However, the Soviet Union's entry into the war certainly made it easier [for us]. It is difficult to tell which event contributed more to the termination of the war: the atomic bombs or the Soviet Union's declaration of war.[35]

On the other hand, Tsuyoshi Hasegawa argues in his book *Racing the Enemy* that the atomic bombs did not scare the military enough to shake their resolve to fight but that the Soviet declaration of war caught the army completely by surprise. Hasegawa cites the diary of Kawabe Torashiro, vice chief of the Army General Staff as evidence. Kawabe wrote only that he had received "a serious jolt [*shigeki*]" from news of the atomic bombing of Hiroshima. But after the Soviet declaration of war Kawabe wrote, "The Soviets have finally risen! My judgment has proven wrong." Hasegawa suggests that the exclamation mark conveys Kawabe's "shock [*shogeki*]" and, therefore, that the Soviet declaration of war was more shocking and devastating to Kawabe than the atomic attacks.[36] However, Kawabe's own postwar memoir offers another explanation: that these two events could be seen as inseparable, as a one-two knockout punch. Kawabe wrote in his memoir, "I felt the atomic bomb struck me hard on one cheek, and immediately afterwards the Soviet declaration of war hit me with full force on the other cheek."[37] Perhaps, historians will never be able to agree on the exact weight to assign to these two extraordinary events. The recollections of Japanese eyewitnesses suggest that the bombings and Soviet declaration of war happened so close together that it was humanly impossible to separate their psychological impacts.

Final arrangements for the emperor's *seidan* were set early on the morning of August 9, sometime between 5:00 and 10:30 AM when the prime minister convened a meeting of the Supreme War Council. Cabinet Chief Secretary Sakomizu went to Prime Minister Suzuki's private residence at around 5:00 AM with news of the Soviet declaration of war against Japan. Foreign Minister Togo also went to see the prime minister. According to Sakomizu, Suzuki said, "What we feared finally came about"; and Suzuki immediately went to the palace to see the emperor.[38] The prime minister soon returned to his official residence and told Sakomizu that he had spoken to the emperor and carefully listened to the emperor's wishes. According to the prime minister, he and the emperor had both agreed that Japan should end the war by accepting the Potsdam Proclamation. Although Kido's diary does not mention Suzuki's audience with the emperor that morning, it is highly unlikely, as journalist Hando Kazutoshi points out, that the prime minister would not speak to the emperor upon receiving the alarming news of the Soviet invasion. It is likely that the prime minister saw the emperor and that the two had reached some sort of understanding, before Kido arrived for his own audience with the emperor at 9:55 AM—a meeting in which Kido first learned about the Soviet entry into the war. Hirohito asked Kido to "consult thoroughly" with the prime minister. Kido happened to have a prearranged meeting with Suzuki that morning, and when the two men met at 10:10 AM Kido conveyed the emperor's desire to terminate the war swiftly by accepting the Potsdam Proclamation.[39]

According to Chamberlain Tokugawa Yoshihiro, who waited upon the emperor and recorded the actions on August 9, the emperor woke up at 7:30 AM and went to the basement shelter at 8:20 AM because of an air-raid warning. According to the chamberlain, the emperor had an audience with General Umezu at 9:37 AM. Therefore, it is possible that Prime Minister Suzuki informally spoke to the emperor in the basement shelter before Umezu arrived.[40]

The Supreme War Leadership Council was convened at 10:30 AM on August 9. Nobody spoke against accepting the Potsdam Proclamation, but participants reached an impasse over what conditions should be attached to Japan's surrender. Foreign Minister Togo and Navy Minister Yonai supported accepting the Potsdam Proclamation with only one condition: preservation of the imperial house and the *kokutai*. However, War Minister Anami and the chiefs of the Army and Naval General Staffs, General Umezu and Admiral Toyoda Soemu, argued for three additional conditions: no occupation of Japan's home islands by the Allies, voluntary self-disarmament of the Japanese forces, and war crimes trials run by a Japanese authority. News of the second atomic bomb dropped on Nagasaki arrived around 11:30 A M, but the council meeting adjourned without reaching any clear decision regarding surrender. The Suzuki cabinet met at 2:00 PM and continued discussions. Although the majority of the cabinet expressed support for the one-condition proposal (supported by Togo and Yonai), this group, too, failed to reach a firm resolution. Six cabinet members supported Togo's one-condition proposal, three supported the four-condition proposal, and five remained undecided (although they generally favored reducing the number of conditions).[41]

During a midnight imperial conference on August 9–10, the prime minister planned to ask the emperor to choose between the two ideas, and he expected that Hirohito would support the one-condition proposal. Although historians, citing different sources, do not agree about when the emperor finally made up his mind to support the one-condition proposal, I consider Foreign Minister Togo's account a reliable record of the events.[42] According to the foreign minister, by the end of August 8, before the Soviet declaration of war on Japan, the emperor, prime minister, and foreign minister had a tacit understanding that they would accept the Potsdam ultimatum with the least conditions. As described earlier, by early May the emperor had already given up his objection to disarmament and punishment of Japanese war leaders by the enemy. According to Togo's memoir, during the morning of August 8, Togo met with the emperor and reported that an atomic bomb had been used against Hiroshima. Togo proposed, "This should be used as an opportunity to decide for the earliest possible termination of the war." The emperor agreed with the foreign minister and said, "Now that this sort of weapon has been used, it is becoming increasingly impossible to continue the war. I do not think it is a good idea to miss an opportunity to end the war by attempting to secure advantageous conditions. Besides, even if we try to discuss terms, I am afraid we won't be able to come to an agreement. Therefore, I hope you will take measures that will conclude the war as soon as possible."[43]

Thus, emphasizing the need to end the war at the earliest possible opportunity, the emperor asked Foreign Minister Togo to convey his opinion to Prime Minister Suzuki. Togo immediately contacted Kido and the prime minister and requested that they convene a meeting of the Supreme War Leadership Council. Togo also testified later that the prime minister responded to the emperor's request: Suzuki "hastily started preparing for a Big Six meeting, but it failed to be convened on August 8. What finally brought it about was the Soviet entry into the war."[44] Therefore, Suzuki should have known before August 9 that the emperor was supporting immediate acceptance of the Potsdam Proclamation with the least conditions attached. The memoir of Grand Chamberlain Fujita, who attended Togo's audience with the emperor, offers an almost identical account of Togo's exchange with the emperor.[45]

Kido's diary entry of August 9 recorded that Prime Minister Suzuki told him that the Big Six meeting in the morning had decided to attach four conditions to acceptance of the Potsdam Proclamation, and Kido reported his own understanding of the meeting to the emperor. Kido was probably led to believe, incorrectly, that the Supreme War Leadership Council had already made a decision in favor of the four conditions, partly because of the ambiguous and alarming way the prime minister explained what happened at the meeting of the Big Six. Kido's misunderstanding was most likely also caused by the alarming reports Kido had received from several people that same day. Prince Konoe, former foreign minister Shigemitsu Mamoru, and Prince Takamatsu, upon learning that War Minister Anami and the chiefs of Army and Naval General Staffs were insisting on four conditions for surrender, all contacted Kido and urged him to request the emperor's intervention in favor of the sole condition for surrender. In any event, Kido spoke to the emperor from 4:35 to 5:10 PM and confirmed that Hirohito fully understood the situation and agreed to express his personal preference at the imperial conference to be held that night. Suzuki and Togo had an audience with the emperor at about 11:00 PM. We can assume that it was during this meeting that participants made final preparations for the emperor's issuance of a *seidan* that accepted the Potsdam Proclamation with one condition.[46]

The imperial conference began at 11:50 PM on August 9 and lasted until 2:20 AM the following day. In the presence of Emperor Hirohito and the president of the Privy Council, Hiranuma Kiichiro, who attended the meeting at the emperor's request, the Big Six repeated the same debate over whether Japan should accept the Potsdam Proclamation with one condition or four. First, Foreign Minister Togo presented the case for one condition—the preservation of the imperial institution—a position that Navy Minister Yonai supported. War Minister Anami defended the four conditions—the position supported by the chiefs of the Army and Naval General Staffs. President of the Privy Council Hiranuma played an important role for the peace party. He expressed support for Togo's one-condition idea, but he proposed that the wording for that condition be changed from the preservation of "His Majesty's legal status established by the [Meiji] Constitution [*tenno no kokuho-jo no chii]*" to the preservation of "the prerogatives of His Majesty as a sovereign ruler." This would clearly guarantee the emperor's position as sovereign ruler but would narrow the definition of the preservation of the *kokutai* to mean the preservation of the imperial court's prerogatives.[47]

After two hours of debate, however, attendees in the imperial conference were again deadlocked: three in favor of the foreign minister's one-condition proposal and the other three in favor of attaching four conditions. Prime Minister Suzuki, who had not yet announced which side he favored, instead of stating his position resorted to an unprecedented measure to solve the impasse. He stood up, walked in front of the emperor, and asked for the emperor's opinion. Hirohito leaned forward and spoke:

> I agree with the foreign minister's proposal. Let me explain my reasons. There have always been discrepancies between plans made by the high command and their executions. Although we are about to engage in a decisive battle on the main island, we are far behind the schedule in fortifying Kujukuri-hama, where American forces are expected to land, and according to the report of the war minister the fortifications won't be completed until the end of August. I hear that equipment for the increased divisions in the inland is insufficient. How can you fight back American forces in such a state? [The number of] air raids is escalating every day. I do not wish my people to fall into deeper distress or destroy our culture, nor do I wish to bring misery to mankind.
>
> The time has come when we must bear the unbearable. It is truly unbearable for me to see my loyal armed forces disarmed and see those who rendered me devoted service punished as war criminals. However, it cannot be helped for the sake of the nation. Now is the time to bear in mind the feelings of the Emperor Meiji at the time of the Triple Intervention. For these reasons, I support the foreign minister's proposal.[48]

The emperor's words had a strong emotional impact on everyone present, but at this point, Hirohito's statement was "little more than an expression of the Emperor's personal desire."[49] To transform the emperor's personal opinion into a decision of state, Prime Minister Suzuki and his cabinet had to accept it as the cabinet's decision. Members of the Suzuki cabinet met at 3:00 AM, and within an hour they unanimously endorsed the emperor's decision.

At dawn on August 10, through the Swiss government, the Japanese Foreign Ministry sent US secretary of state James F. Byrnes Japan's decision to accept the Potsdam Proclamation with the assumption that the emperor's status would not be altered. Tokyo's diplomatic note stated that the Japanese government was ready to accept the terms enumerated in the Potsdam Proclamation "with the understanding that the said declaration does not comprise any demand which prejudices the prerogatives of His Majesty as a Sovereign Ruler." The note asked for a prompt response from the United States, saying, "The Japanese Government sincerely hope that this understanding is warranted and desire keenly that an explicit indication to that effect will be speedily forthcoming."[50]

SECOND *SEIDAN*

However, the wording of Secretary of State Byrnes's response to this diplomatic note forced the Suzuki cabinet to repeat the process, and Emperor Hirohito had to issue a second *seidan* in order to accept the United States' surrender terms. The crux of the issue was whether Japan would be able to maintain the emperor "as a sovereign ruler," with all his prerogatives, if Japan accepted the US offer. The US reply said, "From the moment of surrender the authority of the Emperor and the Japanese Government to rule the state shall be *subject to* the Supreme Commander of the Allied powers who will take such steps as he deems proper to effectuate the surrender terms." It also said, "The ultimate form of government of Japan shall, in accordance with the Potsdam Declaration, be established *by the freely expressed will of the Japanese people*."[51]

Between August 10 and 12, as the contents of the Byrnes Note were unofficially disseminated in Japan through Allied news media, chaotic and frantic discussions ensued in Tokyo. (The Foreign Ministry intercepted unofficial radio announcements of the US response early on the morning of August 12 and received the official US reply at 6:40 PM on the same day but did not release the contents of the reply to the cabinet and supreme command until the following morning.) Foreign Minister Togo and Vice Foreign Minister Matsumoto Shunichi, although initially disappointed and not certain of US intentions regarding the future status of the imperial house, worked resolutely to encourage acceptance of the Byrnes Note. Prime Minister Suzuki was unsure if he could protect the imperial house if the Byrnes Note was accepted, and he appeared to be vacillating. However, according to Sakomizu, Suzuki's first priority was to terminate the war at all costs. Suzuki was eventually persuaded by Togo, Kido, and Sakomizu that accepting the Byrnes Note was the only way to end the war. Thus, with Suzuki's approval, Sakomizu (who had been drafting an imperial rescript for Emperor Hirohito to announce Japan's acceptance of the surrender terms) worked diligently toward the acceptance of the Byrnes Note.[52] Navy Minister Yonai was "not pessimistic" about the US position regarding the imperial house, and he expressed to Rear Admiral Takagi his determination to make the navy go along with the decisions of the peace faction.[53]

At the same time, the president of the Privy Council, Hiranuma, who had sided with the peace party at the August 9 imperial conference, refused to accept the Byrnes Note on the grounds that it proposed to make the emperor subordinate to the authority of the Supreme Commander of the Allied Powers. Hiranuma asked Prime Minister Suzuki to negotiate further with the United States.[54] Many in the War Ministry and the supreme command, especially army officers, were not convinced that the US response guaranteed the preservation of Japan's *kokutai*; these doubters insisted that Japan should continue to fight until receiving clarification regarding the preservation of the emperor's prerogatives as sovereign ruler. War Minister Anami and the chiefs of the Army and Naval General Staffs, General Umezu and Admiral Toyoda, were under pressure from subordinates who were determined to fight to the bitter end. On August 12, Umezu and Toyoda resorted to a direct appeal to the emperor, asking Hirohito to reject the Byrnes Note.[55] Behind the scenes, Navy Minister Yonai was trying hard to mitigate objections from military hard-liners. Yonai protested the delaying tactics of the chiefs of the General Staffs. He also reprimanded Vice Admiral Onishi Takijiro, vice chief of the Naval General Staff, who had expressed sympathy for the army hard-liners and who was encouraging War Minister Anami to stand firm against the US proposal.[56]

But what was the emperor's personal position on the Byrnes Note, and what role did he play in its acceptance? Emperor Hirohito's recorded words and actions show that, during this period, he maintained an unwavering conviction that the war must end immediately. The emperor himself was prepared to accept the Byrnes Note as soon as it was received and was ready to surrender immediately. His firm attitude *did* make a difference in the peace party's efforts to convene the second and final imperial conference on August 14. Even before the arrival of the Byrnes Note, the emperor was preparing himself for what he believed was inevitable: Japan's surrender. While the Foreign Ministry anxiously awaited the US response, Hirohito called for a series of meetings, with Lord Privy Seal Kido's encouragement; the emperor had always been conscientious about following proper procedures and was especially so as he moved to ratify a grave national decision of such magnitude. Between August 10 and 12, Emperor Hirohito made sure that he met with all his distinguished senior advisers and had the opportunity to listen to their opinions. This group included Makino Nobuaki, seven *jushin* (past prime ministers), and all senior members of the imperial house.

On August 11, through Kido, the emperor conveyed to Imperial Household Minister Ishiwata Sotaro his willingness to broadcast an imperial rescript over the radio, presumably to declare Japan's surrender.[57] According to Ishiwata's memoir, on August 12 the emperor also asked the imperial household minister if he could pay a final visit to his mother, the empress dowager. The emperor told Ishwata, "My mother [*haha-miya*] will move to Karuizawa for safety soon, but it seems that she is not coming to the palace. I am not sure what is going to happen to me. Before she leaves, I really wish to see her and bid farewell one last time."[58] In the event of Japan's surrender, the emperor was apparently preparing himself for a worst-case scenario in which he might be arrested by the Allied Powers, even tried and executed as a war criminal.

Once Foreign Minister Togo and his staff came to a consensus that Japan should accept the Byrnes Note and surrender, Togo went to the palace on the morning of August 12, reported to the emperor the contents of the Byrnes Note as he understood it, and recommended its acceptance. Togo mentioned possible concerns about obstacles created by the *kokutai* advocates' objection to the US proposal that "the ultimate form of government of Japan . . . be established by the freely expressed will of the Japanese people." But Togo explained that the Foreign Ministry did not anticipate any danger to the preservation of the imperial house in accepting the Byrnes Note. At this time, the emperor told Togo, "I think the [US] reply is all right. You had better proceed to accept the note as it is."[59] The meeting with Togo strengthened the emperor's conviction that ending the war immediately by accepting the US proposal was the only way to save his country and maintain the existence of the imperial house. In turn, the emperor's support for the Byrnes Note clearly encouraged Togo to continue his uphill battle with the diehards in the military. In an unfinished draft of a postscript Togo intended to add to the memoir he wrote in Sugamo Prison, the foreign minister wrote, "It is not too much to say that His Majesty was the only one I could trust from the beginning to the end. Although there were vacillating opinions within both the cabinet and imperial court, His Majesty alone had a clear constant sense.

Throughout my life, I have never encountered such a noble character: a rarity even in history." Togo also wrote, "His Majesty alone had a pure heart. I felt that he was constantly thinking of his responsibility to his ancestors and the well-being of his people."[60] Foreign Minister Togo considered Emperor Hirohito his strongest ally in his efforts to end the war.

On the same day, August 12, the three Japanese military leaders of the Supreme War Leadership Council who had previously opposed accepting the Potsdam peace terms also came to see the emperor to express their opposition. Hirohito did not want to hear objections from two of these dissenters (the chiefs of the Army and Naval General Staffs) and calmly told them to hold their dissent until Japan received an official reply from the US government. The emperor's response to the third man, War Minister Anami, was slightly different because of the emperor's closer acquaintance with General Anami. (Anami had served as the emperor's military aide-de-camp from 1929 to 1930, and he occasionally had an audience with the emperor in the ensuing years.) Although Hirohito did not agree with the general, he recognized that Anami's objection to the US proposal stemmed from a sincere concern about the future of the imperial house. As a demonstration of his understanding, Hirohito called the war minister by his name, instead of using Anami's title as he normally did in such audiences, and said, "Anami, don't worry. I have confidence in my position." Anami believed that the emperor was trying to console him with comforting words.[61] Later that night, Anami also appealed to Prince Mikasa, the emperor's youngest brother, to intervene; but the prince reprimanded the general, saying, "The army has never acted in compliance with His Majesty's wishes ever since the Manchurian Incident. It is unconscionable to continue the war at this stage." Hearing these words was difficult for General Anami.[62]

In addition to these audiences, Hirohito also called a meeting of all senior members of the imperial house. Thirteen members met with the emperor from 3:00 to 5:20 PM on August 12, in the palace's basement shelter. In this meeting Hirohito explained several reasons for his decision to accept the provisions of the Potsdam Proclamation (and consequently the Byrnes Note), and he asked for the imperial court's united support for his decision. He emphasized that Japan's national resources had been exhausted by the prolonged war; that recently Japan had suffered defeat after defeat; and that there was no prospect for winning a decisive battle on the home island. The eldest member of the imperial house, Prince Nashimoto, spoke for the entire court, pledging unanimous support for the emperor's decision. However, the background for the court support of Hirohito's decision was more complicated than Nashimoto's statement suggests. On the one hand, some members of the imperial house, who had met with Foreign Minister Togo at the residence of Prince Takamatsu the day before, were aware of the implications of accepting the surrender provisions of the Byrnes Note. The emperor knew he could count on these members of the court's peace faction (including two of his younger brothers, Prince Takamatsu and Prince Mikasa, and his uncle, Prince Higashikuni).[63]

On the other hand, some other senior members of the imperial house originally had been more sympathetic to the army hard-liners. One such member, Prince Asaka, who, although in favor of seeking peace, asked the emperor whether Japan should continue to fight if the *kokutai* would be abolished. The emperor answered affirmatively.[64] In this exchange, it became clear that the only terms that Emperor Hirohito would refuse to accept would be the enemy's demand to abolish the imperial house. Thus, the emperor's definition of the *kokutai* by that time was narrowly limited to *koto* (imperial reign). In other words, although Hirohito was determined to protect the imperial house, he did not intend to defend the entire system of the *kokutai* as the ultranationalists and the military advocated.[65]

By the end of August 12, the key figures of the peace party—Foreign Minister Togo, Lord Privy Seal Kido, and Prime Minister Suzuki—had reached a solid consensus that Japan should accept the Byrnes Note and surrender. These men all knew that they had the firm support of the emperor and the court.

The Big Six met at 8:30 A M on August 13 and debated whether or not to accept the Byrnes Note, but again the group reached an impasse, and they adjourned at 3:00 P M. Suzuki, Togo, and Navy Minister Yonai supported accepting the Byrnes Note; War Minister Anami and General Umezu not only argued against its acceptance (because it would endanger the *kokutai*) but even revived their demand that Japan should oversee its own disarmament. Admiral Toyoda sided with the army representatives on the grounds that the Byrnes Note failed to guarantee preservation of imperial rule. The meeting was interrupted when the emperor summoned Umezu and Toyoda at 9:30 A M. According to the diary of the emperor's military aide-de-camp, Colonel Ogata Kenichi, the emperor asked the army and navy chiefs, "In view of the ongoing diplomatic negations, shouldn't we suspend our air attacks?"[66] Ogata observed that on that day the emperor was overburdened with a heavy schedule, was full of worry, and appeared to suffer from mental exhaustion.

Prince Higashikuni also noted in his diary that the emperor looked pale and worn out the day before.[67]

Given Hirohito's obvious stress during this period, was the emperor really confident that he would be able to preserve the imperial house if Japan accepted the Byrnes Note? The emperor's August 13 conversation with his closest adviser, Lord Privy Seal Kido, reveals Hirohito's thoughts. Because Kido had been bombarded with objections to the Byrnes Note from President of the Privy Seal Hiranuma, as well as from War Minister Anami, Kido specifically asked for the emperor's views about the problematic Byrnes Note clause that stated, "The ultimate form of government of Japan shall . . . be established by the freely expressed will of the Japanese people." The emperor responded, "If the Japanese people no longer want the imperial house, even if the United States allows it to continue, there will be no use trying to save it. If the Japanese people still continue to trust the imperial house, I would like them to make that decision through their freely expressed will." In a note written in 1950, Kido emotionally commented, "The emperor's genuine trust in his people made me pause, and I felt as though my eyes were opened."[68] The emperor's clearly expressed thoughts and unshaken conviction strengthened Kido's determination to make peace with the United States.

The emperor's conviction was likely further strengthened when encouraging information about the Byrnes Note reached the palace. Japanese minister Okamoto Suemasa in Stockholm sent a cable to the Foreign Office in Tokyo, reporting the circumstances in which the United States chose to send the Byrnes Note, despite US allies' objections to its contents. Minister Okamoto urged Tokyo to accept the US offer without attempting to extract further concessions, because he believed that the manner in which the Byrnes Note was conveyed to Tokyo indicated the United States' intention to tacitly approve Japan's condition concerning preservation of the imperial house. Vice Foreign Minister Matsumoto Shunichi called the attention of Prime Minister Suzuki to Okamoto's cable. This cable was also communicated to Kido through his secretary. Matsumoto later asserted that the emperor "certainly saw the report."[69]

The emperor's expression of confidence that the war could be ended by accepting the Byrnes Note can be viewed as a reflection of his own resolve to preserve at all costs the imperial house and the nation of Japan. As will be shown, in the final imperial conference of August 14, the emperor declared that he was prepared to sacrifice himself, if necessary, to save his country and the court, which were one and the same in his mind. At the same time, the emperor's determination to end the war reflected his realistic understanding of what was necessary to preserve his country and the court. Although determined to protect the unbroken descent line of the imperial court, Hirohito understood that the only way to do so was to bring an end to the war that was destroying his country from within. The emperor's biggest fear was the disintegration of his country through domestic unrest and the chaos that would result from a devastating defeat after a prolonged war.

When Foreign Minister Togo received an audience with the emperor at 2:00 PM on August 13, the emperor reconfirmed his full support of Togo's position that Japan should accept the surrender provisions of the Byrnes Note. The emperor asked Togo to convey his wish to Prime Minister Suzuki.[70] Fifteen members of the Suzuki cabinet held a meeting from 4:00 to 7:00 PM, in which twelve ministers supported Togo's position and three ministers, including War Minister Anami, opposed it. Suzuki stated his support for accepting the Byrnes Note, declaring that he would report the result of the cabinet discussion to the emperor and ask him for his *seidan*. At this point, both supporters and opponents anticipated that the emperor would speak in favor of accepting the Byrnes Note's without reservation. The question was whether and when the opponents, namely the War Ministry and supreme command, would agree to convene an imperial conference, in which the emperor would choose to make his statement of surrender.

The following day, on August 14, the final push toward holding an imperial conference came from leaflets dropped by US B-29 bombers. The leaflets, which urged Japan's surrender, contained Japan's August 10 diplomatic note accepting the Potsdam Proclamation and a translation of the Byrnes Note into Japanese. The bombers began dropping leaflets at 5:00 PM on August 13 and continued into the following day. On the morning of August 14, Lord Privy Seal Kido, Prime Minister Suzuki, and Cabinet Chief Secretary Sakomizu agreed that they must ask the emperor to summon an imperial conference immediately, before the American leaflets ignited a rebellion among military diehards.

The War Ministry and supreme command both wanted to postpone the imperial conference until 1:30 PM, so Sakomizu resorted to a clever maneuver. Because Sakomizu did not have necessary seals of approval from the chiefs of the General Staffs to convene an imperial conference, he suggested an unprecedented plan: the prime minister would ask Emperor Hirohito to summon an imperial conference, to be attended by all top leaders of the government and supreme command—that is, all members of the Supreme War Leadership Council (including the four secretaries), all ministers of the

Suzuki cabinet, and the president of the Privy Council. At 8:40 AM, Suzuki and Kido jointly asked the emperor to summon this extraordinary conference, and Hirohito readily agreed. Thus, the final imperial peace conference was convened by the emperor at 10:30 AM on August 14. This caught many conference attendees by surprise. Those who were not dressed properly to appear in front of the emperor had to improvise sartorially for the occasion.[71]

Immediately before the imperial conference, at 10:20 AM, the emperor held a short meeting with three marshals (*gensui*). At the meeting, Marshals Nagano Osami and Sugiyama Gen, who had been the General Staff chiefs when Japan decided to go to war with the United States, still insisted on fighting to the bitter end, while Marshall Hata Shunroku, who had just arrived from his command post in Hiroshima, was more conciliatory and recommended further negotiations before accepting the Potsdam Proclamation. The emperor's response was firm. After commenting on the futility of continuing the war, Hirohito expressed his conviction that the imperial court would be secure under the US proposal. With regard to the *kokutai*, he told the marshals that, in the eyes of the United States, Japan's argument for the continuance of imperial prerogatives might look like an extraterritoriality and therefore would not be acceptable. The emperor added that disarmament and punishment of his loyal armed forces by the enemy would be unbearable for him, but this could not be avoided if the country was to be saved. The emperor urged the marshals to cooperate.[72]

Around 10:50 AM, Emperor Hirohito walked into the palace basement shelter, where twenty-three participants were waiting for the imperial conference. Prime Minister Suzuki opened the meeting with a brief summary of events since August 9 and stated that more than 80 percent of the cabinet members supported acceptance of the Byrnes Note, though the cabinet had not been able to reach a unanimous decision. Apologizing for troubling the emperor, the prime minister asked the emperor to issue his *seidan* after hearing the opinions of those who opposed the Byrnes Note. War Minister Anami and General Umezu repeated their argument that Japan must negotiate further to obtain a clear assurance that the *kokutai* would be preserved; otherwise Japan must continue to fight. Admiral Toyoda had milder reservations about the Byrnes Note and spoke mainly to show his sympathy for the army's position. As soon as the three speakers finished, the prime minister turned to the emperor.

Although many attendees recorded their own recollections of Emperor Hirohito's words, the record by Director of Information Shimomura Hiroshi

(Kainan) has long been considered the quasi-official version. Shimomura edited the accuracy of his own recollection of the emperor's words by cross-referencing his notes with those taken by Minister of State Sakonji Seizo, Minister of Education Ota Kozo, and Navy Minister Yonai. Shimomura's final transcript was proofread by Prime Minister Suzuki.

According to this transcript, on August 14, 1945, in a truly historic statement, Emperor Hirohito said,

> If there is no other opinion, I will state my thoughts.
>
> I have listened to the arguments in opposition [to acceptance of the Byrnes Note], but my thoughts have not been changed. I have carefully assessed the situation of the world and conditions within Japan, and I think it is impossible to continue the war.
>
> Although I hear various apprehensions [expressed] about the future of the *kokutai*, judging from the tenor of the [Byrnes] reply, I have concluded that they [the Allies] are approaching the question with favorable intentions. It is certainly understandable to have concerns about their attitude; but I do not want to doubt them. What matters most is the faith and resolution of the [Japanese] people as a whole, and therefore, I believe we should accept their offer. And I would like all of you to agree with me.
>
> I appreciate how difficult it will be for the officers and soldiers of the army and navy to surrender their arms and accept occupation [by the enemy]. However, no matter what happens to me, I want to save the lives of all my people. If we continue the war, the whole country will be reduced to ashes, and I cannot endure the thought of letting my people suffer any longer. I will not be able to carry on the wishes of my imperial ancestors. It is natural to be unable to completely trust an enemy's conduct, even if it is through peaceful means. But compared with an alternative path that would lead to Japan's annihilation, if we can preserve our race, there is a hope for [Japan's] recovery.
>
> As I recall the anguish that Emperor Meiji [my grandfather] had to suffer at the time of the Triple Intervention [by Russia, Germany, and France in 1897], all of us now must bear the unbearable and tolerate the intolerable, and [we must] work together for the recovery and reconstruction [of our nation]. When I think about those who perished in battle and died in the line of duty, and their surviving families, I feel an unbearable grief. I am also deeply concerned about the lives of the people who lost their livelihood because of war injuries and war damage. If there is anything I should do

to deal with this situation, I am willing to do whatever is necessary. If it is deemed necessary for me to appeal to my people, I will stand in front of a microphone. Since ordinary people have remained uninformed, when they hear this decision suddenly, their shock may be great. The shock of military officers and soldiers may be even greater. It may be very difficult to calm their emotion, but I would like the army and navy ministers to understand my thoughts and make efforts to bring them [soldiers and officers] under control. If necessary, I do not mind persuading them directly. It is also necessary to issue an imperial rescript [for the termination of the war]. I want the government to prepare it.[73]

After the imperial conference ended, the emperor's *seidan* needed to be transformed into an official governmental decision. This procedure began with a Suzuki cabinet discussion and approval of the wording of the imperial rescript to be broadcast over the radio. The document was sanctioned by the emperor at around 8:30 PM and signed by the cabinet ministers by 11:00 PM. At that point Japan's decision to accept the Byrnes Note and surrender became official. By 11:00 PM on August 14, the emperor finished recording a public announcement that declared Japan's surrender. This recording was scheduled to be broadcast throughout Japan over the radio at noon the following day. This would be the first time ordinary Japanese people would hear Emperor Hirohito's voice.

It is fortunate that, at this juncture in history, the man who happened to occupy the throne—and who was revered by the Japanese military and ultranationalists as the embodiment of Japan's *kokutai*—was an individual who held moderate, if not democratic, political views, with a realistic sense of patriotism, and who understood what was necessary to preserve the nation and people of Japan. In February 1946, according to Grand Chamberlain Fujita's memoir, the emperor confided that one question had been haunting him: if he (the emperor) could end the war, why could he not prevent the war in the first place? Hirohito rationalized that under the system of constitutional monarchy there was nothing he could have done to prevent the government and military from going to war once they had reached a unanimous decision, but the situation was different in 1945, when the emperor made the decision to end the war. That is, because government and military leaders were divided in 1945 and unable to reach a decision, the prime minister had asked for the emperor's opinion on the best course of action. The emperor told Grand Chamberlain Fujita, "Here, for the first time, I was given an opportunity to speak my own opinion freely without encroaching upon anyone's responsibility or infringing upon anyone's power. So I expressed my own convictions that I had been holding for some time and ended the war."[74]

In the end, as the peace faction had hoped, the emperor's *seidan* worked a "political miracle." Emperor Hirohito's expression of imperial will allowed the Suzuki cabinet and supreme command to force the entire Japanese military to comply with the government's decision to surrender. The emperor's *seidan* played a crucial role in averting a large-scale military coup, which might have resulted in the formation of a military government determined to fight to the bitter end.

AVOIDING A MILITARY COUP

On the morning of August 9, when news of the Soviet declaration of war arrived in Japan, the shocked vice chief of the General Staff, Lieutenant General Kawabe Torashiro, admitted that he had been wrong about the Soviet Union. Kawabe realized that wishful thinking had blinded him and that he had not been able to predict the Soviets' next move. Kawabe's initial reaction to this devastating news, however, did not change his resolve to continue fighting the war, perhaps because of the momentum of events and his own unwillingness to admit Japan's defeat. Kawabe quickly drafted a scenario that morning that included a plan to place the entire nation of Japan under martial law, dissolve the Suzuki cabinet, and establish a military regime. However, neither Army Chief General Umezu nor War Minister Anami would commit themselves to forming a military regime before they attended the August 9 Supreme War Leadership Council.[75]

The following morning, August 10, the emperor's first *seidan* (to accept the Potsdam Proclamation and end the war) had a tremendous psychological impact on the highest-level commanders at the Army General Staff headquarters and in the War Ministry. When General Umezu announced the emperor's decision to the officers at army headquarters, he explained that the emperor could no longer trust the army's strategy to successfully conclude the war. Sharing the deep shock of his military counterparts, General Kawabe wrote in his August 10 diary, "All is over." Realizing that Emperor Hirohito had completely lost his trust in the army's ability to win the war, Kawabe admitted that the emperor's *seidan* was not just a result of ineffective arguments by military leaders at the Supreme War Council. Rather, Kawabe realized that the emperor's decision to issue the *seidan* expressed an increasing distrust of the military, which had built up over the past few years within the court and among the Japanese people.[76] Clearly, the emperor's expression of no confidence in the army was a vital blow to the leaders of the Army General Staff.

By August 11, the Army General Staff officers were in a state of dejected lethargy. Kawabe's diary reveals the anguish he experienced as he gradually accepted that Japan had been utterly defeated. Thinking back over the past fourteen years, Kawabe criticized the arrogance and self-deception, of both the army and himself, that had brought about this disaster. Kawabe called these misguided ambitions "dreadful dreams, sinful dreams." At the same time, during this nightmarish period Kawabe began to search for actions he *could* take, as vice chief of the General Staff, at the moment of "the last gasp of the ruined country [*bōkoku no danmatsuma*]." On August 12, while the Foreign Office waited for an official reply from the United States, and the war minister and General Staff chiefs maintained a tough posture to defend the *kokutai*, Kawabe observed that the army headquarters remained "relatively calm and circumspect." Kawabe's August 12 exchanges with army officers, however, were filled with pessimism, and he noted that some officers in the War Ministry's Military Affairs Bureau and in the Army General Staff were "rattled."[77]

In fact, some officers did refuse to accept Japan's surrender after the first imperial *seidan*. War Minister Anami informed officers of the War Ministry that the emperor had issued a *seidan* in support of the Potsdam Proclamation, with the sole condition being the preservation of the imperial house. At that time, General Anami declared that the army "had no choice but to comply with His Majesty's wish" and emphasized the need for the army's "self-discipline [*jishuku*]." However, Lieutenant Colonel Takeshita Masahiko in the Military Affairs Bureau, brother-in-law of General Anami, recorded in his office diary that he and some other officers in the bureau continued to plot a military coup, possibly by mobilizing the Imperial Guard Division and the Eastern Area Army. Major plotters included Lieutenant Colonel Shiizaki Jiro and Major Hatanaka Kenji; and their superior officer, Colonel Arao Okikatsu (section chief in the Military Affairs Bureau), was sympathetic to their cause. There was even talk of assassination plots against advisers trusted by the emperor, such as Prime Minister Suzuki, Foreign Minister Togo, Navy Minister Yonai, and some others in the peace faction (such as Konoe Fumimaro, Okada Keisuke, and Sakomizu Hisatsune). Hiranuma Kiichi, president of the Privy Council, was also targeted for assassination because of his support of the one-condition proposal. The coup plotters repeatedly urged War Minister Anami to sanction their scheme and lead the coup.[78]

Between August 10 and 14, War Minister Anami played a crucial role in preventing a large-scale army mutiny in defiance of the emperor's *seidan*. General Anami consistently represented the army's hard-line position at the Supreme War Leadership Council and imperial conferences, primarily to keep all officers under his control. After the first *seidan*, Anami patiently listened to defiant junior officers' pleas in the War Ministry. On August 13, upon receiving the Byrnes Note, Takeshita and other plotters in the Military Affairs Bureau finalized a coup plan for the following morning and approached Anami during the night. The general appeared sympathetic to the plot, comparing himself to Saigo Takamori, who in 1877 remained loyal to Emperor Meiji but rebelled against the emperor's government in order to support Saigo's loyal followers from his home domain of Satsuma. But Anami did not make any commitment to the coup scheme. If the general had truly wanted to prevent Japan's surrender, he could have sanctioned his subordinates' coup plan, or he could have resigned as war minister, both of which would have made it impossible for the Suzuki cabinet to reach a decision to end the war. The planned army coup did not take place the next day, August 14, because the historic imperial conference was convened earlier than the plotters expected. They planned to storm the imperial conference at the palace and kidnap Emperor Hirohito, but Chief of the General Staff Umezu refused to sanction the action, and General Anami, who appeared to have anticipated this, did not object to General Umezu's decision.[79]

Although it was not obvious to many Japanese leaders at that time, a few noticed that General Anami held his cards close to the chest. While he maintained a hard-line stance so as not to alienate or radicalize rebellious young officers, the general's true intention was to stay on as war minister in the Suzuki cabinet until the government could conclude the war. (Anami tendered his resignation when part of the imperial palace was burned down during a US air raid on March 25, 1945, but when Emperor Hirohito asked the general to remain in the post to assist Prime Minister Suzuki, Anami complied.)[80] The general softened his position gradually as he learned about the emperor's desire to conclude the war—Anami learned of Hirohito's wishes first through his conversation with Lord Privy Seal Kido on June 18 and then directly from the emperor at the June 22 imperial conference. The latter occasion was probably an important turning point in the general's thinking.

Once the emperor expressed his desire on August 9 to accept the Potsdam Proclamation with one condition, Anami faithfully explained the emperor's wish to officers in the War Ministry. On the afternoon of August 13, while the Suzuki cabinet was engaged in an intense debate over the Byrnes Note, Cabinet Chief Secretary Sakomizu witnessed Anami's act of *haragei* (the art of the hidden psychological technique),[81] which the general employed to accomplish his unspoken objective of complying with the emperor's wishes and surrendering with no military insubordination. The prevailing opinion of the cabinet was to support Foreign Minister Togo's position and to accept the Byrnes Note, a course of action that had the emperor's firm support as well.

During this cabinet meeting, Anami suddenly asked Sakomizu to step aside to the next room, where Anami telephoned the Military Affairs Bureau and said, "The cabinet meeting has just started, and the ministers are moving toward the direction that is receptive to your cause. So I want you to take no action and wait for me calmly until I return there. I have the cabinet chief secretary here with me. If you want to hear about the cabinet meeting, I can put him on the phone." Stunned, Sakomizu wondered why the war minister was giving the Military Affairs Bureau information that was opposite of what was happening at the cabinet meeting. Sakomizu quickly realized that Anami was fighting alone against pressure from his die-hard subordinates and was trying to restrain their hasty violent action through the act of *haragei*.[82]

Prince Higashikuni, who was later asked to assume premiership after Prime Minister Suzuki resigned on August 15, wrote of a curious event in his diary. On August 14 at 8:40 AM, the chief of the Personnel Affairs Bureau, Nukada Hiroshi, went to see Prince Higashikuni on behalf of War Minister Anami and told the prince, "The army has decided to comply with the imperial command and faithfully carry out the Potsdam Proclamation," and that they were studying how to deal with potential problems of insubordination.[83]

In the end, War Minister Anami and General Umezu, along with other top army commanders, fulfilled the long-inculcated virtue of *shōshō-hikkin* (obey the imperial will without fail). As soon as the emperor delivered his second *seidan*, on August 14, accepting the Byrnes Note, General Anami cooperated with General Kawabe and General Umezu and gave his seal of consent to the order that the entire army must obey the emperor's *seidan* and surrender.[84] Thus, an ambiguous mixture of a formal loyalty to the emperor—who served both as commander in chief of the imperial army and as the embodiment of the *kokutai* (or the symbol of state)—and personal loyalty to Emperor Hirohito prevailed over resistance within the entire military. This seemed miraculous to those who had watched the military overwhelm the imperial court's resistance and lead the country to war, first against China in 1937 and later against the United States and Great Britain in December 1941. The emperor's *seidan*, which officially refused to support the army's position, was a decisive blow to hard-liners. The only remaining action left for the supreme command was to maintain the chain of command and make sure that the entire armed forces obeyed the order of the emperor. To do so, the War Ministry and Army General Staff deliberately held a firm public stance to defend the *kokutai* and fight to the bitter end in order to maintain tight control over the entire armed forces until the very end of the war. After the second *seidan*, this strategy allowed the supreme command to swiftly shift its position while holding firm control over the military and using the emperor's *seidan* as a shield to justify their order that the armed forces should surrender.[85] Therefore, the military, as well as the peace faction, found itself using the emperor's *seidan* to carry out the final act of surrender and disarmament.

Most army officers complied with the headquarters' order to surrender, in the tradition of unquestioned loyalty to the emperor. However, a few officers refused. Major Hatanaka and Lieutenant Colonel Shiizaki conspired to mobilize the Imperial Guard Division, take over the imperial palace, seize the record of the emperor's rescript declaring Japan's decision to end the war, and stop the emperor's radio broadcast scheduled for noon of August 15. When these men failed to persuade the commander of the Imperial Guard Division, Lieutenant General Mori Takeshi, to join the coup, Hatanaka shot and killed Mori and issued a false order to cut off the palace from the outside world and seize the record of the emperor's rescript. The insurgents searched the palace and radio station for the emperor's record in vain, which had been hidden in a secure place. Although palace communication with the outside world was cut off, a telephone line between a naval aide-de-camp and the Navy Ministry still worked. General Tanaka Shizuichi, commander of the Eastern Area Army, rushed to the palace and quelled the uprising. By 8:00 AM on August 15, the general had successfully restored order in the palace and other parts of Tokyo held by the insurgents. No political leaders were harmed by the rebellious officers, but the private residences of Prime Minister Suzuki and Privy Council president Hiranuma were burned by other small groups of insurgents.[86]

The basement shelter in the palace where Emperor Hirohito was staying was well shielded, and the insurgents who surrounded the shelter could not enter. However, the emperor could hear the commotion outside. When a chamberlain reported that the Imperial Guard Division had taken over the palace, the emperor said, "It's a coup, isn't it? I want you to gather [rebel] soldiers in the courtyard. I want to talk to them directly. I want to explain my thoughts. I want to go out. Can you call the chief aide-de-camp?" The emperor was dissuaded this plan, but according to Grand Chamberlain Fujita, the emperor spent a sleepless night in his military uniform, looking astonishingly pale and disheartened. He told Fujita, "What on earth are they [the rebels] trying to do? Why can't they understand my sorrow?"[87]

At dawn on August 15, War Minister Anami wrote an apology and committed suicide in the traditional manner of seppuku in his office. Anami was trusted by both Emperor Hirohito and by die-hard military officers. In the Japanese tradition, Anami honorably extricated himself from the dilemma of split loyalty by taking his own life. The last words Anami wrote, as the highest military officer of the land, were very few, but they echoed his deepest emotions: "With my death, I humbly apologize for my great crime, believing our sacred land shall never perish." When the emperor learned of Anami's suicide, he remembered how the general had pleaded for his cause, with tears in his eyes, during the imperial conference. The emperor said, "Anami had Anami's own thoughts. I feel sorry for him."[88] Anami's death, along with the deaths of several other high-level commanders, had considerable influence over the subsequent orderly surrender of the *kogun*, the Japanese imperial army.

In retrospect, the conversation between Kido and Anami on June 18 was highly suggestive regarding the different roles the military commanders and civilian government officials would be expected to play on August 14, 1945. In June, when Kido tried to persuade War Minister Anami to support his efforts to conclude the war diplomatically, the war minister hewed to a military solution through a decisive battle. At one point, Kido became exasperated and told Anami, "You military officers are fortunate. You can make a final assault on the enemy and die in this final desperate act, but politicians cannot do that. We must save the nation of Japan. And we have to do it now before it is too late."[89] At that time, Kido did not realize there could be another way: military leaders like Anami could sacrifice their own lives to help achieve peace. In any case, regardless of how and why these Japanese military leaders died, the age of military rule in Japan was over when Japan surrendered to the Allies.

Emperor Hirohito himself had no idea what would happen to him under the Allied occupation, but he acted in the hope that the imperial court and the new government, with Prince Higashikuni as prime minister, would continue its endeavors to save the nation of Japan and the imperial house. The letter the emperor wrote to his twelve-year-old son, Crown Prince Akihito, on September 6, 1945, reveals not only his candid opinion on Japan's defeat but also his priority at the time of Japan's surrender:

> Let me say a few words about the reasons for our defeat. Our people placed too much confidence in the empire and held England and America in contempt. Our military placed too much emphasis on spirit and forgot science. During the time of Emperor Meiji, there were renowned commanders in the army and the navy, such as Yamagata, Oyama, and Yamamoto. But this time, as in the case of Germany in the First World War, the military ran rampant and failed to take a broad view of the situation; they knew how to advance but did not know how to retreat. If we had continued the war, I would not have been able to protect the Three Sacred Treasures of the Imperial House, and [more Japanese] people would have been killed. I swallowed my tears and tried to save the Japanese race from extinction.[90]

The letter shows the emperor's regret for the war his country waged against the United States and Great Britain. But he was silent about China. He blamed the military's shortsightedness and its inability to retreat. What is most revealing, however, is his preoccupation with the Three Sacred Treasures of the Imperial House (Sanshu-no-jingi)—the imperial mirror, sword, and jewel that he inherited from his ancestors. These treasures symbolized the mythical origins of the imperial house and legitimized the unbroken imperial line. For Hirohito, as the 124th emperor, protection of the three treasures equaled the preservation of the imperial house, hence the *kokutai*.

In his 1946 "Monologue," the emperor repeated that he was prepared to sacrifice himself, if necessary, to end the war and save Japan from national suicide. At the time of Japan's surrender, his priorities were, first, to protect Japanese subjects and save the Japanese race from extinction and, second, to protect the three sacred treasures to preserve the *kokutai*.[91] However, we should not forget the hard reality that the emperor, as a monarch who believed in reason of state, considered the protection of the state and imperial house far more important than the protection of the lives of individual Japanese subjects. After all, since 1890, the Imperial Rescript on Education his grandfather issued had inculcated the Japanese people with the notion of self-sacrifice as part of their patriotic duty. The rescript stated, "Should emergency arise, offer yourselves courageously to the State; and thus guard and maintain the prosperity of Our Imperial Throne coeval with heaven and earth."[92] Emperor Hirohito, no matter how sensible and considerate he might have been, never questioned this precept. In his mind, the imperial house and the state of Japan were one and the same, and without saving the imperial house there was no protecting of the state of Japan and the Japanese people.

EPILOGUE

FROM THE MID-1930S UNTIL JAPAN'S SURRENDER IN 1945, THE nation was engaged in a series of wars in Asia and the Pacific. Throughout these wars, Japan's military-led government steadfastly sought to defend Japan's *kokutai* (national polity) by mobilizing the entire nation for war. During this period, Emperor Hirohito, as divine sovereign of the state and commander in chief of Japanese imperial forces, embodied the essence of the *kokutai* for the entire nation. However, after Japan's surrender, General Douglas MacArthur, Supreme Commander for the Allied Powers (SCAP), approached the issue of the *kokutai* from a different perspective. The general spared Hirohito from being tried as a war criminal and allowed him to reign in postwar Japan as "the symbol of the state" under a new democratic constitution. In the end, the emperor, as the symbol of the nation, became MacArthur's most useful ally in efforts to reform occupied Japan.[1] But this positive outcome could not be divined on the eve of Japan's surrender; at that point, the future of Emperor Hirohito was uncertain. The emperor was prepared to take personal responsibility for the war and to abdicate, but in the end he was persuaded by the Allied occupiers and postwar Japanese leaders to remain on the throne.

During the final days of World War II in the Pacific theater, the Allies' Potsdam Proclamation demanded that Japan surrender unconditionally. But so important was the *kokutai* to the Japanese government, that it began negotiations with the United States to keep the door open for preservation of Japan's *kokutai* and the imperial house. This process was complicated by a serious disagreement between the peace faction and the war faction at the Supreme War Leadership Council (the Big Six) over what kind of *kokutai* to preserve. Their debate was a continuation of arguments based on opposing views of the nature of imperial rule—arguments that had persisted since the early twentieth-century controversy over the emperor organ theory and the *kokutai* clarification movement of the mid-1930s. Emperor Hirohito, who watched how the military abused the concept of *kokutai* to promote a series of aggressive military actions in Asia and the Pacific, did not support the rightist interpretation of the *kokutai*. Taking a more moderate approach, he was willing to accept the Potsdam Proclamation so long as the imperial house was preserved and Japan's sovereignty was maintained. The emperor was willing to continue hostilities only if unconditional surrender to the Allies meant abolition of the imperial house.[2]

Because the prewar Meiji Constitution designated the emperor as sovereign of the state and commander in chief of the Japanese imperial forces, there is no doubt that the emperor, though a ruler in name only, must nevertheless share some responsibility for the war—at least moral responsibility, if not legal or political responsibility. If the authority of the emperor was primarily symbolic, one can argue that, precisely because of his symbolic significance, he should have taken a symbolic action to accept his responsibility for the war (although it might have been necessary to clarify what would constitute symbolic war responsibility).

Contrary to some critics' assertions that the emperor was obsessed with his own survival and "wanted to obfuscate the issue of accountability,"[3] when Japan surrendered, Hirohito was prepared to take personal responsibility for the war and, if necessary, to abdicate. At the crucial imperial conference on August 14 that finalized Japan's decision to surrender to the Allies, the emperor clearly stated that he did not care what happened to him as long as his country, including the imperial house, and his people were saved.[4] On August 12, the emperor notified Ishiwata Sotaro, minister of the imperial household, that he would like to visit his mother, the empress dowager, to bid her a final farewell. This suggests that in the event of Japan's surrender, the emperor was prepared for a worst-case scenario in which he might be captured and tried by the Allied Powers.[5]

Despite Hirohito's disagreement with the military, the emperor agonized over the fate of Japan's wartime leaders, who were to be tried as war criminals by the Allied Powers. According to the diary of Lord Keeper of the Privy Seal Kido Koichi, shortly after Japan's surrender on August 29, the emperor told Kido, "It is truly painful and unbearable to hand over our wartime leaders to the Allies. I wonder if I could assume all the responsibility for the war and abdicate from the throne and [thus] settle the issue [of war responsibility]." Kido strongly advised against the emperor's abdication and urged him to stay on the throne. Kido pointed out that Emperor Hirohito's abdication would probably not satisfy the Allies and "might eventually destroy the foundation of the imperial family, which might result in the ascendancy of advocates for a republican form of government."[6]

Prince Higashikuni, who served as prime minister immediately after Japan's surrender, sought advice from Kido, from former prime minister Konoe Fumimaro, and from Foreign Ministry officials concerning the emperor's war responsibility. They all agreed that the emperor did not have legal responsibility for the war because state ministers with the duty of *hohitsu* (providing advice to the emperor) assumed direct responsibility for all government decisions. However, in his diary, Prince Higashikuni also noted that some officials recommended that the emperor eventually step down because he had moral responsibility for the war. Some officials also suggested that the timing of the abdication should be after promulgation of a new constitution or after the signing of peace treaties with the Allies.[7] In other words, in this scenario, the emperor should step down after the Allied occupation ended and Japan's sovereignty was restored.

Kido was one of those who believed that the emperor should abdicate when peace treaties with the Allied Powers ended their occupation of Japan. After he was named as a "class A" defendant for war crimes, Kido obtained an audience with the emperor on December 10, 1945. Realizing that this would be the last time he would speak directly to the emperor, Kido repeated his recommendation that the emperor stay on the throne until Japan could conclude peace treaties and the country was "restored as a peaceful member of the international community." Kido pleaded with the emperor, "If His Majesty insists on taking some sort of responsibility, His Majesty has a heavy responsibility to guide Japan to that end."[8]

The emperor seems to have followed Kido's advice, because Hirohito did continue to feel responsible for protecting the imperial family and helping restore the sovereignty of Japan. On March 6, 1946, as the opening of the Tokyo war crimes trial drew closer, the emperor admitted to Vice Chamberlain Kinoshita Michio that his abdication would certainly release the emperor from his very difficult position. However, Hirohito told Kinoshita that he did not believe that any of his brothers were qualified to assume the throne. Prince Chichibu was ill; Prince Takamatsu was not fit to serve as regent because of his pro-war stance at the outset of hostilities; and Prince Mikasa was too young and inexperienced.[9]

It turned out that General MacArthur's intervention was a crucial factor in Emperor Hirohito's ultimate decision to stay on the throne. According to Kinoshita's diary, on January 1, 1946, the day the emperor issued his "declaration of humanity," the emperor learned from Kinoshita that the reorganization blueprint drawn up by Brigadier General Ken R. Dyke (head of the Civil Information and Education Section) proposed preservation of the imperial status of Emperor Hirohito and his three brothers without granting them real political power.[10] Sometime between March 18 and April 8, 1946, shortly before the Tokyo war crimes trial began and while the emperor was preparing his "Monologue" in anticipation of the trial, Hirohito received sufficient indications from MacArthur's staff that he would not be prosecuted for war crimes. On March 20, the second day of the emperor's "Monologue" dictation session, Terasaki Hidenari (liaison between the imperial court and Brigadier General Bonner F. Fellers, military secretary of General MacArthur) brought vital information to the emperor. According to Terasaki, General MacArthur had no desire to try the emperor's war responsibility or ask him to abdicate.[11] MacArthur's now-famous January 25, 1946, secret cable to US Army chief of staff General Dwight D. Eisenhower revealed MacArthur's strong determination to persuade Washington to spare Emperor Hirohito from a war crimes trial and keep him on the throne. MacArthur warned, "[Hirohito's] indictment will unquestionably cause a tremendous convulsion among the Japanese people. . . . Destroy him and the nation will disintegrate. . . . A vendetta for revenge will thereby be initiated whose cycle may well not be complete for centuries if ever." To continue a successful Allied occupation, MacArthur warned that "a minimum of a million troops would be required which would have to be maintained for an indefinite number of years."[12]

As the Tokyo Trial concluded in the fall of 1948, and the day of the verdicts for class A war criminals (November 12, 1948) drew closer, the Japanese public engaged in an open discussion of the question of the emperor's abdication. General MacArthur and his staff were seriously concerned about this development, and the general met with Prime Minister Yoshida Shigeru to discuss the issue of abdication on October 28. According to the diary of Tajima Michiji, director from 1948 to 1953 of the Imperial Household Agency (formerly the Imperial Household Ministry), Prime Minister Yoshida came to the palace on October 29 and told Tajima that MacArthur thought the emperor "should never abdicate." Accordingly, Tajima reported to the emperor the general's advice: "[His Majesty] should never abdicate." On November 11, the day before the final rulings in the Tokyo Trial, Prime Minister Yoshida went to see Tajima and asked that the emperor write a reply to MacArthur's message about abdication. Tajima and his staff hurriedly drafted a message from Emperor Hirohito, and the emperor approved this draft. In this letter to MacArthur, dated November 12, 1948, Hirohito told the general that he was committed to staying on the throne in order to work for the reconstruction of Japan.

According to Tajima's diary, the missive contained the following message from the emperor to MacArthur: "I am most grateful for the kind and considerate message Your Excellency was good enough to send me via Prime Minister Yoshida the other day. It is my lifelong desire to serve the cause of world peace as well as to promote the welfare and happiness of my people. I am now determined, more than ever, to do my best in concert with the [Japanese] people to surmount all difficulties and to speed the national reconstruction of Japan."[13]

Kido Koichi, who was imprisoned in Sugamo at that time, was probably unaware of this communication between the emperor and General MacArthur, which had been facilitated by Prime Minister Yoshida. It is not clear whether Kido realized how deeply Yoshida was committed to keeping Emperor Hirohito on the throne. In any event, on October 17, 1951, after the peace treaty with the United States was signed, Kido requested (through his own son, Takahiko) that Matsudaira Yasumasa, the grand master of ceremonies of the imperial household, move forward with abdication plans for Emperor Hirohito. Kido made a strong plea for the emperor's abdication, saying that if the emperor failed to seize this moment to step down, "The end result will be that the imperial family alone will have failed to take responsibility [for the war]; and an unsatisfactory mood will persist, which I am afraid might leave an eternal scar." Matsudaira replied on November 28 that the emperor, Tajima, and Matsudaira all agreed with Kido that the emperor should abdicate; but this letter also stated that Prime Minister Yoshida was not interested in Kido's request. Historian Awaya Kentaro speculates that it would have been extremely difficult for the Yoshida cabinet to reverse its position after the emperor had already committed to staying on the throne in his earlier message to General MacArthur. By the time the peace treaty became effective, Kido realized there was little hope for the emperor's abdication. In fact, Japanese newspapers interpreted the emperor's public statement at the ceremony for the restoration of Japan's sovereignty (May 3, 1952) as putting an end to the controversy over his abdication. Although the emperor's speech expressed his own "deep reflection" on past mistakes, it also emphasized his resolution to bear the heavy burden of the throne for years to come. Kido was obviously disappointed by the emperor's speech. He believed that the emperor should have set the record straight by assuming responsibility for the war and should have publicly apologized to the Japanese people.[14]

Records from the director of the Imperial Household Agency, Tajima Michiji, clearly show that the emperor wanted to issue a public apology to the Japanese people and that Tajima was looking for an opportunity for the emperor to do so. Emperor Hirohito's recently discovered apology, drafted by Tajima but never published, shows that the emperor felt personally responsible for the tragic outcome of the war and regretted his own "lack of virtue."[15] Kato Kyoko, who has been investigating Tajima's papers for many years, suggests that this apology by the emperor was most likely drafted around the time that the verdicts of the Tokyo war crime trials were announced.[16] Tajima's diary notes that he and Prime Minister Yoshida frequently discussed the question of the emperor's public apology but that nothing came of these discussions. In fact, earlier drafts of the emperor's public statement at the restoration of sovereignty ceremony on May 3, 1952, also contained an apology: "I deeply apologize to the nation for my responsibility for the defeat." However, this passage was deleted because of the objection of one of the emperor's advisers.[17]

That the emperor did not abdicate—and that he remained silent about his own responsibility for the war and failed to publicly apologize to the people who suffered from the war—did not necessarily mean that he did not wish to do so. Available historical records indicate the opposite. However, the fact remains that Emperor Hirohito kept silent about these matters for the rest of his reign, and this silence held unfortunate implications. Shortly after the war, the verdicts of the Tokyo Trial had already created a myth in which the emperor and his people were victims of aggression promoted by the military and ultranationalists. One can argue that the emperor's silence and inaction limited an open public discussion of his war responsibility and reinforced the victimization myth of the Tokyo Trial. This, in turn, helped anesthetize personal feelings of war guilt in individual Japanese citizens. Film reviewer Sato Tadao aptly commented in 1959, "Why didn't the Japanese people try to pursue the emperor's war responsibility? I think that the reason is that, for the vast majority of the people, the easiest way to exonerate themselves of war responsibility was to exonerate the emperor."[18]

Historian James Orr suggests that "the emperor, as the preeminent and powerful symbol of both state and people, could have forced such [a] confrontation by publicly asserting his own sense of responsibility and facing the consequences."[19] One can see the virtue of such action and might wonder what would have happened had the emperor done so. However, the past actions of Emperor Hirohito inform us that this kind of bold, even reckless, act conflicted with both his temperament and training. We have seen Hirohito's personal inclination for a cautious and controlled response at critical moments—as on the eve of Japan's 1945 surrender, when the US and Japanese governments were engaged in negotiations over the fate of the emperor and the imperial house. Kido later wrote that the emperor trusted the judgment of the Japanese people, telling Kido there was no use in trying to save the imperial house if the Japanese people did not want it. The emperor added that he was willing to accept the US proposal: "The ultimate form of government of Japan shall . . . be established by the freely expressed will of the Japanese people."[20]

According to a survey conducted among 3,080 Japanese voters by *Yomiuri Shinbun* in August 1948, soon after promulgation of the new constitution, over 90 percent of respondents supported continuation of the emperor system as defined under the new constitution. In the same survey, 68.5 percent responded that Emperor Hirohito should stay on the throne, 18.4 percent preferred his abdication, and only 4 percent favored abolition of the emperor system.[21]

It is quite possible that Emperor Hirohito was convinced that the Japanese people wanted him to stay on the throne and chose to assume a new responsibility as symbolic emperor (*shocho tenno*) and work with his people in rebuilding a peaceful and prosperous Japan. For better or worse, Hirohito chose a path predicted by former prime minister Suzuki Kantaro in the aftermath of Japan's surrender. At that time, Suzuki said, "It is proper that His Majesty should take responsibility for the war. However, in the current chaotic situation in Japan, nobody else will be able to rebuild Japan. He ought not to think of abdication. . . . His Majesty will be willing to make a hard choice and endure hardship with his people. He will have to bear his war responsibility while he [continues to] stay on the throne."[22]

In postwar Japan, Emperor Hirohito never publicly addressed the issue of his own war responsibility. However, the private memos of Tomita Tomohiko, former director of the Imperial Household Agency, indicate that the emperor, privately and in his own way, showed his strong feelings against the actions of some of Japan's wartime leaders. According to Tomita, after the emperor found out in 1978 that the names of seventeen wartime leaders who had been sentenced as class A war criminals by the Tokyo Trial had been quietly added next to the war dead enshrined at Yasukuni Shrine, the emperor stopped visiting the monument. He never set foot in the shrine again.[23]

Emperor Hirohito, who was born into an "inviolable" position that demanded superhuman status as sovereign and commander in chief during the turbulent war years of Showa, emerged as a complex historical figure whose actions could make no difference or decisive impact independent of or because of circumstances and the intentions of the people surrounding him. Regardless of his intentions, he has become a controversial historical figure whose silence and inaction will continue to have divergent and far-reaching impacts, both negative and positive, for generations to come.

NOTES

1   Historians use various names for the wars Japan waged in Asia and the Pacific from 1931 to 1945. The Japanese government called the 1941–45 war in the Pacific the "Greater East Asian War," but most Japanese today, except conservative war apologists, refrain from using this name because of its obvious association with the government's wartime propaganda. The US occupation forces, as part of the War Guilt Information Program, renamed the war the "Pacific War." Although the term is still widely used today, especially in the United States, it reflects the US-centered view of the war that begins with Japan's attack on Pearl Harbor and ends with the verdicts of the Tokyo Trial (officially called the International Military Tribunal of the Far East). Leftist historians who criticize Japan's military aggression, from the 1931 Manchurian Incident to the end of World War II in 1945, refer to all Japanese military actions during this period as the "Fifteen Year War." Some historians who see continuity between Japan's expansionist wars on the Asian continent and the Pacific prefer the name "Asia-Pacific War." This book uses "Pacific War" in a broader sense than that employed by the US occupation forces. The Pacific War refers here to the whole of Japan's turbulent relations, including both a cold war and belligerent acts against the rest of the Pacific powers, from the early 1930s until the end of World War II.

2   According to Article 4 of the Meiji Constitution, "The Emperor is the head of the Empire, combining in Himself the rights of sovereignty, and he exercises them [these rights] in accordance with the provisions of the present Constitution." Article 11 declared that "the Emperor has the supreme command of the army and navy." At the same time, however, Article 55 stipulated that "the respective Ministers of State shall give their advice to the Emperor, and be responsible for it. All laws, public ordinances, and imperial rescripts, of whatever kind, that relate to the affairs of state require the counter-signature of the Minister of State." The Imperial House Act (Koshitsu Tenpan) of 1889 declared that the emperor was *arahito-gami*, which could be literally translated as a "living god" or a "god reincarnate."

3   Shibusawa, *America's Geisha Ally*, 99–100; Janssens, *"What Future for Japan?"*, 375.

4   John Dower argues in *Embracing Defeat: Japan in the Wake of World War II* that General MacArthur and his staff dissuaded Emperor Hirohito from acknowledging his responsibility for the war in order to resituate the emperor as the center of the democratic reforms that MacArthur would try to bring about in postwar Japan.

Dower suggests that in early October 1945, "SCAP's commitment to saving and using the emperor was firm. The pressing, immediate task was to create the most usable emperor possible" (299).

5   This question was originally raised by Brigadier General Bonner F. Fellers, military secretary of General Douglas MacArthur and the chief of his psychological warfare operations, to Terasaki Hidenari, who served as liaison between General Fellers and Emperor Hirohito during the American occupation of Japan. Higashino, *Showa tenno futatsu no "dokuhakuroku"*, 113–16.

6   Kurihara, *Tenno*; Hando, *Seidan*; Hata, *Showa tenno itsutsu no ketsudan*; Shoda, *Jushin-tachi no showa-shi*; Ito Yukio, *Showa tenno den*; Furukawa, *Showa tenno: "Risei no kunshu" no kodoku*. Masumi Junnosuke's *Showa tenno to sono jidai* offers a more balanced and thoughtful reexamination of Emperor Hirohito's role in the war.

7   My use of the term "leftist historians" follows Hatano Sumio's definition in Asada, *Japan and the World, 1853–1952*, chapter 4. Hatano offers a useful historiographical essay on Japanese leftist scholars' works, including Inoue Kiyoshi, Ienaga Saburo, and Fujiwara Akira. Younger scholars who belong to the postwar generation also have published numerous studies on Emperor Hirohito and his responsibility for the war. Awaya Kentaro is best known for his critical works on the Tokyo Trial; Yamada Akira for his studies of Emperor Hirohito as *daigensui* (commander in chief) during the Asia-Pacific War; and Yoshida Yutaka for political, historical, and intellectual studies of the emperor's war responsibility.

8   Butow, *Tojo and the Coming of the War*; Butow, *Japan's Decision to Surrender*; Large, *Emperor Hirohito and Showa Japan*; Titus, *Palace and Politics in Prewar Japan*; Wetzler, *Hirohito and War*; Maruyama, *Thought and Behaviour in Modern Japanese Politics*, chapter 3.

9   Butow, *Tojo and the Coming of the War*, 176.

10   Butow, *Japan's Decision to Surrender*, 232 (italics in original).

11   Japanese names in this book are in their traditional order; that is, family names precede given names. However, when Japanese authors' publications are published in English, their citations follow the Western style.

12   Titus, *Palace and Politics in Prewar Japan*, 261, 263, 272, 313, 333. Wetzler, *Hirohito and War*, chapters 2 and 3.

13   Bix's *Hirohito and the Making of Modern Japan*, which relies heavily on Japanese leftist scholars' works, requires cautious reading because the book contains mistranslations and misleading selective quotations from both primary and secondary Japanese sources. Bergamini's *Japan's Imperial Conspiracy* and Behr's *Hirohio: Behind the Myth* also offer critical accounts of Emperor Hirohito.

14   According to Kido Koichi's diary, shortly after Japan's surrender on August 29, 1945, Emperor Hirohito asked Kido whether he could take responsibility for the war and abdicate if that would stop the Allies from arresting the Japanese war leaders, but Kido advised him to stay on the throne at least until Japan signed a peace treaty that would end the Allied occupation. When the peace treaty became effective in 1952, Prime Minister Yoshida Shigeru rejected Kido's request from Sugamo Prison to allow Emperor Hirohito's retirement. John Dower demonstrates in *Embracing*

Defeat how General MacArthur and his staff intervened to keep the emperor on the throne throughout the occupation. Diary of Kido Koichi in the collection of Kido-ke Bunsho (microfilm), National Diet Library of Japan, August 29, 1945; October 17, 1951; November 28, 1951; April 4, 1952; May 2, 1952. See also Awaya et al., *Kido Koichi jinmon chosho*, 559–62; Dower, *Embracing Defeat*, chapter 9.

15 Kato Kyoko, "Showa tenno: Kokumin eno shazai shosho soko," 94–113; Kato Kyoko, *Showa tenno "shazai shochoku soko" no hakken.*

16 Takeda, *Dual-Image of the Japanese Emperor*, 1.

17 Ibid., 4.

18 Wetzler, *Hirohito and War*, 185.

19 Masumi, *Showa tenno to sono jidai*, 5, 113.

20 Books by Robert Butow and David Titus provide details of the relationship between the emperor, his advisers, and the government. In their Japanese-language books, although Masumi Junnosuke, Fujiwara Akira, and Yamada Akira disagree on the emperor's intentions, they offer useful accounts on the relationship between the emperor and the military. Michael Barnhart, in *Japan Prepares for Total War: The Search for Economic Security, 1919–1941*, illuminates the accelerating interservice rivalry between the Japanese army and the navy.

21 Higashino, *Showa tenno futatsu no "dokuhakuroku"*, 212.

22 Fujiwara, *Tenno-sei to guntai*, 182–207.

23 Butow, *Japan's Decision to Surrender*, 232 (italics in original).

24 Igarashi, *Bodies of Memory*, chapter 1.

25 Hando, Hosaka, and Isoda, "Showa tenno jitsuroku no shogeki," 122.

26 Terasaki and Miller, *Showa tenno dokuhakuroku*. The emperor's "Monologue" was originally published in *Bungeishunju* (December 1990): 94–145.

27 Kinoshita, *Sokkin nisshi*, 211–12.

28 Kido, *Kido Koichi nikki*, 2:1230.

29 This blueprint was created by Brigadier General Ken R. Dyke, the head of the Civil Information and Education Section. Kinoshita, *Sokkin nisshi*, 96–99.

30 Kinoshita, *Sokkin nisshi*, 174–75, 222–23.

31 Masumi, *Showa tenno to sono jidai*, 4; Fujiwara, "Dokuhakuroku no shiryo-teki kachi," 13, in Fujiwara et al., *Tettei kensho Showa tenno dokuhakuroku.*

CHAPTER 1. THE AFTERMATH OF
THE PARIS PEACE CONFERENCE, 1919–1933

1 MacMillan, *Paris 1919*; Baker, *Woodrow Wilson and World Settlement*; Levin, *Woodrow Wilson and World Politics*; Manela, *Wilsonian Moment*; Ambrosius, *Wilsonianism*; Barnhart, *Japan Prepares for Total War*; Kawamura, *Turbulence in the Pacific.*

2 Yamada, *Showa tenno no gunji shiso to senryaku*, 29.

3 Kanroji, *Hirohito*, 127.

4 Makino, *Makino Nobuaki nikki*, 22. On August 17, 1921, Lord Keeper of the Privy Seal Makino Nobuaki received Crown Prince Hirohito's essay, composed in January 1920, from the prince's ethics teacher, Sugiura Jugo.

5   Ibid.

6   Ibid.

7   Ibid.

8   Burkman, *Japan and the League of Nations*.

9   *Genro* traditionally had the final say in selecting the next prime minister.

10 Terasaki and Miller, *Showa tenno dokuhakuroku*, 20.

11 Kinoshita, *Sokkin nisshi*, 211. Terasaki's record on this particular subject is considerably shorter than Kinoshita's, but the contents are very similar, indicating the accuracy of these records.

12 Ibid. (all quotations).

13 Kinoshita, *Sokkin nisshi*, 211–12.

14 Nagai, *Seinen kunshu Showa tenno to genro Saionji*, 9–16.

15 Hara Keiichiro, *Hara Kei nikki*, 5:166.

16 Ibid., 5:276.

17 Matsukata Masayoshi's *naiso* (report to the throne) in Makino Nobuaki Bunsho (Makino Nobuaki Papers), cited in Kishida, *Jijucho no showa-shi*, 19–20.

18 Hara Keiichiro, *Hara Kei nikki*, 5:347.

19 Interview at the Nasu Imperial Villa, August 29, 1979, in Takahashi, *Heika, otazune moshiagemasu*, 279.

20 Crown Prince Hirohito's statement, June 25, 1921, Verdun, cited in Nakao, *Showa tenno hatsugen kiroku shusei*, 1:32.

21 Hara Keiichiro, *Hara Kei nikki*, 5:434.

22 Kishida, *Jijucho no showa-shi*, 31; Takahashi, *Heika, otazune moshiagemasu*, 143.

23 Takahashi, *Heika, otazune moshiagemasu*, 295–96.

24 Nagai, *Seinen kunshu showa tenno to genro Saionji*, 57.

25 Nakao, *Showa tenno hatsugen kiroku shusei*, 1: 39.

26 Ibid., 1:43. Prince Regent Hirohito married Princess Nagako, daughter of Prince Kuninomiya Kunihiko, on January 26, 1924.

27 Makino, *Makino Nobuaki nikki*, 107–8.

28 Nakao, *Showa tenno hatsugen kiroku shusei*, 1:45.

29 Nagai, *Seinen kunshu showa tenno to genro Saionji*, 255–56; Masuda Tomoko, *Tennosei to kokka*, 145.

30 Yamada, *Showa tenno no gunji shiso to senryaku*, 45–46.

31 Terasaki, *Showa tenno dokuhakuroku*, 22.

32 Nagai, *Seinen kunshu showa tenno to genro Saionji*, 311–35. Based on newly available primary sources, such as the diaries of Makino Nobuaki, Nara Takeji, and Kawai Yahachi, Nagai recapitulates the debate among Japanese historians (including Ito Yukio, Masuda Tomoko, Yasuda Hiroshi, Awaya Kentaro, Shibata Shinichi, and Nakazono Hiroshi) over the emperor's role in the resignation of Prime Minister Tanaka Giichi, and Nagai reexamines how and why Emperor Hirohito influenced the course of the event.

33 Kinoshita, *Sokkin nisshi*, 213.

34 Large, *Emperor Hirohito and Showa Japan*, 39.

35 Grand Chamberlain Chinda Sutemi died in 1929 and Admiral Suzuki Kantaro was

appointed as his successor.

36 Burkman, *Japan and the League of Nations.*

37 Makino, *Makino Nobuaki nikki*, 474; Kido Koichi, *Kido Koichi nikki*, 1:100; Nara, *Jijubukancho Nara Takeji nikki-kaikoroku*, 3:359.

38 Fujiwara, *Tennosei to guntai*, 194.

39 Harada, *Saionji-ko to seikyoku*, 2:65.

40 Ibid., 2:69.

41 Kido Koichi, *Kido Koichi nikki*, 1:100; Makino, *Makino Nobuaki nikki*, 474–75.

42 Yamada, *Showa tenno no gunji shiso to senryaku*, 56–57.

43 Nara, *Jijubukancho Nara Takeji nikki-kaikoroku*, 3:359.

44 Ibid.

45 Kido Koichi, *Kido Koichi nikki*, 1:101.

46 Nara, *Jijubukancho Nara Takeji nikki-kaikoroku*, 3:365–66.

47 Yamada, *Showa tenno no gunji shiso to senryaku*, 58.

48 Kido Koichi, *Kido Koichi nikki*, 1:98; Harada, *Saionji-ko to seikyoku*, 2: 21–34; Butow, *Tojo and the Coming of the War*, 49–53.

49 Nakao, *Showa tenno hatsugen kiroku shusei*, 1:149–53; Makino, *Makino Nobuaki nikki*, 540; Nara, *Jijubukancho Nara Takeji nikki-kaikoroku*, 3:353–54; Kawai, *Showa shoki no tenno to kyuchu*, 5:151–53.

50 Kido Koichi, *Kido Koichi nikki*, 1:103.

51 Ibid., 1:102–7; Makino, *Makino Nobuaki nikki*, 477–78; Nara, *Jijubukancho Nara Takeji nikki-kaikoroku*, 3:368–69.

52 Nara, *Jijubukancho Nara Takeji nikki-kaikoroku*, 3:370–71.

53 Ibid., 3:373.

54 Harada, *Saionji-ko to seikyoku*, 2:108.

55 Ibid., 2:115–16.

56 Ibid., 2:160.

57 Nakao, *Showa tenno hatsugen kiroku shusei*, 1:179.

58 Nara, *Jijubukancho Nara Takeji nikki-kaikoroku*, 3:415. The emperor mentioned his direct order to General Shirakawa in his 1946 "Monologue"; see Terasaki and Miller, *Showa tenno dokuhakuroku*, 28–29.

59 Makino, *Makino Nobuaki nikki*, 497–99.

60 Yamada, *Showa tenno no gunji shiso to senryaku*, 62–63; Terasaki and Miller, *Showa tenno dokuhakuroku*, 35; Makino, *Makino Nobuaki nikki*, 534; Harada, *Saionji-ko to seikyoku*, 2:428. Makino's diary entry on January 9, 1933, also stated that the need to hold an imperial conference had come up several times but he had been reluctant to support the idea because the prime ministers, such as Wakatsuki and Inukai, did not favor such a conference.

61 Burkman, *Japan and the League of Nations*, 168–72 (quotations p. 170). Yamada Akira provides details of the emperor's efforts to stop the Kwantung Army from invading Rehe (Jehol) in February 1933, which was hampered by the ambiguity about the emperor's discretionary power; see Yamada, *Showa tenno no gunji shiso to senryaku*, 64–67.

62 Makino, *Makino Nobuaki nikki*, 540–41, 543, 546, 548 (quotation).

63 Takamatsumiya, *Takamatsumiya nikki*, 2:89–90.

64 Kinoshita, *Sokkin nisshi*, 213.

65 Wetzler, *Hirohito and War*, 185 (all quotations).

66 Large, *Emperor Hirohito and Showa Japan*, 54; Kawahara, *Hirohito and His Times*, 58–59.

67 Irokawa, *Age of Hirohito*, 13.

CHAPTER 2. CRISES AT HOME AND ABROAD

1 Fujiwara, *Showa tenno no jugo-nen senso*. Fujiwara laid the foundation for the leftist interpretation of the history of Japan's fifteen-year war in Asia and the Pacific.

2 Kido Koichi, *Kido Koichi nikki*, 1:354 (all quotations).

3 Honjo, *Honjo nikki*, 193–94 (all quotations). Another English translation of the emperor's conversation with Prince Fushimi is in Hane, *Emperor Hirohito and His Chief Aide-de-Camp*, 117.

4 Honjo, *Honjo nikki*, 194–95. See another English translation in Hane, *Emperor Hirohito and His Chief Aide-de-Camp*, 118.

5 Honjo, *Honjo nikki*, 196.

6 Ibid., 198–99.

7 Okada, *Okada Keisuke Kaikoroku*, 98–99 (all quotations).

8 Suzuki Hajime, *Suzuki Kantaro*, 252.

9 Kishida, *Jijucho no showa-shi*, 63.

10 Masuda, *Tenno-sei to kokka*, chapter 6.

11 Masuda, *Tenno-sei to kokka*, 259–73; Butow, *Tojo and the Coming of the War*, 59–63.

12 Honjo, *Honjo nikki*, 203; English translation from Hane, *Emperor Hirohito and His Chief Aide-de-Camp*, 129–30.

13 Honjo, *Honjo nikki*, 203.

14 Okada, *Okada Keisuke Kaikoroku*, 114; Harada, *Saionji-ko to seikyoku*, 4:238.

15 Honjo, *Honjo nikki*, 204. In this paragraph, my English translations are similar to those in Hane, *Emperor Hirohito and His Chief Aide-de-Camp*, 130–31, except for Ito Hirobumi's commentaries on the Meiji Constitution. (Ito led the drafting of the Meiji Constitution.) I translate and italicize Ito's word *ringyo*, which means an imperial visit or presence, as "reign" in order to distinguish it from "rule" or "govern."

16 Honjo, *Honjo nikki*, 205–6; English translation from Hane, *Emperor Hirohito and His Chief Aide-de-Camp*, 133–34.

17 Honjo, *Honjo nikki*, 207. See also Hane, *Emperor Hirohito and His Chief Aide-de-Camp*, 135.

18 Honjo, *Honjo nikki*, 207–8.

19 Ibid., 208; English translation from Hane, *Emperor Hirohito and His Chief Aide-de-Camp*, 136.

20 Masaki Jinzaburo's diary entry, April 24, 1935, cited in Nakao, *Showa tenno hatsugen kiroku shusei*, 1:303.

21 Honjo, *Honjo nikki*, 211 (all quotations).

22   Ibid.; English translation from Hane, *Emperor Hirohito and His Chief Aide-de-Camp*, 140.

23   Masuda, *Tenno-sei to kokka*, 289.

24   Honjo, *Honjo nikki*, 216–17. See also Hane, *Emperor Hirohito and His Chief Aide-de-Camp*, 146–47.

25   Honjo, *Honjo nikki*, 218–19 (all quotations).

26   Ibid., 220, 224 (quotation).

27   Ibid., 228–29 (all quotations). An alternative English translation is in Hane, *Emperor Hirohito and His Chief Aide-de-Camp*, 161–62.

28   Honjo, *Honjo nikki*, 232–33; English translation from Hane, *Emperor Hirohito and His Chief Aide-de-Camp*, 167.

29   Kido Koichi, *Kido Koichi nikki*, 1:440–41.

30   Chadani, *Showa senzen-ki no kyuchu seiryoku to seiji*, 141–47.

31   Ibid.

32   Irie Tametoshi, *Irie Sukemasa nikki*, 1:76.

33   Furukawa, *Showa tenno: "Risei no kunshu" no kodoku*, 205. Furukawa cites an unpublished portion of Honjo Shigeru's diary entry.

34   Hane and Perez, *Modern Japan*, 277.

35   Butow, *Tojo and the Coming of the War*, 63.

36   Ibid., 65–67; Shillony, *Revolt in Japan*, 135–37; Suzuki Hajime, *Suzuki Kantaro-den*, 262–64. Suzuki's wife, Taka, had a special place in Emperor Hirohito's childhood memory, for Taka had served as the future emperor's nurse for eleven years.

37   Kanroji, *Hirohito*, 125–26.

38   Kishida, *Jijucho no showa-shi*, 79.

39   Honjo, *Honjo nikki*, 272.

40   Ibid., 272, 274; Kunaincho, *Showa tenno jitsuroku*, 23:25.

41   Honjo, *Honjo nikki*, 275–76. See another English translation of quotations in this paragraph in Hane, *Emperor Hirohito and His Chief Aide-de-Camp*, 212–14. Also see Harada, *Saionji-ko to seikyoku*, 5:6.

42   Honjo, *Honjo nikki*, 236; English translation from Hane, *Emperor Hirohito and His Chief Aide-de-Camp*, 172.

43   Terasaki and Miller, *Showa tenno dokuhakuroku*, 32.

44   Honjo, *Honjo nikki*, 292; English translation from Hane, *Emperor Hirohito and His Chief Aide-de-Camp*, 234.

45   Honjo, *Honjo nikki*, 292–93; English translations slightly modified from Hane, *Emperor Hirohito and His Chief Aide-de-Camp*, 234–35.

46   Honjo, *Honjo nikki*, 293.

47   Kido Koichi, *Kido Koichi nikki*, 1:474; *Asahi Shinbun*, March 7, 1936.

48   Tsutsui, *Showa ju-nen-dai no rikugun to seiji*, chapter 1.

49   Gaimusho, *Nihon gaiko nenpyo narabini shuyo bunsho*, 2:344–48.

50   Tsunoda, de Bary, and Keene, *Sources of Japanese Tradition*, 2:278–88.

51   Bix, *Hirohito and the Making of Modern Japan*, 319. Bix's argument is not supported by evidence. He simply quotes Japanese historians' assertions from their secondary works, and his use of primary sources is misleading. For example, when he quotes

from Harada Kumao's diary (Harada, *Saionji-ko to seikyoku*, 6:30), he mistranslates it.

52 Shimada Shigetaro's memo of December 5, 1935, in Nakao, *Showa tenno hatsugen kiroku shusei*, 1:327 (all quotations).

53 Takamatsumiya, *Takamatsumiya nikki*, 2:459; Nakao, *Showa tenno hatsugen kiroku shusei*, 1:370–71.

54 Harada, *Saionji-ko to seikyoku*, 6:30.

55 Kido Koichi, *Kido Koichi nikki*, 2:802.

56 Terasaki and Miller, *Showa tenno dokuhakuroku*, 35–36.

57 Gaimusho, *Nihon gaiko nenpyo narabini shuyo bunsho*, 2:365–66.

58 Barnhart, *Japan Prepares for Total War*, 84–88.

59 Shimada Shigetaro's memos of July 21, 1937, in Nakao, *Showa tenno hatsugen kiroku shusei*, 1:374–75.

60 Konoe, *Ushinahareshi seiji*, 14–15 (quotations p. 15); Shimada Shigetaro's memos of July 30,1937, in Nakao, *Showa tenno hatsugen kiroku shusei*, 1:376.

61 Takamatsumiya, *Takamatsumiya nikki*, 2:512–13.

62 Shimada Shigetaro's memos of August 12 and 15, 1937, in Nakao, *Showa tenno hatsugen kiroku shusei*, 1:379–78.

63 Terasaki and Miller, *Showa tenno dokuhakuroku*, 37.

64 Shimada Shigetaro's memos of August 18, 1937, in Nakao, *Showa tenno hatsugen kiroku shusei*, 1:381.

65 Rikugunsho (War Ministry), "Hokushi seimu shido yoko" (The outline of political guidance in northern China), August 12, 1937, in [Misuzu Shobo], *Gendai-shi shiryo: Nicchu senso*, 2:26.

66 *Asahi Shinbun*, September 4, 1937, in Nakao, *Showa tenno hatsugen kiroku shusei*, 1:384.

67 Takamatsumiya, *Takamatsumiya nikki*, 2:537–38.

68 Cabinet decision of August 24, 1937, "Outline of Policy to Mobilize the People's Morale," in Yamada, *Gaiko shiryo*, 257–58.

69 Nakao, *Showa tenno hatsugen kiroku shusei*, 1:392.

70 Harada, *Saionji-ko to seikyoku*, 6:136–37.

71 Yamada, *Showa tenno no gunji-shiso to senryaku*, 100–101.

72 Harada, *Saionji-ko to seikyoku*, 6:140.

73 Ibid., 6:202.

74 Ibid., 6:204.

75 Gaimusho, *Nihon gaiko nenpyo narabini shuyo bunsho*, 2:385–86.

76 Harada, *Saionji-ko to seikyoku*, 6:208.

77 Hata Shunroku's diary, cited in Nakao, *Showa tenno hatsugen kiroku shusei*, 1:400–401.

78 Harada, *Saionji-ko to seikyoku*, 7:8

79 Ibid., 7:32.

80 Gaimusho, *Nihon gaiko nenpyo narabini shuyo bunsho*, 2:407; Yamada, *Gaiko shiryo*, 257.

81 Harada, *Saionji-ko to seikyoku*, 7:50–51. Two other English translations of Harada

diary's entry are in Large, *Emperor Hirohito and Showa Japan*, 93; and Coox, *Nomonhan*, 130.

82 Yamada, *Showa tenno no gunji-shiso to senryaku*, 118–19.

83 Harada, *Saionji-ko to seikyoku*, 7:49.

84 Large, *Emperor Hirohito and Showa Japan*, 94. Japan suffered more than 50,000 casualties; Russia and Mongolia, 9,000 combined. Butow, *Tojo and the Coming of the War*, 128.

85 Hata Shunroku, *Hata Shunroku nisshi*, 229. Hata served as chief aide-de-camp from May 25 to August 30, 1939, and his diary entries during this period contain numerous candid remarks by Emperor Hirohito.

86 Furukawa, *Showa tenno: "Risei no kunshu" no kodoku*, 258.

87 Terasaki and Miller, *Showa tenno dokuhakuroku*, 49.

88 Yamada, *Gaiko shiryo*, 315.

89 For the history of US economic sanctions of Japan, see Barnhart, *Japan Prepares for Total War*; Miller, *Bankrupting the Enemy*; Utley, *Going to War with Japan*.

90 Vice Chief of General Staff Sawada Shigeru's memoir, cited in Nakao, *Showa tenno hatsugen kiroku shusei*, 1:471–74.

91 Kido Koichi, *Kido Koichi nikki*, 2:814.

92 Harada, *Saionji-ko to seikyoku*, 8:311.

93 Ibid., 8:330–31.

94 Chadani, *Showa tenno shokkin-tachi no senso*, 159–64.

95 Kido Koichi, *Kido Koichi nikki*, 2:822.

96 Harada, *Saionji-ko to seikyoku*, 8:346–47; English translation of the emperor's words slightly modified from Large, *Emperor Hirohito and Showa Japan*, 100.

97 Kido Koichi, *Kido Koichi nikki*, 2:825.

98 Terasaki and Miller, *Showa tenno dokuhakuroku*, 52.

CHAPTER 3. THE ROAD TO PEARL HARBOR

A substantial portion of this chapter was originally published as "Emperor Hirohito and Japan's Decision to Go to War with the United States," in *Diplomatic History* 31 (January 2007): 51–79.

1 English translation of "Outline of National Policies in View of the Changing Situation," at the imperial conference, July 2, 1941, in Ike, *Japan's Decision for War*, 77–90.

2 Sanbohonbu, *Sugiyama memo*, 1:276–78.

3 Records of Tanaka Shinichi under the title "Daitoa senso eno dotei" (The road to the Greater East Asian War), the National Institute of Defense Studies, Japan, cited in Nakao, *Showa tenno hatsugen kiroku shusei*, 2:48.

4 Miller, *Bankrupting the Enemy*; Barnhart, *Japan Prepares for Total War*, 229–32; Utley, *Going to War with Japan*, 153–56.

5 Tanaka Shinichi's diary entry of July 30, 1941, quoted in Nakao, *Showa tenno hatsugen kiroku*, 2:49.

6 Sanbohonbu, *Sugiyama memo*, 1:284, 286.

7 Kido Koichi, *Kido Koichi nikki*, 2:895–96.

8   Higashikuni, *Higashikuni nikki*, 74.

9   Sanbohonbu, *Sugiyama memo*, 1:291.

10   English translation of "The Essentials for Carrying Out the Empire's Policy," September 6, 1941, in Ike, *Japan's Decision for War*, 135.

11   Butow, *Tojo and the Coming of the War*, 255–56. Stephen S. Large also argues that the emperor's intervention would have made little difference in the decision of September 6, 1941. Large, *Emperor Hirohito and Showa Japan*, 109.

12   Ito Takashi, *Takagi Sokichi nikki to joho*, 2:557; Bix, *Hirohito and the Making of Modern Japan*, 410–12. See also Koketsu, *Nihon kaigun no shusen kosaku*, 70–73.

13   Terasaki and Miller, *Showa tenno dokuhakuroku*, 62–63.

14   Konoe, *Ushinahareshi seiji*, 120; Konoe, *Heiwa eno doryoku*, 84–85.

15   Sanbohonbu, *Sugiyama memo*, 1:310–11.

16   Butow, *Tojo and the Coming of the War*, 254–55. Butow offers a detailed summary of the event based on the records left by Kido and Konoe.

17   Konoe, *Ushinahareshi seiji*, 121.

18   Ibid.; English translation from Butow, *Tojo and the Coming of the War*, 255.

19   Sanbohonbu, *Sugiyoma memo*, 1:310–11.

20   Konoe, *Ushinahareshi seiji*, 122; Kurihara, *Tenno: Showa-shi oboegaki*, 165; Butow, *Tojo and the Coming of the War*, 255.

21   Tanaka Shinichi, "Daitoa senso eno dotei," cited in Nakao, *Showa tenno hatsugen kiroku shusei*, 2:64.

22   Ito Takashi, *Takagi Sokichi nikki to joho*, 2:693.

23   Kido Koichi, *Kido Koichi nikki*, 2:901.

24   Ibid., 2:905.

25   Sanbohonbu, *Sugiyama memo*, 1:311. The English translation of Emperor Meiji's poem is from Butow, *Tojo and the Coming of the War*, 258.

26   Fujiwara, *Showa tenno no jugo-nen senso*, 25, 28.

27   Ishii Akiho's memoir, in Joho, *Gunmu kyokucho Muto Akira kaisoroku*, 262; also cited in Yamada, *Daigensui showa tenno*, 144–49.

28   Ishii Akiho's memoir in Joho, *Gunmu kyokucho Muto Akira kaisoroku*, 262–63.

29   Boeicho Boeikenshujo Senshishitsu, *Senshi sosho, Daihonei rikugunbu daitoa senso kaisenkeii*, 5:49.

30   Takayama, *Sanbohonbu sakusenka*, 98–122.

31   Yamada, *Daigensui showa tenno*, 150–55; Boeikenkyujo, Daihonei, "Josokankei tsuzuri," vol. 1, "Materials to Be Submitted in Reply to the Throne: The Operational Outlook, Both at the Beginning and Several Years Later, in Regard to a War with the United States, Britain, and Holland," October 20, 1941, by Takayama Shinobu. The entire text is in Yamada, *Showa tenno no senso shido*, 221–31.

32   Yamada Akira and Peter Wetzler suggest that Hirohito saw this particular *hoto shiryo* ("Material to Be Submitted in Reply to the Throne," October 20, 1941) and was influenced favorably toward war, but they do not offer any evidence as proof. Yamada, *Showa tenno no senso shido*, 85–90; Wetzler, *Hirohito and War*, 53–55. According to Takayama Shinobu, the original author of this document, the Army General Staff, never reported it to the emperor as part of a *joso* (report to the

throne), but the document eventually became the basis for the material discussed at the liaison conference in late November. Takayama, *Sanbohonbu sakusenka*, 98

33 Okada Keisuke's notes of his conversation with Prince Fushimi on March 7, 1944, in Takagi, *Takagi kaigun shosho oboegaki*, 21.

34 Kido Koichi, *Kido Koichi nikki*, 2:913.

35 Terasaki and Miller, *Showa tenno dokuhakuroku*, 67.

36 Takagi Sokichi recorded this information from Konoe Fumimaro on October 6, 1941; see Ito Takashi, *Takagi Sokichi nikki to joho*, 2:566. There is a similar report in the diary entry of October 9, 1941, of Vice Minister of the Navy Sawamoto Yorio, in Ito, Sawamoto, and Nomura, "Sawamoto Yorio kaigun-jikan nikki," 463.

37 Kido Koichi, *Kido Koichi nikki*, 2:914. See details in Butow, *Tojo and the Coming of the War*, 276–77.

38 Terasaki and Miller, *Showa tenno dokuhakuroku*, 62–63, 67 (quotation).

39 Tomita Kenji, *Haisen nihon no uchigawa*, 196. Another English translation is in Bix, *Hirohito and the Making of Modern Japan*, 419–20.

40 For the detailed account of how Prime Minister Konoe's disagreement with War Minister Tojo and the General Staffs led to his resignation, including the failure of the Ogikubo conference of October 12, 1941, see Butow, *Tojo and the Coming of the War*, 262–87.

41 Weber, *Wirtschaft und Gesellschaft*, 672, quoted in Maruyama, *Thought and Behaviour in Modern Japanese Politics*, 125 (italics in original).

42 Butow, *Tojo and the Coming of the War*, 297.

43 National Diet Library of Japan, "Kido Koichi seiji danwa rokuon sokkiroku," April 12, 1967, 74–79. Kido was sentenced to life imprisonment by the Tokyo war crimes trial but was released from Sugamo Prison in 1953 because of illness, and in the spring of 1967 he engaged in a series of interviews with the National Diet Library's project team on February 16, March 6, 13, and 27, April 12, and May 29.

44 Kinoshita, *Sokkin nisshi*, 146.

45 Terasaki and Miller, *Showa tenno dokuhakuroku*, 68.

46 The emperor's order read by Kido, quoted in Kido Koichi, *Kido Koichi nikki*, 2:917. The interpretive English translation (including italics) of the Japanese original text is from Butow, *Tojo and the Coming of the War*, 301.

47 Ishii Akiho's memoir, in Joho, *Gunmu kyokucho Muto Akira kaisoroku*, 269.

48 Akamatsu, *Tojo hishokan kimitsu nikki*, 33. Another partial English translation is in Wetzler, *Hirohito and War*, 69.

49 Tanaka Shinichi, *Taisen totsunyu no shinso*, 128.

50 Ugaki Matome, *Sensoroku*, 4.

51 Takamatsumiya, *Takamatsumiya nikki*, 3:307.

52 Kido Koichi, *Kido Koichi nikki*, 918. The English translation for the Japanese saying "Koketsu ni irazunba koji wo ezu" is quoted in Large, *Emperor Hirohito and Showa Japan*, 110–11, also in Butow, *Tojo and the Coming of the War*, 309. Herbert Bix fails to mention the abundant documents and historical studies on the reasons why the emperor and Kido decided to seek Tojo's appointment as prime minister. Eager to suggest that the emperor was prepared to go to war with the United States, Bix

translates the saying as "Nothing ventured, nothing gained" and implies that Hirohito gambled on General Tojo as a "wartime leader" who would take Japan to war. Bix simply states that "the emperor and Kido and those close to them now believed that war was unavoidable." Bix, *Hirohito and the Making of Modern Japan*, 419.

53 Participants of this liaison conference were the prime minister and war minister (Tojo Hideki), foreign minister (Togo Shigenori), finance minister (Kaya Okinori), navy minister (Shimada Shigetaro), director of the Planning Board (Suzuki Teiichi), chief of the Army General Staff (Sugiyama Gen), chief of the Naval General Staff (Nagano Osami), chief cabinet secretary (Hoshino Naoki), chief of the Military Affairs Bureau (Muto Akira), chief of the Naval Affairs Bureau (Oka Takasumi), vice chief of the Army General Staff (Tsukada Osamu), and vice chief of the Naval General Staff (Ito Seiichi). Decisions reached by a liaison conference usually became Japan's national policies, because the standard practice of the imperial conference was to rubber-stamp the liaison conference's resolutions, as in the case of the imperial conference of September 6, 1941.

54 Ike, *Japan's Decision for War*, 198–99 (all quotations).

55 Sanbohonbu, *Sugiyama memo*, 1:370–72.

56 66th Liaison Conference, November 1, 1941, in Ike, *Japan's Decision for War*, 204.

57 See the English translation of Japan's Proposals A and B in Ike, *Japan's Decision for War*, 209–11.

58 Tojo Hideki's testimony in Asahi shinbun hotei kishadan, *Tokyo saiban*, 2:866–67.

59 Record of the imperial conference on November 5, 1941, in Sanbohonbu, *Sugiyama memo*, 2:406–30. An English translation is in Ike, *Japan's Decision for War*, 208–39.

60 Bix, *Hirohito and the Making of Modern Japan*, 424. Bix writes, "Clearly, in the early days of November Hirohito's mind had become fixed on war. He no longer agonized over the deadlocked negotiations with the United States."

61 Yamada, *Daigensui Showa tenno*, 164.

62 In the Battle of Okehazama (1560), the legendary Japanese warlord Oda Nobunaga, outnumbered twenty to one by invading enemy forces, defended his territory through a spectacular surprise attack against the enemy in a driving rain.

63 The entire text of Admiral Nagano's report to the emperor is in Yamada, *Showa tenno no senso shido*, 231–36. See also Wetzler, *Hirohito and War*, 35; Boeicho Boeikenshujo Senshishitsu, *Senshi sosho, Daihonei rikugunbu daitoa senso kaisenkeii*, 5:336–37.

64 Sanbohonbu, *Sugiyama memo*, 1:388.

65 Ibid., 2:525.

66 Ibid., 2:523–25. An English translation is in Ike, *Japan's Decision for War*, 247–49. The document proposed that Japan should create an international environment that would precipitate surrender by the United States. To achieve this goal, Japan would work closely with Germany and Italy to hasten the surrender of Great Britain and at the same time arrange a peace between Germany and the Soviet Union.

67 Ishii Akiho's memoir, in Joho, *Gunmu kyokucho Muto Akira kaisoroku*, 273–74.

68 Sanbohonbu, *Sugiyama memo*, 2:387.

69 Kido Koichi, *Kido Koichi nikki*, 2:923–24.

70 Gunji-shi Gakkai, *Daihonei rikugunbu senso shidohan: Kimitsu senso nisshi*, 1:192, entry on November 27, 1941.

71   Kido Koichi, *Kido Koichi nikki*, 2:926.

72   Terasaki and Miller, *Showa tenno dokuhakuroku*, 71.

73   Butow, *Tojo and the Coming of the War*, 363.

74   Kanroji, *Hirohito*, 127.

75   Sanbohonbu, *Sugiyama memo*, 2:533.

76   Kido Koichi, *Kido Koichi nikki*, 2:926–27.

77   Terasaki and Miller, *Showa tenno dokuhakuroku*, 74.

78   Kido Koichi, *Kido Koichi nikki*, 2:927–28. According to Terasaki and Miller, Emperor Hirohito told Prince Takamatsu, "I am afraid that we might not win." Terasaki and Miller, *Showa tenno dokuhakuroku*, 74.

79   Shimada, "Shimada Shigetaro taisho kaisen nikki," 367–68 (all quotations). Admiral Shimada, who had been away from the supreme command in Tokyo since he left the position of vice chief of the Naval General Staff in 1937, was unfamiliar with the top-secret decisions surrounding the September 6 imperial conference. Shimada's diary shows his surprise at his appointment as the new navy minister and his reservations about war with the United States. However, like the emperor, by November 30, 1941, Shimada--under pressure from the military bureaucracy--eventually accepted the argument for the inevitability of war.

80   Kido Koichi, *Kido Koichi nikki*, 2:927–28. The English translation of "soto no kakushin" as "reasonably confident" is from Butow, *Tojo and the Coming of the War*, 358.

CHAPTER 4. AN UNEASY COMMANDER IN CHIEF

1   Kanroji, *Hirohito*, 128. Kanroji grew up as playmate and classmate of Emperor Hirohito's father (Emperor Yoshihito). He became a trusted member of the imperial household and served Emperor Hirohito until 1959.

2   Hando, "Tenno to daihonei" in Miyake, *Showa-shi no gunbu to seiji*, 77–78.

3   "Draft Proposal for Hastening the End of the War against the United States, Great Britain, the Netherlands, and Chiang [Kai-shek in China]," adopted on November 15, 1945, in Sanbohonbu, *Sugiyama memo*, 2:523–25. An English translation is in Ike, *Japan's Decision for War*, 247–49.

4   Yamada, *Showa tenno no gunji shiso to senryaku*, 186–87.

5   Matsutani, *Daitoa senso shushu no shinso*, 22.

6   Kido Koichi, *Kido Koichi nikki*, 2:943–45.

7   Matsutani, *Daitoa senso shushu no shinso*, 22–23; diary entries of April 13 and September 7, 1942, in Tanemura, *Daihonen kimitsu nisshi*, 120, 134.

8   Matsutani, *Daitoa senso shushu no shinso*, 24–25.

9   Kido Koichi, *Kido Koichi nikki*, 2:949.

10   Drea, *In the Service of the Emperor*, 187.

11   Yamada, *Showa tenno no gunji shiso to senryaku*, 195–99.

12   Nakao, *Showa tenno hatsugen kiroku shusei*, 2:117, 119–20, 123–25; Yamada, *Showa tenno no gunji shiso to senryaku*, 202–5.

13   Nakao, *Showa tenno hatsugen kiroku shusei*, 2:137. See also Yamada, *Showa tenno no gunji shiso to senryaku*, 201.

14   Diary entry of May 6, 1942, in Tanemura, *Daihonen kimitsu nisshi*, 122; Nakao, *Showa*

tenno hatsugen kiroku shusei, 2:130–31. The emperor commented in his 1946 "Monologue" that those three American POWs who had been executed should have been spared. Terasaki and Miller, *Showa tenno dokuhakuroku*, 89.

15 Kido Koichi, *Kido Koichi nikki*, 2:966–67 (quotation p. 967); Kido Nikki Kenkyu-kai, *Kido Koichi kankei bunsho*, 128.

16 Yamada, *Showa tenno no gunji shiso to senryaku*, 214–17; Tanaka Shinichi's operational diary, in Boeicho Boeikenshujo Senshishitsu, *Senshi sosho, Daihonei rikugunbu*, 5:45.

17 Colonel Ogata Kenichi's diary entry of December 11, 1942, in Nakao, *Showa tenno hatsugen kiroku shusei*, 2:169–70.

18 Yamada, *Showa tenno no gunji shiso to senryaku*, 223–24; Boeicho Boeikenshujo Senshishitsu, *Senshi sosho, Daihonei rikugunbu*, 5:562–64 (all quotations).

19 Yamada, *Showa tenno no gunji shiso to senryaku*, 227–33; Boeicho Boeikenshujo Senshishitsu, *Senshi sosho, Daihonei rikugunbu*, 6:248–49.

20 National Diet Library of Japan, "Kido Koichi seiji danwa rokuon sokkiroku"; Kido's reference to his conversation with the emperor in March 1943 appears on p. 93.

21 Kido's conversations with the emperor on February 5 and March 30, 1943, are confirmed by his diary entries on these days in Koichi Kido, *Kido Koichi nikki*, 2:1010, 1020. See also National Diet Library of Japan, "Kido Koichi seiji danwa rokuon sokkiroku."

22 Kido Nikki Kenkyu-kai, *Kido Koichi kankei bunsho*, 128–29.

23 Kido Koichi, *Kido Koichi nikki*, 2:1020.

24 Operational diary of Colonel Sanada Joichiro, June 6, 1943, in Sanbohonbu, *Sugiyama memo*, 2:20 (all quotations). In June 1942, the Japanese navy occupied Attu as part of the operation to secure Midway, but the navy did not have a clear plan to defend the island after the disastrous failure at Midway. When American forces landed on Attu on May 12, the Japanese navy was unable to send reinforcements and had to abandon its men on the island.

25 Operational diary of Colonel Sanada Joichiro June 8, 1943, in Sanbohonbu, *Sugiyama memo*, 2:20–21.

26 Ibid., 2:21.

27 Yamada, *Showa tenno no gunji shiso to senryaku*, 239–41.

28 Kido Koichi, *Kido Koichi nikki*, 2:1033.

29 Sanbohonbu, *Sugiyama memo*, 2:22 (all quotations).

30 Nakao, *Showa tenno hatsugen kiroku shusei*, 2:218–20; Takamatsumiya, *Takamatsumiya nikki*, 6:411.

31 Yamada, *Showa tenno no gunji shiso to senryaku*, 248–52 (quotation p. 250).

32 Kido Nikki Kenkyu-kai, *Kido Koichi kankei bunsho*, 129.

33 Kido Koichi, *Kido Koichi nikki*, 2:1043; Shigemitsu, *Shigemitsu Mamoru shuki*, 382–83.

34 Diary entry of August 2, 1943, by Colonel Ogata Kenichi, in Nakao, *Showa tenno hatsugen kiroku shusei*, 2:229.

35 Sanbohonbu, *Sugiyama memo*, 2:24–26 (all quotations).

36 Terasaki and Miller, *Showa tenno dokuhakuroku*, 102. In his essay "Chasing a Decisive

Victory: Emperor Hirohito and Japan's War with the West (1941–1945)," Edward Drea argues that Hirohito began to believe in a decisive battle to extricate Japan from the losing war against the Allies as early as the fall of 1942; see Drea, *In the Service of the Emperor*, 188–89. However, Drea's argument is based on the unpersuasive conjecture that the emperor lost hope of victory in September 1942 when he learned of Japan's failure to repel the Allied forces along the Owen Stanley Range in eastern New Guinea.

37 Sanbohonbu, *Sugiyama memo*, 2:473; Yamada, *Showa tenno no gunji shiso to senryaku*, 256–59.

38 Memo of October 1, 1943, by Admiral Shimada Shigetaro, in Nakao, *Showa tenno hatsugen kiroku shusei*, 2:247.

39 Diary entries of October 10 and 26, 1943, by Major General Sanada Joichiro, in Nakao, *Showa tenno hatsugen kiroku shusei*, 2:248, 249.

40 Yamada, *Showa tenno no gunji shiso to senryaku*, 272, 274.

41 Takamatsumiya, *Takamatsumiya nikki*, 7:259.

42 Kido Koichi, *Kido Koichi nikki*, 2:1084–85.

43 Ibid., 2:1087.

44 Ibid., 2:1089–90.

45 Sanbohonbu, *Sugiyama memo*, 2:31.

46 Hosokawa, *Hosokawa nikki*, 1:172.

47 Butow, *Japan's Decision to Surrender*, 29.

48 Diary of Sanada Joichiro, June 18, 1944, in Nakao, *Showa tenno hatsugen kiroku shusei*, 2:276.

49 Irie, *Irie Sukemasa nikki*, 2:294.

50 Terasaki and Miller, *Showa tenno dokuhakuroku*, 88–92.

51 Ito Takashi, *Takagi Sokichi nikki to joho*, 2:739–49.

52 Matsutani, *Daitoa senso shushu no shinso*, 66–68.

53 Gunji-shi Gakkai, *Daihonei rikugunbu senso shidohan: Kimitsu senso nisshi*, 2:552.

54 Hosokawa, *Hosokawa nikki*, 1:229–30.

55 Takamatsumiya, *Takamatsumiya nikki*, 7:514.

56 Kido's diary shows that after Japan's defeat in the Marianas on June 19–20, Kido had frequent talks with Prince Takamatsu, Admiral Okada, Konoe Fumimaro, Matsudaira Yasumasa, Professor Yabe Teiji, Professor Amakawa Nobuo, and Fujiyama Aiichiro, as well as Foreign Minister Shigemitsu and Minister without Portfolio Kishi Nobusuke: all of them were critics of continuing the war.

57 Yoshimatsu, *Tojo Hideki ansatsu no natsu*.

58 Ito Takashi, *Takagi Sokichi nikki to joho*, 2:751–52.

59 Kido Koichi, *Kido Koichi nikki*, 2:1115.

60 Ibid., 2: 1116–18.

61 Detailed record of the *jushin's* meeting on July 17 and the subsequent events that led to Tojo's resignation, in Kido Koichi, *Kido Koichi nikki*, 2:1119–28

62 Terasaki and Miller, *Showa tenno dokuhakuroku*, 95.

63 Ibid., 95–96 (all quotations).

CHAPTER 5. IMBROGLIO

1   Butow, *Japan's Decision to Surrender*, 231.

2   Igarashi, *Bodies of Memory*, chapter 1.

3   Iriye, *Power and Culture*, 259, 261.

4   Terasaki and Miller, *Showa tenno dokuhakuroku*, 97–98.

5   Kido Koichi, *Kido Koichi nikki*, 2: 1127.

6   Ibid., 2:1128.

7   Imoto, *Daitoa senso sakusen nisshi*, 562.

8   Yamada, *Showa tenno no gunji shiso to senryaku*, 289–303 (quotation p. 291).

9   Ibid., 308–10; Terasaki and Miller, *Showa tenno dokuhakuroku*, 100; Nakao, *Showa tenno hatsugen kiroku shusei*, 2:312–13; Kido Koichi, *Kido Koichi nikki*, 2:1163.

10 Kido Koichi, *Kido Koichi nikki*, 2:1164.

11 Takamatsumiya, *Takamatsumiya nikki*, 8:19.

12 Fujita, *Jijucho no kaiso*, 43–44. Grand Chamberlain Fujita Hisanori attended almost all these meetings with the *jushin*--except for Prince Konoe's audience with the emperor, which was attended by Kido (instead of Fujita) at Kido's request.

13 Terasaki and Miller, *Showa tenno dokuhakuroku*, 102.

14 Prince Konoe's memorandum submitted to the emperor on February 14, 1945, in Gaimusho, *Nihon gaiko nenpyo narabini shuyo bunsho*, 2:608–11.

15 Record of Konoe Fumimaro's audience with the emperor on February 14, 1945, in Kido Nikki Kenkyu-kai, *Kido Koichi kankei bunsho*, 495–98 (all quotations). According to Fujita Hisanori, Kido volunteered to attend Konoe's meeting with the emperor. Fujita, *Jijucho no kaiso*, 55–56.

16 Diary of Colonel Ogata Kenichi, military aide-de-camp, February 14, 1945, in Nakao, *Showa tenno hatsugen kiroku shusei*, 2:323.

17 Fujita, *Jijucho no kaiso*, 72.

18 Takagi, *Takagi kaigun shosho oboegaki*, 101.

19 Ito Takashi, *Takagi Sokichi nikki to joho*, 2:765–66; Takagi, *Takagi kaigun shosho oboegaki*, 105–6. According to the diary of Prince Takamatsu, the prince met Takagi on September 16, 1944. Takamatsumiya, *Takamatsumiya nikki*, 7:547.

20 Ito Takashi, *Takagi Sokichi nikki to joho*; Takamatsumiya, *Takamatsumiya nikki*.

21 Ito Takashi, *Takagi Sokichi nikki to joho*, 2:816–17.

22 Takagi, *Takagi Sokichi nikki to joho*, 2:822.

23 Kido Nikki Kenkyu-kai, *Kido Koichi kankei bunsho*, 497–98. According to Takagi's record of Harada Kumao's statement on March 21, 1945, with regard to Konoe's audience with the emperor, Konoe employed the term *seidan*. Ito Takashi, *Takagi Sokichi nikki to joho*, 2:831.

24 Kido Koichi, *Kido Koichi nikki*, 2:1176.

25 Kido Nikki Kenkyu-kai, *Kido Koichi kankei bunsho*, 132.

26 Ibid.

27 Shigemitsu, *Shigemitsu Mamoru shuki*, 441–42. Shigemitsu used the word *kōtō* (imperial reign) to mean the *kokutai*.

28   Ibid., 442.

29   Ibid., 442–43.

30   Ibid., 443–44.

31   Ito Takashi, *Takagi Sokichi nikki to joho*, 2:829–30 (all quotations).

32   Spector, *Eagle against the Sun*, 504–5.

33   Nakao, *Showa tenno hatsugen kiroku shusei*, 2:339–40; Fujita, *Jijucho no kaiso*, 78 (quotation), 86–87.

34   National Diet Library of Japan, "Kido Koichi seiji danwa rokuon sokkiroku," 121–22; Fujita, *Jijucho no kaiso*, 95–101 (quotations p. 100); Terasaki and Miller, *Showa tenno dokuhakuroku*, 110–11; Togo, *Togo Shigenori gaiko shuki*, 320–22; Butow, *Japan's Decision to Surrender*, 63–67; Eto, Kurihara, and Hatano, *Shusen kosaku no kiroku*, 2:49.

35   Terasaki and Miller, *Showa tenno dokuhakuroku*, 113–14.

CHAPTER 6. THE "SACRED DECISION" TO SURRENDER

1   *The End of the Pacific War: Reappraisals*, edited by Tsuyoshi Hasegawa, elevated this historical debate.

2   Hasegawa, "The Atomic Bombs and the Soviet Invasion: Which Was More Important in Japan's Decision to Surrender?" in Hasegawa, *End of the Pacific War*, 142.

3   This question was originally raised by Brigadier General Bonner F. Fellers, military secretary to General Douglas MacArthur and chief of his psychological warfare operations, to Terasaki Hidenari, who served as liaison between Fellers and Emperor Hirohito during the American occupation of Japan. Higashino, *Showa tenno futatsu no "dokuhakuroku"*, 113–16.

4   Bix, *Hirohito and the Making of Modern Japan*, chapters 12 and 13.

5   Asada, "Shock of the Atomic Bomb and Japan's Decision to Surrender," 477–512; Drea, *In the Service of the Emperor*, chapter 12; Hasegawa, *Racing the Enemy*.

6   Butow, *Japan's Decision to Surrender*, 231.

7   Hasegawa, "Shusen no kikai wo nogashi tsuzuketa shidoshatachi no sekinin," 100–117.

8   Hasegawa, "The Atomic Bombs and the Soviet Invasion: Which Was More Important in Japan's Decision to Surrender?" in Hasegawa, *End of the Pacific War*, 144.

9   National Diet Library of Japan, "Kido Koichi seiji danwa rokuon sokkiroku," 150.

10   Butow, *Japan's Decision to Surrender*, 232 (italics in original).

11   Titus, *Palace and Politics in Prewar Japan*.

12   Ito Takashi, *Takagi Sokichi nikki to joho*, 2:854–55. Konoe's secretary, Hosokawa Morisada, also recorded in his diary part of the Konoe-Kido conversation that Konoe told him; see Hosokawa, *Hosokawa nikki*, 2:114.

13   Shigemitsu, *Shigemitsu Mamoru shuki*, 442–43.

14   The liaison conference between the top leaders of the government and supreme command was renamed the Supreme War Leadership Council (Saiko Senso Shido Kaigi, lit., "supreme council for the guidance of the war") when General Koiso Kuniaki

became prime minister in July 1944. The council consisted of the prime minister, foreign minister, war minister, navy minister, and chiefs of the Army and Naval General Staffs.

15 Terasaki and Miller, *Showa tenno dokuhakuroku*, 115–19; Admiral Hasegawa's report in Butow, *Japan's Decision to Surrender*, 115–16.

16 Togo, *Togo Shigenori gaiko shuki*, 340.

17 National Diet Library of Japan, "Kido Koichi seiji danwa rokuon sokkiroku," 127–36; record of Harada Kumao's statements on March 21, 1945, in Ito Takashi, *Takagi Sokichi nikki to joho*, 2:831; Terasaki and Miller, *Showa tenno dokuhakuroku*, 123–24n.

18 Terasaki and Miller, *Showa tenno dokuhakuroku*, 122–24.

19 Ito Takashi, *Takagi Sokichi nikki to joho*, 2:855.

20 "Jikyoku shushu no taisaku shian" (A working plan to terminate the war), in Kido Kochi, *Kido Koichi nikki*, 2:1208–9

21 Kido Koichi, *Kido Koichi nikki*, 2:1208–11; Kido Nikki Kenkyu-kai, *Kido Koichi kankei bunsho*, 75–79; Yomiuri Shinbunsha, *Showa-shi no tenno*, 2:134–37, 151–53.

22 Anami, Anami Korechika Kankei Bunsho, file 59, p. 52.

23 Terasaki and Miller, *Showa tenno dokuhakuroku*, 118.

24 Butow, *Japan's Decision to Surrender*, 120.

25 Terasaki and Miller, *Showa tenno dokuhakuroku*, 118.

26 Nakao, *Showa tenno hatsugen kiroku shusei*, 2:377–82.

27 For the entire text of the Yalta Agreement signed on February 11, 1945, by Franklin D. Roosevelt, Winston S. Churchill, and J. Stalin, see appendix B in Butow, *Japan's Decision to Surrender*, 242.

28 The most recent study to demonstrate this point is Hasegawa, *Racing the Enemy*, especially chapter 3.

29 Konoe, *Ushinahareshi seiji*, 153.

30 For the entire text of the Potsdam Proclamation, see appendix C in Butow, *Japan's Decision to Surrender*, 243–44.

31 Hasegawa, *Racing the Enemy*, 168–70; Kido Nikki Kenkyu-kai, *Kido Koichi nikki: Tokyo saibanki*, 441–42; Sakomizu, "Shusen no shinso, 52–53. The latter is a partial reprint from *Shusen no shinso*, privately published by Sakomizu between 1960 and 1961.

32 Weber, *Wirtschaft und Gesellschaft*, 672, quoted in Maruyama, *Thought and Behaviour in Modern Japanese Politics*, 125.

33 Masumi, *Showa tenno to sono jidai*, 207.

34 Kido Nikki Kenkyu-kai, *Kido Koichi nikki: Tokyo saibanki*, 415.

35 Ibid., 444.

36 Hasegawa, *Racing the Enemy*, 200.

37 Kawabe Torashiro Bunsho Kenkyu-kai, *Shosho-hikkin*, 172.

38 Sakomizu, "Shusen no shinso," 56.

39 Ibid., 56–57; Kido, *Kido Koichi nikki*, 2:1223; Hando, *Seidan: Tenno to Suzuki Kantaro*, 336–39.

40 Tokugawa, *Jijucho no yuigon*, 90.

41 Eto, Kurihara, and Hatano, *Shusen kosaku no kiroku*, 2:370–93.

42   Asada argues that Foreign Minister Togo's meeting with the emperor on August 8 was a turning point in both men's decision to pursue an immediate peace with the one condition. However, Hasegawa relying on Kido's diary, argues that the emperor was not firmly committed to the one-condition proposal until the evening of August 9, after the Soviet war declaration and the atomic bomb dropped on Nagasaki. Asada, "Shock of the Atomic Bomb and Japan's Decision to Surrender," 488–495; Hasegawa, *End of the Pacific War*, 117–18; Hasegawa, *Racing the Enemy*, 205–6. There is reason to question Hasegawa's interpretation.

43   Togo, *Togo Shigenori gaiko shuki*, 355–56 (all quotations).

44   Hatano, "The Atomic Bomb and the Soviet Entry into the War: Of Equal Importance," in Hasegawa, *End of the Pacific War*, 98.

45   Togo, *Togo Shigenori gaiko shuki*, 355–56. Fujita quotes the emperor's remarks to Togo: "Now that such a new weapon has been used, we can no longer continue war. It is impossible. We must not miss an opportunity by trying to obtain favorable terms. You must make efforts to terminate the war as soon as possible. Convey this to Lord Privy Seal Kido and Prime Minister Suzuki." Fujita, *Jijucho no kaiso*, 127.

46   Shigemitsu, *Shigemitsu Mamoru shuki*, 522–25; Kido Koichi, *Kido Koichi nikki*, 2: 1223; military aide-de-camp Colonel Ogata Kenichi's diary, in Boeicho Boeikenshujo Senshishitsu, *Senshi sosho, Daihonei rikugunbu*, 10:447.

47   Eto, Kurihara, and Hatano, *Shusen kosaku no kiroku*, 2:389–403; Gaimusho, *Nihon gaiko nenpyo narabini shuyo bunsho*, 2:627–31.

48   This English translation of Emperor Hirohito's words are based on notes taken by Ikeda Sumihisa, who attended the meeting, in Eto, Kurihara, and Hatano, *Shusen kosaku no kiroku*, 2:400. Besides the six members of the Supreme War Leadership Council and Hiranuma Kiichiro, five people attended as aides but did not participate in the deliberations: Sakomizu Hisatsune (chief cabinet secretary), Yoshizumi Masao (chief of the Military Affairs Bureau), Hoshina Zenshiro (chief of the Naval Affairs Bureau), Ikeda Sumihisa (chief of the General Planning Office), and Hasunuma Shigeru (chief aide-de-camp). The following also contain records of Hirohito's statement at the imperial conference almost identical to Ikeda's notes: Sakomizu, *Kikanju-ka no shusho kantei*, 264–66; Sakomizu, *Daihihon teikoku saigo no yon-kagetsu*, 197–98; Hoshina, *Daitoa senso-hishi*, 147; Kido Koichi, *Kido Koichi nikki*, 2:1223–24. The emperor's words at the conference were also re-created by Butow in *Japan's Decision to Surrender*, 175.

49   Butow, *Japan's Decision to Surrender*, 183.

50   See the entire text of Japan's first surrender offer on August 10, 1945, in appendix D in Butow, *Japan's Decision to Surrender*, 244. The Japanese government also contacted Great Britain, the Soviet Union, and China through the Swiss and Swedish governments.

51   See the reply from US secretary of state James F. Byrnes on August 11, 1945, in appendix E in Butow, *Japan's Decision to Surrender*, 245 (emphasis added).

52   Kido Koichi, *Kido Koichi nikki*, 2:1225; Sakomizu, *Daihihon teikoku saigo no yonkagetsu*, 206–8, 239–42.

53   Ito Takashi, *Takagi Sokichi nikki to joho*, 2:926.

54 Sakomizu, *Dainihon teikoku saigo no yonkagetsu*, 212; Sakomizu, *Kikanju-ka no shusho kantei*, 277–78.

55 Eto, Kurihara, and Hatano, *Shusen kosaku no kiroku*, 2:434–46.

56 Ito Takashi, *Takagi Sokichi nikki to joho*, 2:926–27; Vice Navy Minister Hoshina Zan-shiro's testimony, in Eto, Kurihara, and Hatano, *Shusen kosaku no kiroku*, 2:446–49.

57 Kido Koichi, *Kido Koichi nikki*, 2:1224.

58 Nakao, *Showa tenno hatsugen kiroku shusei*, 2:395.

59 Kido Koichi, *Kido Koichi nikki*, 2:1225; Togo, *Togo Shigenori gaiko shuki*, 363 (quotation).

60 Hagihara, *Togo Shigenori: Denki to kaisetsu*, 296–97.

61 Lieutenant Colonel Takeshita Masahiko's diary entry of August 12, 1945, in Gunji-shi Gakkai, *Daihonei rikugunbu senso shidohan kimitsu senso nisshi*, 2:757. According to Takeshita (Anami's brother-in-law), the emperor told Anami, "Chin niwa kakusho ga aru."

62 Testimony by Colonel Hayashi Saburo, War Minister Anami's secretary, in Eto, Kuri-hara, and Hatano, *Shusen kosaku no kiroku*, 2:458.

63 Higashikuni, *Higashikuni nikki*, 198–201.

64 Terasaki and Miller, *Showa tenno dokuhakuroku*, 129.

65 As discussed in chapter 2, since the controversy about the emperor organ theory and the subsequent *kokutai* clarification movement in the mid-1930s, Emperor Hirohito had been fully aware of the serious disagreement over the meaning of the *kokutai*. He knew very well that the ambiguity of the *kokutai* was being exploited by the ultranationalists and the military, especially the army. The emperor did not support the way the military used the concept of *kokutai* and the imperial court as part of its propaganda to mobilize the entire nation toward aggressive wars in Asia and the Pacific. The emperor had often exhibited his frustration and distrust of the army since the Kwantung Army's invasion of Manchuria in 1931.

66 Boeicho Boeikenshujo Senshishitsu, *Senshi sosho, Daihonei rikugunbu*, 10:491.

67 Higashikuni, *Higashikuni nikki*, 201.

68 Kido Nikki Kenkyu-kai, *Kido Koichi nikki: Tokyo saibanki*, 445 (all quotations).

69 Matsumoto Shunichi's note of August 13, 1945, in Eto, Kurihara, and Hatano, *Shusen kosaku no kiroku*, 2:461.

70 Togo, *Togo Shigenori gaiko shuki*, 366.

71 Gunji-shi Gakkai, *Daihonei rikugunbu senso shidohan kimitsu senso nisshi*, 2:761–62; Kido Koichi, *Kido Koichi nikki*, 2:1226; Kido Nikki Kenkyu-kai, *Kido Koichi kankei bunsh*, 135–36; Sakomizu, *Dainihon teikoku saigo no yonkagetsu*, 227–28; Boeicho Boeikenshujo Senshishitsu, *Senshi sosho, Daihonei rikugunbu*, 10:506.

72 Hata Shunroku's memoir, in Boeicho Boeikenshujo Senshishitsu, *Senshi sosho, Dai-honei rikugunbu*, 10:505.

73 Shimomura, *Shusen hishi*, 140–41. See also an English reconstruction of Emperor Hirohito's statement in Butow, *Japan's Decision to Surrender*, 207–8.

74 Fujita, *Jijucho no kaiso*, 205–7.

75 Kawabe Torashiro Bunsho Kenkyu-kai, *Shosho-hikkin*, 170–73.

76 Kawabe Torashiro Bunsho Kenkyu-kai, *Shosho-hikkin*, 178–79. See the more com-

plete quotation from Kawabe's diary in Boeicho Boeikenshujo Senshishitsu, *Senshi sosho, Daihonei rikugunbu*, 10:453.

77 Kawabe Torashiro Bunsho Kenkyu-kai, *Shosho-hikkin*, 179–80, 193–95.

78 Gunji-shi Gakkai, *Daihonei rikugunbu senso shidohan kimitsu senso nisshi*, 2:753–58. In "The Perils and Politics of Surrender," Barton Bernstein offers a concise account of how, between August 10 and 14, the US refusal to accept the preservation of the Japanese imperial house risked inciting further resistance by Japanese militarists.

79 Gunji-shi Gakkai, *Daihonei rikugunbu senso shidohan kimitsu senso nisshi*, 2:759–61.

80 Oki, *Anami Korechika-den*, 283–84.

81 An example of the act of *haragei* is provided in Butow, *Japan's Decision to Surrender*, 70.

82 Sakomizu, *Dainihon teikoku saigo no yonkagetsu*, 214–17 (quotation p. 217).

83 Higashikuni, *Higashikuni nikki*, 202. General Nukada later denied this statement, according to Boeicho Boeikenshujo Senshishitsu, *Senshi sosho, Daihonei rikugunbu*, 10:504.

84 Gunji-shi Gakkai, *Daihonei rikugunbu senso shidohan kimitsu senso nisshi*, 2:751–68; Kawabe Torashiro Bunsho Kenkyu-kai, *Shosho-hikkin*, 178–87.

85 Yamada, *Showa tenno no gunji-shiso to senryaku*, 334–35.

86 Gunji-shi Gakkai, *Daihonei rikugunbu senso shidohan kimitsu senso nisshi*, 2:764–65; Butow, *Japan's Decision to Surrender*, 213–18; Hasegawa, *Racing the Enemy*, 245–47.

87 Nakao, *Showa tenno hatsugen kiroku shusei*, 2:403–4; Fujita, *Jijucho no kaiso*, 152.

88 Takeshita's account of Anami's suicide, in Gunji-shi Gakkai, *Daihonei rikugunbu senso shidohan kimitsu senso nisshi*, 2:765–68. The photo of Anami's suicide note is in Oki, *Anami Korechika-den*; another English translation of Anami's note is in Butow, *Japan's Decision to Surrender*, 219–20. The emperor's quotation is from Fujita, *Jijucho no kaiso*, 158.

89 National Diet Library of Japan, "Kido Koichi seiji danwa rokuon sokkiroku," 134.

90 Nakao, *Showa tenno hatsugen kiroku shusei*, 2:414–15. Another English translation is in Large, *Emperor Hirohito and Showa Japan*, 132.

91 Terasaki and Miller, *Showa tenno dokuhakuroku*, 126–27.

92 Tsunoda, de Bary, and Keene, *Sources of Japanese Tradition*, 2:140.

EPILOGUE

1 Dower, *Embracing Defeat*, chapters 9–11.

2 Terasaki and Miller, *Showa tenno dokuhakuroku*, 129.

3 Bix, *Hirohito and the Making of Modern Japan*, 527.

4 Shimomura, *Shusen hishi*, 140–41; Butow, *Japan's Decision to Surrender*, 207–8.

5 Nakao, *Showa tenno hatsugen kiroku shusei*, 2:395.

6 Kido Koichi, *Kido Koichi nikki*, 2:1230–31. Another partial English translation is available in Large, *Emperor Hirohito and Showa Japan*, 132.

7 Higashikuni, *Higashikuni nikki*, 235, diary entry of September 14, 1945.

8 National Diet Library of Japan, "Kido Koichi seiji danwa rokuon sokkiroku," 161.

9   Kinoshita, *Sokkin nisshi*, 165.

10   Ibid., 96–99.

11   Kinoshita, *Sokkin nisshi*, 174–75, 222–23.

12   US Department of State, *Foreign Relations of the United States*, 1946, 8:395–97.

13   Kato Kyoko, *Showa tenno to Tajima Michiji to Yoshida Shigeru*, 34–35. A photocopy of Tajima's letter of November 12, 1948, is in Hata, *Showa tenno itsutsu no ketsudan*, 240.

14   Diary of Kido Koichi in the collection of Kido-ke Bunsho (microfilm), National Diet Library of Japan, October 17, 1951 (quotation); November 28, 1951; April 4, 1952; and May 2, 1952. See also Awaya et al., *Kido Koichi jinmon chosho*, 559–62.

15   Kato Kyoko, "Showa tenno: Kokumin eno shazai shosho soko," 94–113 (quotation p. 95); Kato Kyoko, *Showa tenno shazai shochoku soko no hakken*, 10.

16   Kato Kyoko, *Showa tenno to Tajima Michiji to Yoshida Shigeru*, 37.

17   Awaya et al., *Kido Koichi jinmon chosho*, 562.

18   Sato Tadao, "Hirohito no bisho" (Hirohito's smile), *Chuo koron* (September 1959), quoted in Ruoff, *People's Emperor*, 136.

19   Orr, *Victims as Hero*, 34.

20   Kido Nikki Kenkyu-kai, *Kido Koichi nikki: Tokyo saibanki*, 444–45.

21   Yoshida, *Nihonjin no senso-kan*, 46.

22   Kishida, *Jijucho no showa-shi*, 111.

23   Takahashi, *Ningen: Showa tenno*, 2:314–17.

BIBLIOGRAPHY

PRIMARY SOURCES

Akamatsu Sadao. *Tojo hishokan kimitsu nisshi* (Confidential diary of Tojo's secretary). Tokyo: Bungeishunju, 1985.

Anami Korechia. Anami Korechika Kanken Bunsho (Anami Korechika Papers). Files 43, 58, 59. National Diet Library of Japan, Tokyo.

Asahi Shinbun Hotei Kishadan. *Tokyo saiban* (Tokyo Trial). 3 vols. Tokyo: Tokyo Saiban Kankokai, 1962.

Awaya Kentaro, Iko Toshiya, Otabe Yuji, Miyazaki Akira, and Okada Nobuhiro, eds. *Kido Koichi jinmon chosho* (Protocol of the interrogation of Kido Koichi). 1st ed. Tokyo: Otsuki Shoten, 1987.

Baker, Ray Stannard. *Woodrow Wilson and World Settlement.* 3 vols. Garden City, NY: Doubleday, Page, 1923.

Boeicho Boeikenshujo Senshishitsu (National Institute for Defense Studies, War History Office). *Senshi sosho* (War history series), vol. 63. *Daihonei rikugunbu* (Imperial Headquarters, Army Department), vol. 5. Tokyo: Asagumo Shinbunsha, 1973.

———. *Senshi sosho* (War history series), vol. 66. *Daihonei rikugunbu* (Imperial Headquarters, Army Department), vol. 6. Tokyo: Asagumo Shinbunsha, 1973.

———. *Senshi sosho* (War history series), vol. 76. *Daihonei rikugunbu daitoa senso kaisenkeii* (Imperial Headquarters, Army Department, particulars on the beginning of the greater East Asian War), vol. 5. Tokyo: Asagumo Shinbunsha, 1974.

———. *Senshi sosho* (War history series), vol. 82. *Daihonei rikugunbu* (Imperial Headquarters, Army Department), vol. 10. Tokyo: Asagumo Shinbunsha, 1975.

Eto Jun, Kurihara Ken, and Hatano Sumio, eds. *Shusen kosaku no kiroku* (The records of the engineering of the termination of the war). 2 vols. Tokyo: Kodansha, Kodanshabunko, 1986.

Fujita Hisanori. *Jijucho no kaiso* (Memoir of a grand chamberlain). Tokyo: Chuokoronsha, Chuko Bunko, 1987.

Gaimusho (Foreign Ministry of Japan). *Nihon gaiko nenpyo narabini shuyo bunsho* (A chronology and a collection of major documents of Japanese foreign policy). 2 vols. Tokyo: Hara Shobo, 1965.

Grew, Joseph C. *Ten Years in Japan: A Contemporary Record Drawn from the Diaries and Private and Official Papers of Joseph C. Grew, United States Ambassador to Japan, 1932–1943.* New York: Simon and Schuster, 1944.

——. *Turbulent Era: A Diplomatic Record of Forty Years, 1904–1945.* 2 vols. Edited by Walter Johnson, assisted by Nancy Harvison Hooker. Boston: Houghton Mifflin, 1952.

Gunji-shi Gakkai (Association of Military History), ed. *Daihonei rikugunbu senso shidohan: Kimitsu senso nisshi* (Imperial Headquarters, Army Department, War Guidance Section: Confidential war diary). 2 vols. Tokyo: Kinseisha, 1998.

Hane, Mikiso, trans. *Emperor Hirohito and His Chief Aide-de-Camp: The Honjo Diary, 1933–36.* Tokyo: University of Tokyo Press, 1982.

Harada Kumao. *Saionji-ko to seikyoku* (Prince Saionji and the political situation). 8 vols. Tokyo: Iwanami Shoten, 1950–52, 1956.

Hara Keiichiro, ed., *Hara Kei nikki* (Diary of Hara Kei). 6 vols. Tokyo: Fukumura Shuppan, 1965.

Hata Shunroku. *Hata Shunroku nisshi: Zoku gendai-shi shiryo dai-yon-kan rikugun* (Diary of Hata Shunroku: Supplement to the sources of modern history, volume 4, the army). Tokyo: Misuzu Shobo, 1983.

Higashikuni Naruhiko. *Higashikuni nikki* (Diary of Higashikuni). Tokyo: Tokuma Shoten, 1968.

Honjo Shigeru. *Honjo nikki* (Diary of Honjo). Tokyo: Hara Shobo, 1967.

Hoshina Zenshiro. *Daitoa senso-hishi* (A secret history of the Greater East Asian War). Tokyo: Hara Shobo, 1975.

Hosokawa Morisada. *Hosokawa nikki.* 2 vols. Tokyo: Chuokoronsha, Chukobunko, 1979.

Hull, Cordell. *The Memoirs of Cordell Hull.* 2 vols. New York: Macmillan, 1948.

Ike, Nobutaka, ed. *Japan's Decision for War: Records of the 1941 Policy Conferences.* Stanford, CA: Stanford University Press, 1967.

Imoto Kumao. *Daitoa senso sakusen nisshi* (A strategy journal of the Greater East Asian War). Tokyo: Fuyo Shobo, 1998.

Irie Tametoshi, ed. *Irie Sukemasa nikki* (Diary of Irie Sukemasa). 6 vols. Tokyo: Asahi Shinbunsha, 1990–191; 12 vols. Asahi Bunko, 1994–95.

Ito Takashi, ed. *Takagi Sokichi nikki to joho* (The diary and intelligence reports of Takagi Sokichi). 2 vols. Tokyo: Misuzu Shobo, 2000.

Ito Takashi, Sawamoto Tsuneo, and Nomura Minoru, eds. "Sawamoto Yorio kaigun-jikan nikki" (Diary of Vice Minister of the Navy Sawamoto Yorio). *Chuokoron* (January 1988): 434–80.

Joho Yoshio, ed. *Gunmu kyokucho Muto Akira kaisoroku* (Chief of the Military Affairs Bureau Muto Akira's memoirs). Tokyo: Fuyo Shobo, 1981.

Kanroji, Osanaga. *Hirohito: An Intimate Portrait of the Japanese Emperor.* Los Angeles: Gateway Publishers, 1975.

Kawabe Torashiro Bunsho Kenkyu-kai, ed. *Shosho-hikkin* (Obey the imperial will without fail). Tokyo: Toshokankokai, 2005.

Kawai Yahachi. *Showa shoki no tenno to kyuchu: Jijujicho Kawai Yahachi nikki* (The emperor and the court in early Showa: Diary of Vice Grand Chamberlain Kawai Yahachi). 6 vols. Tokyo: Iwanami Shoten, 1993–94.

Kido Koichi. *Kido Koichi nikki* (Diary of Kido Koichi). 2 vols. Tokyo: Tokyo Daigaku Shuppan, 1966.

Kido Nikki Kenkyu-kai, ed. *Kido Koichi kankei bunsho* (Papers of Kido Koichi). Tokyo: Tokyo Daigaku Shuppankai, 1966.

——. *Kido Koichi nikki: Tokyo saibanki* (Diary of Kido Koichi: The period during the Tokyo Trial). Tokyo: Tokyo Daigaku Shuppankai, 1980.

Kido Takahiko. *Tokyo saiban to Kido nikki* (The Tokyo Trial and Kido diary). Tokyo: Private publication by Dopposhorin, 1993.

Kinoshita Michio. *Sokkin nisshi* (A chamberlain's diary). Tokyo: Bungeishunju, 1990.

Konoe Fumimaro. *Heiwa eno doryoku* (Efforts for peace). Tokyo: Nihon Dempo Tsushin, 1946.

——. *Ushinahareshi seiji* (Lost politics). Tokyo: Asahi Shinbunsha, 1946.

Kunaincho (Imperial Household Agency), ed. *Showa tenno jitsuroku: Hoteibon genko* (The annals of Emperor Showa: Identical draft of the original dedicated to the emperor). Vols. 23–34. Tokyo, 2014.

Makino Nobuaki. *Makino Nobuaki nikki* (Diary of Makino Nobuaki). Tokyo: Chuokoronsha, 1990.

Matsutani Sei. *Daitoa senso shushu no shinso* (The truth about the conclusion of the Greater East Asian War). Tokyo: Fuyo Shobo, 1984.

Minear, Richard H, ed. and trans. *War and Conscience in Japan: Nambara Shigeru and the Asia-Pacific War*. Lanham, MD: Rowman and Littlefield, 2010.

[Misuzu Shobo]. *Gendai-shi shiryo: Nicchu senso* (Documents of modern history: The Sino-Japanese War). 5 vols. Tokyo: Misuzu Shobo, 1964–66.

Nakao Yuji, ed. *Showa tenno hatsugen kiroku shusei* (A collection of the records of the Showa emperor's statements). 2 vols. Tokyo: Fuyo Shobo, 2003.

Nara Takeji. *Jijubukancho Nara Takeji nikki·kaikoroku* (Diary and memoir of Chief Aide-de-Camp Nara Takeji). 4 vols. Tokyo: Kashiwa Shobo, 2000.

National Diet Library of Japan, ed. "Kido Koichi seiji danwa rokuon sokkiroku" (Stenographic records of conversations on politics with Kido Koichi). February 16, March 6, 13, 27, April 12, May 29, 1967. National Diet Library of Japan, Tokyo.

——. "Sakomizu Hisatsune seiji danwa rokuon sokkiroku" (Stenographic records of conversations on politics with Sakomizu Hisatsune). November 7, 1969, October 4, 1972. National Diet Library of Japan, Tokyo.

Nomura Minoru, ed. *Jijubukan Jo Eiichiro nikki* (Diary of Naval Aide-de-Camp Jo Eiichiro) Tokyo: Yamakawa Shuppansha, 1982.

Okabe Nagaakira. *Aru jiju no kaiso: Gekido-jidai no Showa tenno* (A chamberlain's memoir: The Showa emperor in the turbulent years). Tokyo: Asahi Sonorama, 1990.

Okada Keisuke. *Okada Keisuke Kaikoroku* (Memoir of Okada Keisuke). Tokyo: Mainichi Shinbunsha, 1950.

Sakomizu Hisatsune. *Dainihon teikoku saigo no yonkagetsu* (The last four months of the Greater Japanese Empire). Tokyo: Oriento Shobo, 1973.

——. *Kikanju-ka no shusho kantei* (The prime minister's residence under machine guns). Tokyo: Kobunsha, 1964.

——. "Shusen no shinso" (The truth about the termination of the war). *Seiron* (September 2003): 44–67.

Sanbohonbu (General Staff), ed. *Sugiyama memo* (Sugiyama memoranda). 2 vols. Tokyo: Hara Shobo, 1967.

Shigemitsu Mamoru. *Shigemitsu Mamoru shuki* (Shigemitsu Mamoru's memos). Tokyo: Chuokoronsha, 1986.

Shimada Shigetaro. "Shimada Shigetaro taisho kaisen nikki" (Admiral Shimada Shigetaro's diary of the outbreak of war). *Bungeishunju* 54 (December 1976): 358–72.

Shimomura Kainan. *Shusen hishi* (A secret history of the termination of the war). Tokyo: Kodansha, 1950; reprint, Kodansha Gakujutsubunko, 1985.

Suzuki Hajime, ed. *Suzuki Kantaro-den* (Autobiography of Suzuki Kantaro). Tokyo: Jijistushinsha, 1968.

Takagi Sokichi. *Takagi kaigun shosho oboegaki* (Notes of Rear Admiral Takagi). Tokyo: Mainichi Shinbunsha, 1979.

———. *Takagi Sokichi nikki: Nichi-doku-i sangokudomai to tojo-naikaku dato*. Tokyo: Mainichi Shinbunsha, 1985.

Takamatsumiya Nobuhito. *Takamatsumiya nikki* (Diary of Prince Takamatsu). 8 vols. Tokyo: Chuokoronsha, 1996–97.

Takayama Shinobu. *Sanbohonbu sakusenka* (The Operations Bureau of the General Staff). Tokyo: Fuyo Shobo, 1985.

Tanaka Shinichi. *Taisen totsunyu no shinso* (The truth behind the plunge into the great war). Tokyo: Gengensha, 1955.

Tanemura Sako. *Daihonei kimitsu nisshi* (Imperial Headquarters confidential diary). Tokyo: Daiyamondosha, 1952.

Terasaki Hidenari, and Mariko Terasaki Miller. *Showa tenno dokuhakuroku: Terasaki Hidenari, goyo-gakari nikki* (The Showa emperor monologue: And the diary of the liaison officer of the imperial household, Terasaki Hidenari). Tokyo: Bungeishunju, 1991.

Togo Shigenori. *Togo Shigenori gaiko shuki: Jidai no ichimen* (Diplomatic memoirs of Togo Shigenori: An aspect of the times). Tokyo: Hara Shobo, 1967.

Tokugawa Yoshihiro. *Jijucho no yuigon* (Grand chamberlain's last words). Tokyo: Asahi Shibunsha, 1997.

Tomita Kenji. *Haisen nihon no uchigawa: Konoe-ko no omoide* (An inside story of defeated Japan: Reminiscences of Prince Konoe). Tokyo: Kokin Shoin, 1962.

Toyoda Soemu. *Saigo no teikoku kaigun* (The end of the imperial navy). Tokyo: Sekai no Nihonsha, 1950.

Tsunoda, Ryusaku, William Theodore de Bary, and Donald Keene, eds. *Sources of Japanese Tradition*. 2 vols. New York: Columbia University Press, 1958.

Ugaki Matome. *Sensoroku* (War diary). Tokyo: Hara Shobo, 1996.

US Department of State. *Papers Relating to the Foreign Relations of the United States*. 1946, vol. 8. Washington, DC: Government Printing Office, 1971.

Yamada Akira, ed. *Gaiko shiryo: Kindai nihon no bocho to shinryaku* (Diplomatic documents: Modern Japan's expansion and aggression). Tokyo: Shinnihon Shuppansha, 1997.

Yamagiwa Akira, Nakamura Masanori, and Okada Ryonosuke, eds. *Shiryo nihon senryo 1: Tenno-sei* (Primary sources on the occupation of Japan 1: The emperor system). Tokyo: Otsuki Shoten, 1990.

SECONDARY SOURCES

Agawa Hiroyuki. *Takamatsumiya to kaigun* (Prince Takamatsu and the navy). Tokyo: Chuokoronsha, 1996.

Alperovitz, Gar. *The Decision to Use the Atomic Bomb: And the Architecture of an American Myth*. New York: Alfred A. Knopf, 1995.

Ambrosius, Lloyd D. *Wilsonianism: Woodrow Wilson and His Legacy in American Foreign Relations*. New York: Palgrave, 2002.

Asada, Sadao, ed. *Japan and the World, 1853–1952: A Bibliographical Guide to Japanese Scholarship in Foreign Relations*. New York: Columbia University Press, 1989.

——. "The Shock of the Atomic Bomb and Japan's Decision to Surrender—A Reconsideration." *Pacific Historical Review* 67 (November 1998): 477–512.

Awaya Kentaro. *Jugo-nen senso-ki no seiji to shakai* (Politics and society during the Fifteen Year War). Tokyo: Otsuki Shoten, 1995.

——. *Tokyo saiban-ron* (On the Tokyo Trial). Tokyo: Otsuki Shoten, 1989.

Barnhart, Michael A. *Japan Prepares for Total War: The Search for Economic Security, 1919–1941*. Ithaca, NY: Cornell University Press, 1987.

——. "Review Article: Hirohito and His Army." *International History Review* 21, no. 3 (September 1999): 696–703.

Beasley, W. G. *Japanese Imperialism, 1894–1945*. Oxford: Oxford University Press, 1987.

Behr, Edward. *Hirohito: Behind the Myth*. New York: Vintage Books, 1989.

Bergamini, David. *Japan's Imperial Conspiracy*. New York: William Morrow, 1971.

Berger, Gordon Mark. *Parties Out of Power in Japan, 1931–1941*. Princeton, NJ: Princeton University Press, 1977.

Bernstein, Barton. "The Perils and Politics of Surrender: Ending the War with Japan and Avoiding the Third Atomic Bomb." *Pacific Historical Review* 46 (January 1977): 1–27.

Bix, Herbert P. *Hirohito and the Making of Modern Japan*. New York: Harper Collins, 2000.

——. "Inventing the 'Symbol Monarchy' in Japan, 1945–52." *Journal of Japanese Studies* 21, no. 2 (Summer 1995): 319–63.

——. "Japan's Delayed Surrender: A Reinterpretation." *Diplomatic History* 19, no. 2 (Spring 1995): 197–225.

——. "The Showa Emperor's 'Monologue' and the Problem of War Responsibility." *Journal of Japanese Studies* 18, no. 2 (Summer 1992): 295–363.

Borg, Dorothy. *The United States and the Far Eastern Crisis of 1933–1938: From the Manchurian Incident through the Initial Stage of the Undeclared Sino-Japanese War*. Cambridge, MA: Harvard University Press, 1964.

Borg, Dorothy, and Shumpei Okamoto, with Dale K. A. Finlayson. *Pearl Harbor as History Japanese American Relations, 1931–1941*. New York: Columbia University Press, 1973.

Brooks, Lester. *Behind Japan's Surrender: The Secret Struggle That Ended an Empire*. With a foreword by Fumihiko Togo. New York: McGraw-Hill, 1968.

Burkman, Thomas W. *Japan and the League of Nations: Empire and World Orders, 1914–1938*. Honolulu: University of Hawai'i Press, 2008.

Burns, James MacGregor. *Roosevelt: The Lion and the Fox*. New York: Smithmark, 1996.

——. *Roosevelt: The Soldier of Freedom*. New York: Harcourt Brace Jovanovich, 1970.

Butow, Robert J. C. *Japan's Decision to Surrender*. Stanford, CA: Stanford University Press, 1954.

——. *The John Doe Associates: Backdoor Diplomacy for Peace, 1941*. Stanford, CA: Stanford University Press, 1974.

——. "Marching Off to War on the Wrong Foot: The Final Note Tokyo Did *Not* send to Washington." *Pacific Historical Review* 63, no. 1 (February 1994): 67–79.

——. *The Tojo and the Coming of the War*. Stanford, CA: Stanford University Press, 1961.

Chadani Seiichi. *Showa senzen-ki no kyuchu seiryoku to seiji* (The court influence and politics in prewar Showa). Tokyo: Yoshikawa Kobunkan, 2009.

——. *Showa tenno shokkin-tachi no senso* (A war of the Showa emperor's advisers). Tokyo: Yoshikawa Kobunkan, 2010.

Chimoto Hideki. *Tenno-sei no shinryaku sekinin to sengo sekinin* (Responsibility for invasion and postwar responsibility of the emperor system). Tokyo: Aoki Shoten, 1990.

Conroy, Hilary, and Harry Wray, eds. *Pearl Harbor Reexamined: Prologue to the Pacific War*. Honolulu: University of Hawai'i Press, 1990.

Coox, Alvin D. *Nomonhan: Japan against Russia, 1939*. Stanford, CA: Stanford University Press, 1985.

Coox, Alvin D., and Takahashi Hisashi. "Showa tenno to senso sekinin (The Showa emperor and his responsibilities for the war)." *Gunji Shigaku* 31 (September 1995): 79–89.

Cook, Haruko Taya, and Theodore F. Cook. *Japan at War: An Oral History*. New York: New Press, 1992.

Dallek, Robert. *Franklin D. Roosevelt and American Foreign Policy, 1932–1945*. New York: Oxford University Press, 1995.

Dower, John W. *Embracing Defeat: Japan in the Wake of World War II*. New York: W. W. Norton, 1999.

——. *War without Mercy: Race and Power in the Pacific War*. New York: Pantheon Books, 1986.

Drea, Edward J. *In the Service of the Emperor: Essays on the Imperial Japanese Army*. Lincoln: University of Nebraska Press, 1998.

——. *Japan's Imperial Army: Its Rise and Fall, 1853–1945*. Lawrence: University Press of Kansas, 2009.

Duus, Peter, Ramon H. Myers, and Mark R. Peattie, eds. *The Japanese Informal Empire in China, 1895–1937*. Princeton. NJ: Princeton University Press, 1989.

——. *The Japanese Wartime Empire, 1931–1945*. Princeton, NJ: Princeton University Press, 1996.

Frank, Richard B. *Downfall: The End of the Imperial Japanese Empire*. New York: Random House, 1999.

Fujitani, Takashi. *Splendid Monarchy: Power and Pageantry in Modern Japan*. Berkeley: University of California Press, 1998.

Fujiwara Akira. *Showa tenno no jugo-nen senso* (The Showa emperor's Fifteen Year War). Tokyo: Aoki Shoten, 1991.

——. *Tenno no guntai to nicchu senso* (The emperor's military and the Sino-Japanese War). Tokyo: Otsuki Shoten, 2006.

——. *Tenno-sei to guntai* (The emperor system and the military). Tokyo: Aoki Shoten, 1978.

Fujiwara Akira, Awaya Kentaro, Yoshida Yutaka, and Yamada Akira. *Tettei kensho Showa tenno dokuhakuroku* (Thorough examination of the Showa Emperor's "Monologue"). Tokyo, Otsuki Shoten, 1991.

Furukawa Takahisa. *Showa tenno: "Risei no kunshu" no kodoku* (Emperor Showa: Solitude of a "rational monarch"). Tokyo: Chuokoron Shinsha, 2011.

Garon, Sheldon. *Molding Japanese Minds: The State in Everyday Life.* Princeton, NJ: Princeton University Press, 1997.

Gluck, Carol, and Stephen R. Graubard, eds. *Showa: The Japan of Hirohito.* New York: W. W. Norton, 1992.

Hagihara Nobutoshi. *Togo Shigenori: Denki to kaisetsu* (Togo Shigenori: Biography and commentaries). Tokyo: Hara Shobo, 2005.

Hando Kazutoshi. *Nihon no ichiban nagai hi* (Japan's longest day). Rev. ed. Tokyo: Bungenshunju, 1995.

——. *Seidan: Tenno to Suzuki Kantaro* (Sacred decision: The emperor and Suzuki Kantaro). Tokyo: Bungeishunju, 1985; reprint, Bunshunbunko, 1988.

Hando Kazutoshi, Hosaka Masayashu, and Isoda Michifumi. "Showa tenno jitsuroku no shogeki" (Impacts of the annals of Emperor Showa). *Bungeishunju* (October 2014): 94–123.

Hane, Mikiso, and Louis G. Perez. *Modern Japan: A Historical Survey.* 5th ed. Boulder: Westview Press, 2013.

Hara Takeshi. *Showa tenno* (Emperor Showa). Tokyo: Iwanami Shoten, 2008.

Hasegawa, Tsuyoshi, ed. *The End of the Pacific War: Reappraisals.* Stanford, CA: Stanford University Press, 2007.

——. *Racing the Enemy: Stalin, Truman, and the Surrender of Japan.* Cambridge, MA: Harvard University Press, 2005.

——. "Shusen no kikai wo nogashi tsuzuketa shidoshatachi no sekinin" (The responsibilities of the leaders who kept missing the opportunities to end the war). *Chuokoron* (September 2006): 100–117.

Hata Ikuhiko. *Showa-shi no nazo wo ou* (Pursuing mysteries of Showa history). 2 vols. Tokyo: Bungeishunju, 1999.

——. *Showa tenno itsutsu no ketsudan* (The Showa emperor's five decisions). Tokyo: Kodansha, 1984; reprint, Bunshunbunko, 1994.

Hattori Takushiro. *Daitoa senso zenshi* (A complete history of the Greater East Asian War). Tokyo: Hara Shobo, 1965.

Higashino Makoto. *Showa tenno futatsu no "dokuhakuroku"* (Two "monologues" by the Showa emperor). Tokyo: Nihon Hoso Shuppan Kyokai, 1998.

Hoshina Zenshiro, Oi Atsushi, and Suekuni Masao. *Taiheiso senso hishi* (A secret history of the Pacific War). Tokyo: Nihon Kokubo Kyokai, 1987.

Hori Eizo. *Daihonei sanbo no johosenki* (A record of intelligence war by a staff of the Imperial Headquarters). Tokyo: Bungeishunju, 1996.

Ienaga, Saburo. *The Pacific War, 1931–1945: A Critical Perspective on Japan's Role in World War II.* New York: Pantheon Books, 1978.

Igarashi, Yoshikuni. *Bodies of Memory: Narratives of War in Postwar Japanese Culture, 1945–1970*. Princeton, NJ: Princeton University Press, 2000.

Inoue Kiyoshi. *Tenno no senso sekinin* (The emperor's war responsibility). Tokyo: Gendai Hyoron-sha, 1975; reprint, Tokyo: Iwanami Shoten, 1991.

Iriye, Akira. *The Origins of the Second World War in Asia and the Pacific*. New York: Longman, 1987.

———. *Power and Culture: The Japanese-American War, 1941–1945*. Cambridge, MA: Harvard University Press, 1981.

Irokawa, Daikichi. *The Age of Hirohito: In Search of Modern Japan*. Translated by Mikiso Hane and John K. Urda, with a foreword by Carol Gluck. New York: Free Press, 1995.

Ito Yukio. *Showa tenno den* (Biography of the Showa Emperor). Tokyo: Bungeishunju, 2011.

———. *Showa tenno to rikken kunshusei no hokai: Mutsuhito, Yoshihito, kara Hirohito he* (Emperor Showa and the collapse of constitutional monarchy: Mutsuhito, Yoshihito, to Hirohito). Nagoya: Nagoya Daigaku Shuppankai, 2005.

Janssens, Rudolf V. A. *"What Future for Japan?" U.S. Wartime Planning for the Postwar Era, 1942–1945*. Amsterdam: Rodopi, 1995.

Jeans, Roger B. *Terasaki Hidenari, Pearl Harbor, and Occupied Japan: A Bridge to Reality*. Lanham: Lexington Books, 2009.

Joho Yoshio. *Rikugunsho gunmukyoku-shi* (A history of the Bureau of Military Affairs of the War Ministry). 2 vols. Tokyo: Fuyo Shobo Shuppan, 2002.

Kato Kyoko. "Showa tenno: Kokumin eno shazai shosho soko" (The Showa Emperor: A draft apology to his people). *Bungeishunju* (July 2003): 94–113.

———. *Showa tenno "shazai shochoku soko" no hakken* (The discovery of "the draft of the [Showa] emperor's apology"). Tokyo: Bungeishunju, 2003.

———. *Showa tenno to Tajima Michiji to Yoshida Shigeru: Shodai kunaicho chokan no "nikki" to "bunsho" kara* (The Showa Emperor, Tajima Michiji, and Yoshida Shigeru: From the "diary" and "papers" of the First Director of the Imperial Household Agency). Tokyo: Jinbun Shokan, 2006.

Kato Yoko. *Senso no ronri: Nichi-ro senso kara taiheiyo senso made* (Argument for war: From the Russo-Japanese War to the Pacific War). Tokyo: Keiso Shobo, 2005.

———. *Showa tenno to senso no seiki* (Emperor Showa and the century of war). Tokyo: Kodansha, 2011.

Kawahara, Toshiaki. *Hirohito and His Times: A Japanese Perspective*. Tokyo: Kodansha International, 1990.

Kawamura, Noriko. "Emperor Hirohito and Japan's Decision to Go to War with the United States: Reexamined." *Diplomatic History* 31, no. 1 (January 2007): 51–79.

———. *Turbulence in the Pacific: Japanese-U.S. Relations during World War I*. Westport, CT: Praeger, 2000.

Kimball, Warren F. *The Juggler: Franklin Roosevelt as Wartime Statesman*. Princeton, NJ: Princeton University Press, 1991.

Kishida Hideo. *Jijucho no Showa-shi* (Grand chamberlains' history of Showa). Tokyo: Asahi Shinbunsha, 1982.

Kojima Noboru. *Tenno to senso sekinin* (The emperor and war responsibility). Tokyo: Bungeishunju, 1988; reprint, Bunshunbunko, 1991.

Koketsu Atsushi. *Nihon kaigun no shusen kosaku* (The Japanese navy's scheme to end the war). Tokyo: Chuokoronsha, Chukoshinsho, 1996.

———. "Seidan" kyoko to Showa tenno (Fabrication of the sacred imperial decision and Emperor Showa). Tokyo: Shinnihon Suppansha, 2006.

Koshiro, Yukiko. *Imperial Eclipse: Japan's Strategic Thinking about Continental Asia Before August 1945.* Ithaca, NY: Cornell University Press, 2013.

Kurihara Ken. *Tenno: Showa-shi oboegaki* (The emperor: Notes on Showa history). Tokyo: Yushindo, 1955; reprint, Tokyo: Hara Shobo, 1985.

Kushner, Barak. *The Thought War: Japanese Imperial Propaganda.* Honolulu: University of Hawai'i Press, 2006.

LaFeber, Walter. *The Clash: U.S.-Japanese Relations throughout History.* New York: W. W. Norton, 1997.

Large, Stephen S. *Emperor Hirohito and Showa Japan: A Political Biography.* London: Routledge, 1992.

Levin, N. Gordon, Jr., *Woodrow Wilson and World Politics: America's Response to War and Revolution.* New York: Oxford University Press, 1968.

MacMillan, Margaret. *Paris 1919: Six Months That Changed the World.* New York: Random House, 2001.

Manela, Erez. *The Wilsonian Moment: Self-Determination and the International Origins of Anticolonial Nationalism.* New York: Oxford University Press, 2007.

Manning, Paul. *Hirohito: The War Years.* New York: Dodd, Mead, 1986.

Mauch, Peter. *Sailor Diplomat: Nomura Kichisaburo and the Japanese-American War.* Cambridge, MA: Harvard University Press, 2011.

Maruyama, Masao. *Thought and Behaviour in Modern Japanese Politics.* Edited by Ivan Morris. London: Oxford University Press, 1963.

Masuda Tomoko. *Tenno-sei to kokka: Kindai nihon no rikken kunshusei* (The emperor system and state: The constitutional monarchy of modern Japan). Tokyo: Aoki Shoten, 1999.

Masumi Junnosuke. *Showa tenno to sono jidai* (The Showa emperor and his era). Tokyo: Yamakawa Shuppansha, 1998.

Miller, Edward S. *Bankrupting the Enemy: The U.S. Financial Siege of Japan before Pearl Harbor.* Annapolis: Naval Institute Press, 2007.

Minear, Richard H. *Japanese Tradition and Western Law.* Cambridge, CA: Harvard University Press, 1970.

Mitani Taichiro. *Kindai nihon no senso to seiji* (War and politics of modern Japan). Tokyo: Iwanami Shoten, 1997.

Mitchell, Richard H. *Thought Control in Prewar Japan.* Ithaca, NY: Cornell University Press, 1976.

Miyake Masaki, ed. *Showa-shi no gunbu to seiji* (The military and politics in the history of Showa). Tokyo: Daiichihoki Shuppan, 1983.

Morley, James William, ed. *Japan Erupts: The London Naval Conference and the Manchurian Incident, 1928–1932.* (Selected translations from *Taiheiyo senso e no michi: Kaisen gaiko-shi*). New York: Columbia University Press 1984.

Murakami Shigeyoshi. *Tenno no saishi* (The emperor's rites). Tokyo: Iwanami Shoten, 1977.

Myers, Ramon H., and Mark R. Peattie, eds. *The Japanese Colonial Empire, 1895–1945.* Princeton, NJ: Princeton University Press, 1984.

Nagai Kazu. *Seinen kunshu Showa tenno to genro Saionji* (Young monarch Emperor Showa and Genro Saionji). Kyoto: Kyoto Daigaku Gakujutsu Shuppan, 2003.

Nakamura, Masanori. *The Japanese Monarchy: Ambassador Joseph Grew and the Making of the "Symbol Emperor System," 1931–1991.* Translated by Herbert P. Bix, Jonathan Baker-Bates, and Derek Brown. Armonk, NY: M. S. Sharpe, 1992.

Nakamura, Takafusa. *A History of Showa Japan, 1926–1989.* Translated by Edwin Whenmouth. Tokyo: University of Tokyo Press, 1989.

Oe Shinobu. *Gozen kaigi* (Imperial Conference). Tokyo: Chuokoronsha, 1991.

Ogata, Sadako N. *Defiance in Manchuria: The Making of Japanese Foreign Policy, 1931–1932.* Berkeley: University of California Press, 1964.

Ogura Kazuo. *Yoshida Shigeru no jimon: Haisen, soshite hokokusho "Nihon gaiko no kago"* (Yoshida Shigeru's question to himself: Defeat, and report on "Japanese diplomacy's mistakes"). Tokyo: Fujiwara Shoten, 2003.

Oka Yoshitake. *Kindai nihon no seijika* (Politicians of modern Japan). Tokyo: Iwanami Shoten, 1990.

———. *Konoe Fumimaro: "Unmei" no seijika* (Konoe Fumimaro: A politician of "fate") Tokyo: Iwanami Shoten, 1972.

Oki Shuji. *Anami Korechika-den* (A biography of Anami Korechika). Tokyo: Kodansha, 1995.

Orr, James J. *The Victim as Hero: Ideologies of Peace and National Identity in Postwar Japan.* Honolulu: University of Hawai'i Press, 2001.

Packard, Jerrold M. *Sons of Heaven.* New York: Scribner's, 1987.

Pelz, Stephen E. *Race to Pearl Harbor: The Failure of the Second London Naval Conference and the Onset of World War II.* Cambridge, MA: Harvard University Press, 1974.

Prange, Gordon W. *At Dawn We Slept: The Untold Story of Pearl Harbor.* New York: McGraw-Hill, 1981.

Prange, Gordon W., with Donald M. Goldstein and Katherine V. Dillon. *Pearl Harbor: The Controversial Sequel to "At Dawn We Slept."* New York: Penguin, 1986.

Ruoff, Kenneth J. *Imperial Japan at Its Zenith: The Wartime Celebration of the Empire's 2,600 Anniversary.* Ithaca, NY: Cornell University Press, 2010.

———. *The People's Emperor: Democracy and the Japanese Monarchy, 1945–1995.* Cambridge, MA: Harvard University Press, 2001.

Sato Kenryo. *Tojo Hideki to taiheiyo senso* (Tojo Hideki and the Pacific War). Tokyo: Bungeishunju Shinsha, 1960.

Sherwin, Martin J. *A World Destroyed: Hiroshima and the Origins of the Arms Race.* New York: Vintage, 1987.

Shibusawa, Naoko. *America's Geisha Ally: Reimagining the Japanese Enemy.* Cambridge, MA: Harvard University Press, 2006.

Shillony, Ben-Ami. *Politics and Culture in Wartime Japan.* New York: Oxford University Press, 1981.

———. *Revolt in Japan: The Young Officers and the February 26, 1936 Incident.* Princeton, NJ: Princeton University Press, 1973.

Shoda Tatsuo. *Jushin-tachi no Showa-shi* (Jushin's history of Showa). 2 vols. Tokyo: Bungeishunju, 1981.

Sigal, Leon V. *Fighting to a Finish: The Politics of War Termination in the United States and Japan, 1945.* Ithaca, NY: Cornell University Press, 1988.

Spector, Ronald H. *Eagle against the Sun: The American War with Japan.* New York: Random House, 1985.

Takahashi Hiroshi. *Heika, otazune moshiagemasu* (His Majesty, I would like to ask you). Tokyo: Bungeishunju, 1988.

———. *Ningen: Showa tenno* (A man: Emperor Showa). 2 vols. Tokyo: Kodansha, 2011.

———. *Shocho tenno* (Symbol emperor). Tokyo: Iwanami Shoten, 1987.

Takayama Shinobu. *Futari no sanbo Hattori Takushiro to Tsuji Masanobu.* Tokyo: Fuyo Shobo Shuppan, 1970; reprint, Tokyo: Fuyo Shobo Shuppan, 1999.

———. *Sanbohonbu sakusenka no daitoasenso.* Tokyo: Fuyo Shobo Shuppan, 2001.

Takeda, Kiyoko. *The Dual-Image of the Japanese Emperor.* With a foreword by Ian Nish. New York: New York University Press, 1988.

Titus, David A. *Palace and Politics in Prewar Japan.* New York: Columbia University Press, 1974.

Totani, Yuma. *The Tokyo War Crimes Trial: The Pursuit of Justice in the Wake of World War II.* Cambridge, MA: Harvard University Press, 2008.

Tsutsui Kiyotada. *Showa ju-nen-dai no rikugun to seiji* (The army and politics during the second decade of the Showa era). Tokyo: Iwanami Shoten, 2007.

Utley, Jonathan G. *Going to War with Japan, 1937–1941.* Knoxville: University of Tennessee Press, 1985.

Wetzler, Peter. *Hirohito and War: Imperial Tradition and Military Decision Making in Prewar Japan.* Honolulu: University of Hawai'i Press, 1998.

Yamada Akira. *Daigensui Showa tenno* (The Showa Emperor as commander in chief). Tokyo: Shin-nihon Shuppan, 1994.

———. *Rekishishusei-shugi no kokufuku* (Overcoming revisionism of history). Tokyo: Kobunken, 2001.

———. *Showa tenno no gunji shiso to senryaku* (The Showa Emperor's military ideology and strategy). Tokyo: Azekura Shobo, 2002.

———. *Showa tenno no senso shido* (The Showa Emperor's war leadership). Tokyo: Showa Shuppan, 1990.

Yamada Akira and Koketsu Atsushi. *Ososugita seidan: Showa tenno no senso shido to senso Sekinin* (Delayed imperial decision: The Showa Emperor's war leadership and war responsibility). Tokyo: Showa Shuppan, 1991.

Yamamoto Tomoyuki. *Shusen ka Kowa ka: Teikoku rikugun no himitsu shusen kosaku* (War or peace: The imperial army's secret scheme to end the war). Tokyo: Shinchosha, 2013.

Yomiuri Shinbunsha, ed. *Showa-shi no tenno* (The emperor in the history of Showa). 30 vols. Tokyo: Yomiuri Shinbunsha, 1967–76.

Yoshida Yutaka. *Gendai rekishigaku to senso sekinin* (Modern history and war responsibility). Tokyo: Aoki Shoten, 1997.

———. *Nihonjin no senso-kan: Sengoshi no nakano henyo* (Japanese views of the war: Transformation in the postwar history). Tokyo: Iwanami Shoten, 1995.

———. *Showa tenno no shusen-shi* (The Showa Emperor's history of the end of the war). Tokyo: Iwanami Shoten, 1992.

Yoshimatsu Yasuhiro. *Tojo Hideki ansatsu no natsu* (The summer of the assassination attempt against Tojo Hideki). Tokyo: Shinchosha, 1984: reprint, Shinchobunko, 1989.

INDEX

Note: page numbers followed by "n" indicate endnotes.